Prison Reform in Lancashire, 1700-1850

A STUDY IN LOCAL ADMINISTRATION

Margaret DeLacy

MANCHESTER
Printed for the Chetham Society
1986

Copyright ©1986 by the Board of Trustees
of the Leland Stanford Junior University

Published in Great Britain by
Manchester University Press
Oxford Road, Manchester M13 9PL

ISBN 0 7190 1341 0

British Library cataloguing in publication data
applied for

Printed in U.S.A.

To my parents

Acknowledgments

I would like to thank, in addition to the libraries listed in the Document Sources, the following institutions for giving me access to numerous secondary works and for other assistance: in Oregon, the Clackamas County Library, the Multnomah County Library, the Oregon Health Sciences University, Reed College, and the University of Oregon; in Washington, D.C., the Library of Congress and the National Library of Medicine; in London, the Institute of Historical Research and the Society of Friends' Library; and in England, the Essex, Oxford, and West Yorkshire County Record Offices.

I would also like to thank the following librarians and archivists for their time and patience in giving me personal assistance: Ms. Gaddes at the Lancaster City Library; Mr. David Jones, Mr. David Smith, Ms. Janet Parkinson, and Mr. George Fisher at the Lancaster County Record Office; Ms. Glenise Matheson at the John Rylands University Library in Manchester; Ms. Margaret DeMotte at the Manchester Central Library; Ms. Nancy Hanks at the National Library of Medicine; and Ms. Alice Prochaska at the Public Record Office.

Mr. Kenneth Neale, Mr. M. Butters, and Colonel J. S. Haywood of the Home Office made it possible for me to visit Lancaster and Preston Prisons and helped me track down Lancashire records that had not been deposited in government archives. I would like to thank Mr. Fall, the governor at Lancaster, Mr. G. W. Morrall, the deputy governor at Preston, and the staff at each prison for giving me tours of their respective prisons and answering numerous questions. I would also like to thank the Governor of HM Prison, Bedford, for his assistance.

I will always be grateful to the numerous scholars working in this field who very generously shared both their own work and their sources with me. They include Dr. Marguerite Dupree, Dr. Robin Evans, Dr. Tony Howe, Dr. Walter Joseph King, Ms. Valerie Johnston, Dr. Sean Mc-Conville, Mr. Malcolm Ramsey, Dr. Wayne Joseph Sheehan, Judge Eric Stockdale, Dr. Heather Tomlinson, Dr. Richard Trainor, Dr. John Styles, and Dr. John Walton.

Finally, I am especially grateful to those scholars who not only shared their own work with me but also read and criticized portions of this book. They include Dr. Victor Bailey, Dr. John Dinwiddy, Mr. Michael Collinge, Dr. V. A. C. Gatrell, Dr. Michael Ignatieff, Ms. Joanna Innes, Dr. Margaret Pelling, Sir Leon Radzinowicz, and Dr. David Smith. Dr. Lawrence Stone and Dr. Robert Darnton, who served as advisers for the thesis that formed the basis for this book, also provided valuable editorial advice, as did the anonymous readers for Stanford University Press, who undertook an often unrewarding task with patience and understanding.   Margaret DeLacy

Contents

Tables and Figures

Prison Reform in Lancashire, 1700-1850

Introduction

There are several reasons for the recent scholarly interest in the history of prisons. First, like asylums, workhouses, and reformatory schools, prisons are examples of what Erving Goffman has called "total institutions."[1] Sociologists have become interested in the effect that these closed institutions have on their inmates, both by separating them from the outside world and by creating a different sort of community inside. These institutions all attained their modern form within the past hundred years.

Second, the subject has contemporary political importance. In both England and America the prison system is now under severe strain, as a rapidly rising crime rate crams more and more prisoners into old, deteriorating buildings. The resulting prison revolts and riots have attracted widespread attention and become political issues in their own right, as has the treatment of political prisoners both at home and abroad. At such a time it seems useful to try to understand how the modern prison system developed, how we treated our own prisoners in the past, and how previous generations coped with their own rising crime rates and political prisoners.

Third, developments within historiography have encouraged a renewed interest in the administrative history of prisons. Ever since Dicey's lectures on law and public opinion, but more especially within the past generation, historians have debated the origin of the "welfare state" and the reasons for the legislation of the "Age of Reform" in the first half of the nineteenth century.[2] Prison reform was part of this movement and shared the characteristics of other reforms: a gradual shift of initiative from local to central power, the establishment of a central commission and of a national inspectorate to enforce and superintend governmental decisions, and support from a small group of "middle-class" agitators. Unlike the New Poor Law, the Victorian prison system is still alive; very few English prisons were built after 1877, and the discipline that the old buildings still dictate would still be recognizable to the man of 1840. If the continued existence of the English prison system gives the English some reason to be interested in its past, it concerns Americans for another reason: the United States is now debating whether to continue along a path similar to that taken by England a century ago. By giving the central government increasing power to intervene in local administration and by turning to it for revenue, Americans are gradually shifting control from local to national government.

Like many of the other reforms of the past century, prison reform has evoked mixed feelings among historians. The more traditional see the story as one of progress. This, in general, has been the attitude of local historians and of the biographers of such great reformers as John Howard and Elizabeth Fry. The most important historians of the subject, Sidney and Beatrice Webb, also adopted this view, at least for the period before 1877, although they tempered it with sharp criticism of certain decisions and concluded that "it is probably quite impossible to make a good job of the deliberate incarceration of a human being in the most enlightened of dungeons."[3]

To radical writers—such as Bernard Shaw, who wrote a lengthy preface to the Webbs' book—imprisonment was a fundamental mistake: an institution best abandoned entirely. Among certain recent authors, imprisonment symbolizes everything that is most detestable in the modern state; it is a "totalitarian" instrument of power, used to hammer men into a new image when they are inside and to maintain a repressive structure of power among those outside. To these thinkers, every innovation of the Age of Reform simply put more nails into a coffin built round living men.

This attitude toward the institutions of the modern state in general and toward the prison in particular is by no means new:[4] books expressing this view have always had a relatively wide circulation among the reading public. They did not have much effect on working historians, however, until the appearance of a series of specialized works written for an academic audience. The first of these was Gertrude Himmelfarb's essay, "The Haunted House of Jeremy Bentham" (1965). This account of the failure of Bentham's Panopticon largely amounted to an attack on its author. The Panopticon, Himmelfarb argued, began as an apparently liberal innovation in prison discipline but rapidly degenerated into an exercise in cost-cutting exploitation, as Bentham was carried away by the beautiful image of himself as the all-powerful and enriched Contractor.[5] Especially important was Himmelfarb's use of the Panopticon as a departure point for a total reevaluation of "philosophical radicalism." Bentham, she argued, elevated the "greatest happiness of the greatest number" above all other social desiderata, including rights, liberty, and the guarantees provided by common law. With Bentham, she wrote, "There was no question of the 'rights' of prisoners and paupers, for there was no such thing as rights at all. There were only interests, and the interests of the majority had to prevail. The greatest happiness of the greatest number might thus require the greatest misery of the few." She added that Bentham was as uninterested in the idea of liberty as he was in that of fundamental rights, because they "obscured the real issues, which were happiness, security and good government."[6]

Himmelfarb's disquiet about the effect of utilitarian beliefs on social policy had a great impact on the authors who followed her. Her view of Bentham as a self-interested manipulator of the poor, a "spider in his web," has been echoed by other writers on the Panopticon and extended to other reformers, such as Howard. It has become common to assume that prison reformers were motivated by self- or class-interest in the furtherance of "social control"—an assumption that Himmelfarb herself might not endorse.[7]

This article was also important because of the strength of its imagery. For the historians who have followed Himmelfarb, the Panopticon—that "machine" for "grinding men good" with its "big brother" inspection system, its exploitative work, its codified rules, its fertile inventions for manipulating both body and soul—has entirely eclipsed as a cautionary symbol those two great "gothic" monuments to royal caprice and official neglect, the Bastille and Newgate. For many, the squalor of early modern life is preferable to the automated management of 1984. Himmelfarb has provided thinkers such as Foucault with an appropriate symbol for the modern state. It may be important to remember, therefore, that whatever the Panopticon represents, English society persistently balked at adopting it.

Six years after Himmelfarb's article appeared, David Rothman published a complete reevaluation of the history of American custodial institutions in *The Discovery of the Asylum*. In this wide-ranging intellectual history, Rothman described the transition from the small, familial institutions of the Colonial period to the large, highly regimented institutions of the early nineteenth century, which were organized on a military model. According to Rothman, reformers in Jacksonian America attempted to compensate for the family's perceived failure to act as a stabilizing force by providing institutional discipline for the mad, the poor, the criminal, and the young. "The reformers' original doctrines," he concludes, "were especially liable to abuse, their emphasis on authority, obedience, and regularity turning all too predictably into a mechanical application of discipline. And by incarcerating the deviant and dependent, . . . they discouraged—really eliminated—the search for other solutions that might have been less susceptible to abuse." Rothman ends with a call to avoid institutional responses to social problems because "proposals that promise the most grandiose consequences often legitimate the most unsatisfactory developments."[8]

This is also the position taken by Michel Foucault, whose book *Discipline and Punish* appeared in 1975, following his earlier *Madness and Civilization*. *Discipline and Punish* centers on the transition from a society based on representative torture in the name of the monarch to one of systematic incarceration in the name of public order. When Foucault speaks of incarceration he refers not merely to prisons but also to all modern residential institutions, from reform schools and insane asylums to schools and hospitals. These "carcerals" all maintain order by systematically manipulating their residents. To this end, they make regular divisions and classifications not only in space (e.g., cells) and time but also in the character of their inmates. Foucault considers this last division of particular importance, because it employs the methods on which such modern disciplines as medicine, psychiatry, and sociology are based: a preliminary "examination" and a continuing and inescapable observation or surveillance. The information gained thereby is used to establish standards of normality and deviancy: concepts that were unknown before these institutional methods appeared. Carcerals actually create deviancy and deviants, both by labeling them as such and by separating the deviants from the rest of society.[9]

Foucault argues that the creation of deviancy is a deliberate ploy on the part of the bourgeoisie: first, because it separates the more active and intelligent malefactors from their natural sympathizers among the lower classes; second, because it diverts attention from the greater illegalities perpetrated by the middle and upper classes; and third, because the dependent and easily controlled deviants can be turned into informers and make useful tools for spying on the lower classes. By these means, political radicalism and social unrest are controlled. The high recidivism rate of prisons, therefore, is not an accident or a sign of failure, but the very purpose of their existence.

Prison reform was built into the prison system from the start; it serves the prisons rather than changing them. Far from failing, prison reform has succeeded in keeping the prison firmly rooted in our society. It was never intended to change the way prisons function, but to make them more "corrective" and more "rigorous." "For a century and a half," Foucault writes, "the prison had always been offered as its own remedy: the reactivation of the penitentiary techniques as the only means of overcoming their perpetual failure."[10]

Foucault's arguments have served as the starting point for several young historians. Especially important is a recent book by Michael Ignatieff, *A Just Measure of Pain: The Penitentiary in the Industrial Revolution, 1750-1850*, which applies many of Foucault's theories to an account of a specific era in English penal history. Ignatieff's conclusion contains deliberate echoes of Foucault. Foucault had asked, "Is it surprising that the cellular prison, with its regular chronologies, forced labour, its authorities of surveillance and registration, its experts in normality, who continue and multiply the functions of the judge, should have become the modern instrument of penality? Is it surprising that prisons resemble factories, schools, barracks, hospitals, which all resemble prisons?"[11] Ignatieff in turn concludes, "Humanitarianism was inextricably linked to the practice of domination. . . . It was no accident that penitentiaries, asylums, workhouses, monitorial schools, night refuges, and reformatories looked alike, or that their charges marched to the same disciplinary cadence. Since they made up a complementary and interdependent structure of control, it was essential that their diets and deprivations be calibrated on an ascending scale, school—workhouse—asylum—prison, with the pain of the last serving to undergird the pain of the first. Nor was it accidental that these state institutions so closely resembled the factory."[12]

Ignatieff agrees with Foucault that prison reform and incarceration served each other in a complicated way: "To interpret the history of reform as a cycle of good intentions confounded by unintended consequences is to see it as a history of failure. But reform was a success. . . .

Yet . . . it is a success full of paradox. The movement . . . established among a skeptical, middle-class public the ideal that prisons ought to reform, without ever having to convince them that penitentiaries actually did so. . . . Typically, few reformers ever bothered to torture the recidivism rates into a validation of the penitentiary."[13]

Ignatieff supports his conclusion with an account of the initial development of the penitentiary and of the motives that underlay the reformers' efforts. He fixes this development firmly in its specific historical context: economic (the Industrial Revolution), social (changes in the crime rate and in the behavior of crowds), legal (changes in the jurisdiction of justices of the peace), military (the disruption of penal transportation overseas), political (the battle between Whigs, Tories, and Radicals), and intellectual (the development of "materialist" psychology). He leans toward Rothman's thesis that the reformers were motivated by concern over the apparent disintegration of the social order and by their desire for "a social order based on deferential reconciliation." These factors combined with a sense of guilt (produced by the feeling that "the rich bore some responsibility for the social genesis of crime"), political interests, and religious beliefs to produce a special blend of attitudes affecting penal policies. The end result of these interlinked changes was the experimental national prison at Pentonville, and Ignatieff vividly describes the harsh and solitary regime enforced there. Ignatieff's argument has been echoed by several other radical historians and has been widely accepted by historians in general.[14]

The present book was designed as a test of the radical view, to which it is heavily indebted. I have several objections, however, to the radicals' attempt to explain complex events as merely the history of the domination of one group by another. The first objection is that the approach is based on a theory of "social control"—a phrase that is, unfortunately, so highly charged and yet so vague that it obscures more than it reveals. Many authors who use it really mean "socialization," that is, the way a society acculturates its members. Others use it as a rough synonym for "discipline," so that, for example, the discipline exercised in a school is seen as a form of "social control." Lurking behind the phrase, and all the more potent because tacit, is a more or less Marxist class theory. "Social control" is useless as a tool unless one knows who is being controlled and who is doing the controlling. The usual, although often unproven, assumption is that it is the lower, or working, class that is being controlled, and the aristocracy, the upper class, the middle class, or the bourgeoisie that is doing the controlling. Although authors vary in the care with which they delineate the parties to this relationship, many radical writers assume that any system that furthers the stability of an unequal society necessarily benefits those toward the top, and was, therefore, deliberately created for this purpose.

This assumption may make sense when the right to exercise power is clearly at issue, and when the two sides to a conflict are well delineated, as in debates over politics or the right to vote. It becomes more dubious when the identities of the parties to the conflict are unclear. Anyone who lives in society is subject to communal controls, but not all controls, even those that apply differentially to members of different status groups, are "social controls" in the generally accepted sense of the phrase. An example would be the control exercised by guilds or trade unions over the right to work and over working practices. Another would be the control exercised by the old over the young in establishing minimum drinking, driving, and voting ages. If the theory of social control is shorn of its basis in class theory, it loses its bite and its meaning: to say that a school exercises "social control" in this sense is not an explanation but a tautology. If by social control we mean that an upper class is engaged in controlling a lower one, then the classes must be carefully specified and the divergence in their interests demonstrated. This is particularly important when cultural values rather than material goods are in question. Such values may percolate up and down without any proselytizing by the class that holds them—often, indeed, to its dismay.

In a recent review article, Michael Ignatieff has conceded this point. As he eloquently wrote:

The "social control" model of the prison's function which informed my own work assumed that capitalist society was systematically incapable of reproducing itself without the constant interposition of state agencies of control and repression. . . . Important as the penal sanction may have been in sustaining discipline in pauperized labor markets, or in constituting wage discipline itself in the face of worker resistance, we ought not to take these instances as typical of the role of state force once the wage bargain has been widely accepted. . . . Even in objectively exploitative . . . conditions of labor, one can conceive of men and women voluntarily coming to work. . . . By describing all social relations as relations of domination, Foucault neglects the large aspects of human sociability, in the family and in civil society generally, which are conducted by the norms of cooperation, reciprocity, and the "gift relationship."[15]

This is not to say that a theory based on cultural consensus or imitation is necessarily more appropriate than one based on social conflict, but merely that there are circumstances in which one or the other may be the more plausible alternative. Ideally, we will search for a reasonable balance between the consensual and the coercive while recognizing that this balance is constantly changing.

The problem becomes particularly acute in the case of the penal system, because the admitted purpose of this institution is control. Radical writers have tended to assume that the Victorian habit of distinguishing between the respectable and unrespectable poor was disingenuous, that it served the wish to divide and conquer. They have, therefore, tended to associate the poor and the criminal in order to place them in opposition to the middle or upper classes, feeling that both could only gain from an overthrow of the established order. For example, Peter Linebaugh has suggested that in imposing especially severe penalties on murderers, the members of Parliament who passed the Murder Act were expressing their class hatred.[16]

A class-based approach to penal law is not necessarily incorrect, but it requires demonstration in every specific case. A consensual model may be equally useful in understanding a particular series of decisions, as may a theory based on social conflicts that have other dividing points than those of class. As much as anything, prison, like war, is an institution created by the old but experienced by the young.

Even laws governing property crimes, such as larceny, met with a generally favorable response, even from the poor, who, after all, were the most frequent victims as well as the most frequently imprisoned perpetrators of such crimes. David Philips, in an investigation of criminal prosecution in the Black Country in the mid-nineteenth century, has pointed out that

large numbers of workingmen prosecuted other workingmen for thefts . . . from themselves; they did not simply exact informal retribution from them, but invoked the whole formal and cumbersome process of the law. . . . This suggests two things. First, they must have believed that the system of law had at least some element of justice and fairness about it. . . . Secondly, whatever their feelings about the law and its agents, they cannot have been totally opposed to the idea of invoking the law to prosecute thefts of private property. . . . By making use of the law in this way, they showed an acceptance of its basic legitimacy as applied to themselves and their affairs.[17]

As is quite evident from even the most skeptical reading of their comments, criminals themselves often accepted most of the premises of the ethical system that surrounded them, however much they may have resented heavy-handed attempts to drive the message home.

If the poor were not always antagonistic toward the rules that created the prison, they were also often ambivalent about the rules that were introduced within it. Perhaps the most unpleasant and frightening aspect of imprisonment is the imposition of an unavoidable and unprotected intimacy with serious and often dangerous criminals. Prisoners are afraid of each other. They are also frightened by the possibility of brutality from the staff and, in the early nineteenth century, they were afraid of dying from hunger or disease. The Hulks gained their reputation for brutality partly because of their appalling disease rate, but also because the staff battened down the hatches at the end of the day and left the convicts within to their own devices. While prison reform received a mixed response from prisoners, many welcomed at least moderate controls on behavior, which offered them a measure of protection from each other. Among them were the rules governing general cleanliness and hygiene, rules preventing extortion of food, and rules providing for classification of prisoners according to their sex, age, and offense. How consistently these rules were enforced is open to some doubt. It also seems clear in retrospect that the silent and separate systems went too far in preventing mutual "contamination."

Nevertheless, prisoners themselves often invoked the rules governing classification and strongly resented being confined with more serious offenders. They also expected a degree of protection from prison staff and were increasingly likely to protest if they felt a turnkey had failed to intervene in a fight or had responded too slowly to an illness. Though many prisoners probably welcomed the improved provisions for their health and comfort, some bitterly regretted the loss of freedom and autonomy this necessarily entailed. There was an inevitable trade-off between freedom and protection, and though historians may decide for themselves which they would prefer, they cannot do so with assurance for others.

The story of prison reform, therefore, is not simply the story of the repression of one group, consisting of prisoners, by another group, consisting of administrators. Prisoners themselves were deeply divided over the issue of prison reform as a whole and over the desirability of any particular reform. Even politically radical prisoners like Henry Hunt, John Knight, and John Doherty not only accepted the need for penal imprisonment for (nonpolitical) criminal offenses but also insisted that the authorities enforce a division between them and other convicts. They wished to remove themselves from prison and to control the corruption of prison officers that prevented the system from working "properly"—but not to eliminate imprisonment as an institution. Indeed, they were often strong proponents of the belief that imprisonment ought to be reformative.[18]

The radical argument also raises a problem in ethics. Some authors claim that the solution to the dilemma of choosing between dangerous freedom and corrupting control is to abandon imprisonment entirely. The worst thing about prison reform, for them, is not its content but the fact that it legitimizes imprisonment. If prisons were allowed to decay, without the constant investment of effort, money, and good intentions, perhaps they would be used less often, thus producing a clear benefit to those thousands of potential inmates no longer jailed. This theory applies a deterrent to the judge, who is prevented from sentencing offenders to prison by the absolute wretchedness of those already there. This rather backward deterrent is subject to the same objections originally raised against the eighteenth-century defenders of the "bloody code" of exemplary capital punishment: is it just to punish one man beyond his deserts in order to affect the behavior of someone else? Although the convict population is rising rapidly, both the English and the Americans have deliberately avoided building new prisons, at least partly from a desire to encourage alternatives to incarceration. This is all very well for the convicted robber who now receives a year's probation, but what of the convicted burglar or rapist who is serving out his time jammed into a Victorian cell with three other men, unable even to take a shower for weeks on end? In any case, it is by no means evident that excess prison capacity produces excessive convictions, as the declining conviction rate in England after 1855 suggests. In the late nineteenth century, prisons all over England were shut down for want of inmates.

Moreover, it is doubtful whether even the most appalling prison conditions, even when accompanied by riots, would do much to interest the public in an alternative "decarceration" policy. What evidence there is suggests the opposite. If imprisonment can be changed only if our social structure changes fundamentally, then there seems no reason why we should not make what improvements we can while awaiting that (surely distant) event. Rothman has suggested that reformed institutions are particularly liable to abuse; this may be true, but there were plenty of abuses in the more casual administration of the eighteenth century as well. Furthermore, I cannot help wondering what sort of institutions we will end up with if we make it clear that we will do nothing at all to improve them and really do not care how they are run.

A final objection is purely practical. We do not, in fact, know to what extent the reforms discussed by Ignatieff, Foucault, and others were actually carried out in the prisons. Foucault pays no attention whatever to this problem. Ignatieff concentrates on the "national" prisons, Pentonville and Millbank. Yet these institutions are by no means typical English prisons; from the start they were designed as special experimental places for particularly dangerous offenders. Life in even the largest of the provincial prisons was a world apart. Is it useful to write about how the middle classes were preoccupied with maintaining social order, if they never did much about it? There is a parallel between this controversy and the one about the effects of the New Poor Law; recently some researchers, such as Eric Midwinter, have pointed out that in many regions of England this controversial reform largely amounted to cosmetic changes in the titles of poor law officers. As Midwinter has written, "The continuum between old and new in the country's Poor Law management comes as no surprise. Nevertheless, it must be demonstrated, or the general significance attached to a dramatic Act of Parliament may be allowed to conceal the character of its humdrum practice at the local level."[19]

If we are ever to weigh the costs of prison reform against its benefits, we must know what both were. Despite lengthy arguments, we still know very little about what English prisons were actually like. Many scholars have written about reforms, but we do not know what it was that was being reformed. It is easy to find prison scandals but less easy to reach an understanding of day-to-day life. The only way to uncover the character of the "humdrum practice" of prison administration at a local level is through patient case studies based on archival research in local records. This book undertakes such a case study of a single county prison system, bearing in mind the radical picture of nineteenth-century prisons as sterile, highly regimented institutions that imposed a strict regime on their cowed inmates. We will follow a single county prison system over a long period in order to determine what the system was like before it was reformed; what led local administrators to embark on reform; just what reforms were in fact made; the political, economic, and social context that defined the reforms; and what sort of prison system they created.

One result of a molehill view of history is that many variations appear in a terrain that, viewed from the mountain, might look like a smooth plain. Prisons that might seem quite similar when encompassed in a study of national penal policy based on central records emerge as very diverse when viewed separately, just as the statistically similar families of the demographer take on individuality as the subjects of biography. Historians need both approaches, even though the angle of view may help determine the final conclusion. Certainly, one of the chief conclusions of this study is that though policy choices and new ideas played an important role in the character and quality of the English prison system, on the whole it was impossible for anyone to control that system by making comprehensive policy decisions at the top. Even within a single county, prisons were diverse. Lancashire alone had four prisons, each of which differed radically from the others. They ranged from Lancaster Castle, which was more or less a model of the "unreformed" system, to Preston, as close to a model of the new system as any county prison, to Salford, reformed but embodying all the abuses of the old system—corrupt, crowded and brutal—to Kirkdale, brand-new but nearly ungoverned.

The overall character of these institutions was determined chiefly by three factors: the nature and number of their inmates, the quality of their staff, and the extent of their day-to-day administrative supervision. English prison staffs were comparatively small, and interference by overseers like the justices or the inspectors was comparatively infrequent, so even after the Age of Reform had broken the autonomy of prisoners, the general character of the inmates and of the culture they brought with them into the prison determined many facets of daily life, such as the extent of violence. The level of serious violence in nineteenth-century English prisons was comparatively low because most of the prisoners were not violent and had not been committed for serious, violent offenses—and because mid-nineteenth-century England was a comparatively nonviolent society.

The prison administrators had little control over the character of the inmates, but they exercised some indirect control over their numbers. Though the question of prosecution rates is at the edge of this study, the size of prison populations was a critical element in the quality of prison life. Even more important, however, was the direct control that administrators exercised over the quality of the prison staff, and particularly over the governor. The choice of governor was the single most important decision that could consciously be made in prison affairs, and one made even more significant by prison reform. Eighteenth-century reformers emphasized the need to choose good gaolers, and success in this area was far more important for the realization of their ambitions than were the disciplinary codes they drew up or the buildings they created. While Lancashire's records do not reveal how gaolers were chosen, they do, as this book shows, reveal how the character of particular gaolers affected their prisons. In many ways prison reform made controlling the behavior of the gaoler even more difficult than it had been before.

Unlike Foucault and other radical authors, I do not see the proliferation of institutions in the modern period as in itself a matter for concern. Institutions unavoidably circumscribe freedom, but so do many other dispositions; a cruel "foster family" may be as confining as stone walls and iron bars for the involuntary resident. Though the quality of a prison's food, shelter, and medical care is important, the overall quality of prison life and of the penal system in general depends far more on humane administration than on the adoption of any particular scheme for reform.

Nevertheless, Foucault and Ignatieff are correct in maintaining that the "reformative" prison of the nineteenth century survived despite its complete failure to fulfill its ostensible goal of rehabilitation. Nothing can force people to reform. They can change, but only if they themselves wish to. We can sometimes make it to their advantage to change, or remove barriers in the way of change, but no kindly counseling or carceral "archipelago" can produce true conversion. Most prisoners do indeed reform, because most wish to. John Clay found that about two-thirds of his prisoners did not return to gaol within a reasonable period; today, after a further century and a half of constant dedicated effort, in almost any prison about two-thirds of a typical assortment of prisoners will not return. Certain sorts of offenders may have a higher or lower propensity to repeat their offense, but there is no evidence that any system, any program, any effort, will change the propensity of any given offender to return by more than a marginal amount. Reformation and "rehabilitation" can take place—indeed, they take place more often than not—but it is beyond our power to impose them, as it was beyond the power of earlier reformers. We cannot wrest grace from providence.

Like their inmates, prisons have a life of their own, and they can also prove to be remarkably resistant to reformation imposed from outside. The history of prison reform is far more complicated than a simple history of ideologies or of the dominance of one class by another could suggest. It is a story of mixed motives, intractable problems, and unintended consequences. The Lancashire prison system, as this book shows, was produced by the interaction of many factors: political events, such as the Luddite disturbances; economic problems, such as the postwar inflation; contemporary preoccupations with such issues as the value of free speech, representative government, and reformative punishment; scientific theories, such as a contagionist model of disease; technical constraints, such as prison architecture; particular personalities, such as individual gaolers; and a shifting balance of power between the people of the county, the justices, the inspectors, the prison staff, and Parliament. It seems likely that a similarly complex interaction characterizes all prison systems and that all prison administrators must juggle with the conflicting demands of limited financial resources, administrative inertia, corruption, political conflict, and recalcitrant inmates—indeed, with all the problems of government in an imperfect world.

CHAPTER I

The Eighteenth-Century Gaol

To most authors of general histories, English prison history begins with John Howard. Before that, despite a few flickering ideas, prisons were sunk in Gothic darkness, ruled by cruelty and corruption. With the exception of Pugh's book on medieval imprisonment and a few recent monographs, many still unpublished, most writing on the subject has dismissed the first millennium of English prison life as a single unchanged and unchanging world of squalor, violence, and disease. The Webbs set the tone by devoting seventeen pages of their history of local prisons to the institutions of the sixteenth, seventeenth, and eighteenth centuries, and a further fourteen pages to the period from 1700 to 1773, under such headings as "filth and stench," "cruelty," "licentiousness," and "public apathy." They concluded that "the state of prisons seemed an evil for which there was no remedy," before turning with relief to "John Howard," "his character," "his journeys," and "his policy."[1]

Several recent works have followed the same pattern. W. L. Burn, in the *Age of Equipoise*—until recently the only widely read general history to examine seriously the subject of prison reform—wrote that "the reforms in the management of prisons ought not, in fairness, to start with Howard," but then devoted only half a sentence to the SPCK and Oglethorpe before returning to Howard.[2] Although Ursula Henriques, in her textbook, *Before the Welfare State*, devotes an entire section to a discussion of prison reform based on recent research, she still closely follows the Webbs, seeing the eighteenth-century gaol as a place of unrelieved squalor, extortion, and endemic gaol fever. She attributes these conditions to the prevalence of the fee system, claiming that "the eighteenth-century collapse in administration was nowhere more apparent than in the management of prisons."[3] In another recent book, Bryan Keith-Lucas, while acknowledging the central place of penal institutions in county budgets, confines himself to emphasizing the "appalling" condition of many gaols, the herding together of prisoners, and the fee system. There is no suggestion that any change took place in the years before Howard.[4]

A few young radical historians have attacked this view on two fronts. First, they show that Howard was by no means unique. Robin Evans's recent monograph provides an extensive account of the intellectual history of prison architecture and of *encellulement* in particular. Michael Ignatieff has emphasized the role of some of Howard's contemporaries, especially Jonas Hanway and the mid-century medical reformers whom Howard knew in London and whose advice on the prevention of gaol fever was the key element in the early reforms.[5]

Second, after identifying a larger group of reformers and conceding that they did bring about substantial changes, these critics have gone on to question the value of those so-called reforms. Gertrude Himmelfarb and several followers have succeeded in depicting Bentham as a greedy, power-hungry, and totalitarian "manipulator." Other historians have portrayed Howard and his "circle" (e.g., Paul, Hanway, Whitbread, and Neild) as bourgeois dissenters who wanted above all to control the lower classes—to bring criminals' behavior into conformity with the sanctimonious dictates of middle-class morality. In doing so they built "total institutions," destroyed the prison community, and created "machines" far less humane than the casual residences they had found. As Rod Morgan recently wrote: "In the eighteenth century the prison was transformed from being a mere container . . . to a carefully planned environment for the moral reconstitution of the convicted and sentenced. If the prison was to deter and reform, prisoners had to be separated from those community influences which had been productive of crime. Prisoners were to be stripped of their social identities, all traces of individuality systematically eradicated, normality suppressed. . . . The reformist vision with which Howard's name has been inextricably linked has . . . been productive of as much cruelty, misery and vice as it prevented."[6]

The logic of this argument should entail a more sympathetic attitude toward the eighteenth-century gaol, but this has in fact been lacking, even though recent monographs in local history have provided material that might sustain such an interpretation.* Local prison administration in the eighteenth century has continued to be largely neglected. In fact, the earlier eighteenth century presents serious difficulties for the radical historians because they tend to accept the radical class-based interpretation of eighteenth-century law advanced by the followers of E. P. Thompson. According to this view, the criminal law of the eighteenth century was wielded by the aristocracy, which used it as a weapon to maintain its power in the countryside.[7] This negative view of the aristocracy that was responsible for local administration has impeded what would otherwise be a natural tendency among those protesting nineteenth-century changes to paint the eighteenth-century gaol in rosy colors. In general, the radicals have accepted the contention of earlier historians that the late eighteenth century marked a radical break from what had gone before, without themselves engaging in the sort of local research that could show what the institutions had been like before they changed or how great the change was.

No one would deny that the Age of Reform saw a significant break with the past, nor that the growth of large residential "total" institutions is an important feature of the modern world. Nevertheless, the argument can be overdone. By neglecting the fact that the unreformed prison has its own history of reform and by concentrating heavily on certain types of sources—particularly those that are national in scope, such as the memoirs of reformers and the *Parliamentary Papers*—historians have distorted if not entirely misdrawn the picture.

First, this approach has exaggerated the problem of the inception of

*See, for example, Eric Stockdale, "John Howard and Bedford Gaol," in John C. Freeman, ed., *Prisons Past and Future* (papers given at the Howard Bicentenary Conference; London, 1978), pp. 15-24: "It would . . . be a mistake to think that Howard was the first Sheriff to interest himself in the prison building itself. . . . Various minor modifications and improvements had been made in earlier years [and] many sick prisoners received a degree of sympathetic consideration from the magistrates. There are many references to extra food being provided for such prisoners. . . . The documents relating to the appointment of the gaoler are relatively few, but they demonstrate once again that the gaol was important in the community; and that the identity of the man appointed and his qualifications for office were matters of concern to magistrates and other citizens, as well as to the High Sheriff himself" (pp. 19-21). See also Wayne Joseph Sheehan, "The London Prison System, 1666-1795" (Ph.D. dissertation, University of Maryland, 1975); Robin Evans, "A Rational Plan for Softening the Mind: Prison Design, 1750-1842" (Ph.D. dissertation, University of Essex, 1975).

Information on the major manuscript collections and parliamentary papers consulted by the author, together with the abbreviations used in citing documents, can be found in Document Sources, pp. 255-59. For dating, see p. 231.

reform in the late eighteenth century. Jennifer Hart's question—Why did abuses suddenly appear "intolerable" to certain groups in the early nineteenth century?—becomes especially difficult to answer if one begins by assuming that these abuses had existed and been widely tolerated for many centuries.[8] The events associated with the Industrial Revolution obviously affected the severity of the problems involved, yet that fact does not explain the emergence of a wholly new sensitivity to social problems among some members of local elites. To explain that sensitivity, as Ursula Henriques has conceded, one must turn to such "special circumstances" as personal suffering, a "violent shock to the consciousness," and "participation in a conflicting sub-culture." In addition, she hypothesizes a complete change in culture, from a "traditional" to a "forward-looking" outlook within the nation at large.[9]

The problem becomes less severe if it can be shown that by the end of the eighteenth century a well-established tradition of social concern and of responsible and relatively humane administration already existed. In that case, one might assume that exceptional situations, such as the size of London or the rise of a market economy, could have caused a breakdown in the administrative system and eventually necessitated drastic new solutions, without any sudden and independent change in culture, consciousness, or sense of responsibility among the landed gentry. This hypothesis accords more closely with what we know of the best-documented branch of local administration, the Poor Laws. In that area a tradition of relatively humane administration continued throughout the eighteenth century—including the "Speenhamland years"—before it began to disintegrate and was replaced by the stringencies of the New Poor Law. For both prisons and Poor Laws, by the early nineteenth century a new response had emerged that included a new reliance on large institutions—but this response did not necessarily require a sudden and unprecedented sensitivity to the problems themselves.

A second and related effect of the distorted view of prison reform is that it has led historians to place an undue emphasis on the thoughts and activities of "middle-class" reformers, and on their London-based pressure groups. This bias is shared by the traditional writers and the radicals, for whom it fits neatly into a class-based theory of social control. To quote Ursula Henriques again: "Most reforms were pre-empted by middle-class activists," who were "members of middle-class minority groups."[10]

This approach has led to the neglect of the institutions of local, particularly county, government, in which "middle-class" and largely urban "minority group" reformers played a small part. (Evangelicals in particular are notable only for their complete absence from any role in Lancashire prison reform during the entire period covered by this study.) This approach has also led to an implicit but bewildering discontinuity in the radical argument, by which that well-entrenched landed aristocracy that had been manipulating the legal system with such success suddenly and inexplicably disappears, to be replaced—both in its concern for social control and in its ability to manipulate the system—by an urban bourgeoisie. In fact, throughout the early nineteenth century it was the aristocratic, Anglican, and often Tory county bench that bore the responsibility for running the prisons and for implementing any reforms. An understanding of the attitude, problems, and administrative traditions of the eighteenth-century bench, therefore, is vital to an understanding of the implementation of reforms in the Howardian period. It can, moreover, provide an element of continuity lacking in most historical accounts.

This chapter will examine some of these administrative traditions to see what effect they had on prison life. Did the justices, in fact, simply abandon prisoners to the tender mercies of cruel and extortionate gaolers, to die of disease, neglect, and starvation? Or were prisons administered along the lines of the old Poor Law: often rough, capricious, and inadequate but offering real safeguards in a dangerous and unreliable world? Did the unreformed prison remain forever unchanged?

Prisons and County Government

Lancashire is one of England's largest and most remote counties. Because of its great size the county was divided into six hundreds: West Derby (which included Liverpool), Amonderness (which included Preston), Salford (which included Manchester and several other large textile towns), Leyland, Blackburn, and Lonsdale (which included Lancaster, the county town). These hundreds were further divided into divisions, each with its own high constable. The divisions were split into parishes, and, because Lancashire parishes also tended to be very large, the parishes were further subdivided into townships, the basic unit of county administration.

The Lancashire justices, like their colleagues in Yorkshire, had evolved a system to deal with the county's large size. The Quarter Sessions, the chief judicial and administrative body, met every quarter at

Lancaster and then followed a fixed series of adjournments to Preston, to Ormskirk or Wigan, and to Manchester. Each adjournment administered the business of its own hundreds and was usually, although not invariably, attended by its own set of justices. Unless a special adjournment was called in an emergency, there were, therefore, sixteen Quarter Sessions meetings each year. The names of each quarter's session varied somewhat; I have reduced this to four standard seasonal names: Easter, Trinity, Michaelmas, and Epiphany.

At the beginning of the eighteenth century, Lancashire was a very poor county; isolated and lawless, it was distinguished by a long history of rebellion and recusancy. The county contained a great variety of terrains, but much of the countryside was rough and hilly, making communication difficult. Agriculture was inefficient and unproductive. For centuries one of the poorest and most backward counties in England, and then, suddenly, one of the most developed, wealthy, and densely populated, Lancashire cannot claim to be "typical." It can, however, claim to be entirely different from London, the source of most of our information on prisons, and to be important in its own right. By the middle of the nineteenth century its municipal and county prisons contained nearly one-fifth of all the prisoners in England and Wales. Its four county prisons were among the largest in the country. The criminal classes of Manchester, Liverpool, and the smaller textile towns were attracting national attention—as were the methods used in the county prisons to deter and, it was hoped, to "reform" criminals. Moreover, from the time of the Industrial Revolution, Lancashire experienced in magnified form all the difficulties and dislocations caused by industrial development. It thus provides a graphic example of problems that the rest of England would confront more gradually.*

Prisons appeared before justices and Sessions. They are among the oldest local institutions in England, going back to Anglo-Saxon times. By the later Middle Ages there were many different sorts of prisons, corresponding roughly to the large number of different courts entitled to use imprisonment as a sanction. The county gaols may be seen as a product of the Norman legal system: they were used by the king's judges for breaches of the king's law. The king's civil representative in the county,

---

*The only municipal prison of any significance in Lancashire during this period was the Liverpool borough gaol. For some time after its incorporation, Manchester sent its borough prisoners to the New Bailey under contract. Municipal prisons and local police or village lockups are not considered in this study.

the sheriff, was responsible for the gaols' administration; justices of the peace had little legal authority in prison affairs. It was the sheriff who, legally, acted as gaoler, appointed prison officers, had custody of the prisoners, was responsible for bail and escapes, and answered for any breaches of discipline.

The sheriff's jurisdiction, an artifact of the system's antiquity, was unfortunate. After 1340, sheriffs held office for only one year; after 1377, they could be reappointed only after the lapse of three years. The result was that sheriffs had little opportunity to become familiar with their responsibilities and lacked the experience to administer prisons effectively. Ordinarily, they appointed a deputy to act as the real gaoler, sometimes paying him a salary. But since each sheriff could appoint whom he pleased, the gaoler's tenure of office was insecure, and the practice of bribing successive sheriffs to retain the office became common, although it was strictly prohibited by law.[11]

As justices of the peace took on more responsibility for the financial, legal, and civil administration of the counties, the sheriff increasingly became a figurehead, with little interest in day-to-day duties. He continued to be responsible for the collection of certain revenues due the Crown and for certain expenditures, including the building of gaols, the maintenance of condemned prisoners awaiting transportation or execution, and the costs of execution. Occasionally, conscientious sheriffs such as John Howard and John Wilkes took a serious interest in the prisons under their charge, but these men seem to have been exceptional.

Despite the erosion of the sheriff's role, one important shrieval institution survived in Lancashire long after it had disappeared from other counties. This was the Sheriff's Court or Tourn, known in Lancashire as the Sheriff's Board, a local parliament attended by county dignitaries in town for the Assizes. The justices used this body to make joint decisions that would be binding on all the adjourned sessions. In the late seventeenth and early eighteenth centuries this was the chief administrative body of the county; unfortunately, most of its records for this period have been lost.[12]

One other person also exercised important authority over prison administration, although he possessed few official powers. This was the Assize judge. The judge made twice-yearly circuits to "deliver" the county gaol; unlike the justices, who often sent prisoners to the houses of correction, he committed to the gaol alone. When the county prison required major renovation, a grand jury "presented" the gaol to the judge at Assizes. The judges felt a proprietary interest in the gaols and successfully intervened in their management. Long before the nineteenth-century act that empowered them to review the legality of prison regulations made by the justices, judges in open court were hearing the complaints of prisoners about their accommodations and demanding that conditions be improved.[13]

Nevertheless, by the eighteenth century the justices were the real rulers of the counties. Whether or not they had a legal mandate in prison affairs, they were the only group in a position to exercise authority over prison management on a regular basis. It was the justices who committed offenders to gaol to await trial, and it was the justices who levied the county rates. The evidence shows that by the eighteenth century they were prepared to intervene in a wide range of prison problems.

Until the late eighteenth century, the main use of imprisonment was to hold persons who might be needed for trial. Laws permitting courts to use it as a penalty in itself dated as far back as the Middle Ages, but its expense always discouraged its use. Although many petty offenders found themselves in gaol because they could not or would not pay fines, debts, or recognizances, imprisonment as an initial penalty in criminal cases was usually reserved for serious offenders whom the government was reluctant to execute: the powerful who had committed political offenses, the knowing who might betray others under pressure, and the religious, who might be considered martyrs. Most prisoners, however, were awaiting some event rather than serving fixed terms.

Over the years, a large body of statute law, common law, ordinance, and custom had grown up to protect prisoners from extortion, cruelty, and neglect. On the whole, these laws defined the rights of prisoners rather than prescribed the conduct of the gaoler. Instead of providing for the supervision of administrators, the laws granted prisoners rights to redress in the courts and rewards for successful prosecution. Most important were the attempts to control extortion. Though some gaolers received salaries, most of their income came from fees. A long series of statutes set strict limits on admission fees, though gaolers were free to provide extra goods and services at any price they chose. Municipal corporations, such as Coventry and Bristol, sometimes issued special regulations fixing the prices of commodities for sale in the prison and requiring good conduct from the gaoler. The London prisons were regulated especially closely; in the late seventeenth century zealous aldermen went so far as to prohibit unauthorized female visitors, misbehavior in chapel, gambling, and drinking.[14]

Tudor legislation permitted justices of the peace to collect rates for building gaols and to provide financial support for prisoners. Especially important was the legislation passed under Edward VI that for the first time created separate institutions for penal incarceration after conviction.[15] The new houses of correction (Lancashire's were erected by the early seventeenth century) were intended to serve as real prisons in the modern sense of the word: places for the deterrence, punishment, and rehabilitation of inmates after trial. While the distinction between gaols and houses of correction was not observed in practice, it is important to note that the houses of correction were under the superintendence of the justices, not of the sheriffs. Historians who speak of "prisons" run by irresponsible fee-taking gaolers are entirely neglecting those institutions that were actually intended for post-trial custody. In this context the relaxed regime of the gaols that were intended to provide pre-trial detention is more understandable.

In Lancashire, geography frustrated the intent of this legislation; it was so expensive and time-consuming to arrest, convey, and prosecute petty offenders that rural townships seldom considered compliance worthwhile. The distance between the houses at Preston and Manchester and the gaol at Lancaster led Lancashire's justices to commit to the nearest institution whenever legally possible, thus blurring the distinction between them. The county houses of correction remained very small until the nearby population exploded in the late eighteenth century.[16]

There is evidence that prison conditions deteriorated in the later seventeenth century, leaving some inmates to face starvation unassisted either by the abundant private charity of the Middle Ages or the experimental public support of the Tudors. There is also evidence of corruption and of political jobbery in prison administration, paralleling a similar degeneration in national and local government. Nevertheless, this period also saw a national effort to improve prison conditions, including new legislation, new financing, and new building. Probably the most important achievement of the Restoration period was the act of 1670 that established a procedure for the release of insolvent debtors and that protected imprisoned debtors from extortion and contact with felons.[17]

In the few counties that have been studied, such as Oxfordshire, Yorkshire, and Lancashire, the last two decades of the century saw a flood of petitions from prisoners, suggesting a decline in conditions, a raising of expectations, or a change of administrative procedures. Possibly all three were involved. In Lancashire, the hard years that came at the end of the century increased the strain on the gaol, resulting in complaints and outbreaks of sickness. But this period also saw a slow but steady and, ultimately, successful effort by the justices to bring the situation under control.

The Buildings

By the end of the seventeenth century, all three of Lancashire's county institutions were well established. During the Civil War, Lancaster Castle was occupied and damaged, but most of its medieval towers, joined by the curtain wall in a rough ring around the keep, survived. The Quaker leader George Fox, imprisoned in the Castle in the late seventeenth century, complained about conditions there to the Assize judge, who ordered that extensive repairs be made.[18] The Dungeon Tower was torn down during construction of a women's prison in the early nineteenth century, but most of the rest of the Castle, including the curtain wall, keep, well tower, court complex, gatehouse, and one other ancient round tower, still stands. As a prison, the Castle had serious deficiencies. Parts were extremely old. Moreover, it had not been intended for the custody of miscreants, and its rambling design made the separation of prisoners difficult, security fragile, and supervision almost impossible. With their small deep windows (in the case of the lower cells, no windows at all) and their stone-flagged floors, the cells could be cold, dark, and uncomfortable. Few of the rooms had originally possessed fireplaces.[19]

By the standards of London prisons of the same time, however, Lancaster had many advantages. By 1703, after extensive repair work, only one debtors' room in the Castle lacked a fireplace. Overcrowding in the 1720's led to further complaints by the debtors about smoky chimneys, the housing of prisoners in rooms without fireplaces, and leaking roofs, but these problems were rapidly repaired by the justices. Moreover, the Castle could claim a large and attractive courtyard, a clean water supply from its own wells, and many large rooms. The worst off were the penniless convicted felons; they were often lodged in subterranean rooms under the Dungeon and Well towers that were large and dry but unheated, unventilated, and windowless.

The history of the Salford house of correction is obscure, partly because its administration was largely left to the Salford justices while the other three sessions decided jointly on any changes made at Preston. The bridewell opened in Manchester in 1657, but the building itself may have served as a prison for recusants in the sixteenth century. A surviving picture shows a small house with a pitched roof and cells overlooking the street. From the windows of these, inmates lower bags to passersby for charity. The house and its outbuildings received extensive repairs in 1700, 1720, 1746-47, and 1757. It was completely rebuilt once more in 1774.[20] John Howard visited Manchester shortly after this last transformation and described it as follows: "Separate Court-yards and Apartments for Men and Women. The former have Work-rooms, over which are Chambers. Their Night-rooms or Dungeons, in a passage or long room forty-five feet by six are close; eleven feet by eight; eleven steps below the yard; but not properly under ground being on the declivity of a hill. —Women have three rooms on the ground-floor, and three chambers: here is also a dungeon, down nine steps, fourteen feet by thirteen; but women are not put there."[21]

Preston's history is a little clearer. Located a little out of town on the banks of the Ribble, it had been a convent of the Grey Friars until the dissolution of the monasteries. In 1618, after years of steady pressure from the government, the Lancashire justices finally agreed to purchase this property for the county house of correction. They appropriated £700 for erecting and finishing the house and for furnishing it with working implements and gardens.[22] Like Manchester, Preston underwent major renovation in the 1740's. Expenditures of £40 or more are also recorded in 1724, 1762, 1768, 1772, and 1774, and at frequent intervals thereafter. Howard wrote that no water was available to prisoners, although there is evidence of a pump in earlier years. He found a large room on the ground floor, "in which are eleven Closets, called *Boxes*, to sleep in; and another Room, the Dungeon." Above it was a large workroom for the men and a smaller one for the women. All the rooms were dirty at the time of his visit and the prison was in disrepair.[23]

The frequency of repairs at all three of these institutions makes it clear that the eighteenth-century justices did not neglect them. Although the keeper was responsible for minor repairs, Quarter Sessions frequently raised money for improvements. For example, the justices ordered the collection of rolls for more than £5 for repairs at the Castle twenty-eight times between 1704 and 1769. These rolls were often for more than £100.[24]

The comfort of prisoners, however, depended as much on the quality of the original buildings as on the frequency of repairs. On the whole, prisoners in the Castle were fortunate, although the felons must frequently have been wretched. Preston, however, despite frequent repairs, was probably uncomfortable from the beginning. With only four rooms, it was ill equipped for any significant expansion in the number of prisoners. There can be no question that the bridewells needed attention even more urgently than the gaols.

Prison Life

Since the raison d'être of the gaols was to restrict the liberty of their inmates, the first question for a study of prison life is the extent to which prisoners were confined. Some so-called prisoners were not imprisoned at all, or were frequently let out. While "imprisoned" in the Castle in the late seventeenth century, the Quaker Roger Haydock visited churches in Westmoreland and attended two debates in Cheshire.[25] Roger Kenyon, the clerk of the peace, admitted to the Earl of Derby in 1683 that of sixteen Quaker and Catholic prisoners officially in the Castle, eleven were lodging elsewhere.[26]

Prisoners of conscience, who were rare after 1700, were not the only ones to gain a measure of liberty. Some debtors enjoyed a similar freedom. In London the practice of freeing debtors for a fee became well established; in Lancashire ordinary debtors normally remained within the Castle walls, but late-seventeenth-century evidence suggests that the many mesne-process debtors were allowed the liberty of the town and could even work outside the gaol. (These were people arrested on mesne process for failing to provide bail for their appearance at the hearing that would officially establish their debt. Until this hearing was held, they were not "in execution.") Thomas Fell, a perennial and irascible prisoner, complained to Quarter Sessions in 1693 that debtors working in the town were coming up to the Castle on Saturday morning and collecting prison allowances.*

---

*For a more detailed description of arrest on mesne process, see Wayne Joseph Sheehan, "The London Prison System, 1666-1795" (Ph.D. dissertation, University of Maryland, 1975), pp. 7-8, and the *House of Commons Journals* 47 (1792): 640-52. See also LCRO, QSP, Lanc. M 1693, no. 15. Thomas Fell was imprisoned in 1692 and could not gain release because he refused to make his property over to his creditors and was, therefore, not insolvent. In 1693 he applied for an allowance of 3s. per week, stating that the entire income from his estate was going to his creditors. He was refused, but received an allowance in 1702. He died in the Castle in 1722. He may be the same man as the Thomas Fell, yeoman, of Aughton (near Hindpull) who was presented in 1687 for riotous assembly and for throwing a man into the river Lune.

Lax or venal keepers of the houses of correction may also have granted some liberty, although the justices did not approve. One of the terms imposed on the keeper when the Preston house first opened was that the master would see that "the prisoners goe not abroade to the charge or trouble of the towne or cuntrie where they are, or to converse abroade or have anie meetings but to bee kept close to their worke."[27] Among the articles against the corrupt keeper of Preston in 1703 was one complaining that he had allowed some prisoners to escape without pursuit and "others to goe abroad at their free will and pleasure."[28] A prisoner supposedly confined in Salford witnessed a murder in another house in 1749.[29]

Though keepers may have been rather lax from time to time, gaolers could not afford to allow convicted felons or debtors in execution to escape. Escapes did take place at rare intervals, but they were attended with very high penalties for the gaoler, particularly if the fugitive was not recaptured. Lancashire's most corrupt gaoler, John Ellitson, allowed at least five prisoners to escape. At least one, Robert Arrowsmith, was recaptured and punished by being chained to a post during the day.[30]

The mid-century gaoler Edward Styth also suffered an escape. A group of debtors had sued for release under an insolvency act and had been granted their discharge in court when a technicality came up about the indemnification of the sheriff against actions of escape by creditors. When the Quarter Sessions refused to free the debtors, a group of them broke prison. All but two were recaptured, but Styth found it necessary to post an armed guard around the gaol for six months, "the Debtors being very Riotous having knocked down the Turn Key and threatening to Murder him and the Gaoler and to make their Escapes apprehending they were detained there Contrary to the sence of the Legislator."[31]

To prevent escapes and to identify prisoners for the guards, felons were usually placed in irons, although a wealthy criminal could avoid irons by paying a fee to compensate the gaoler for the greater risk. Critics of eighteenth-century prisons maintain that gaolers often loaded new prisoners with especially heavy fetters in order to extort greater fees. John Ellitson did attempt this, but he was clearly an exceptionally cruel and extortionate gaoler. After Ellitson's reign, no complaints on this issue have been found; in fact, there are few complaints of any sort of extortion. Judging from the prisoners' readiness to petition about other matters, it seems likely either that gaolers were not in fact ironing prisoners unreasonably or that the practice was so widely accepted that no one thought to complain. Ordinary ironing was both practiced and accepted; to this day the popular image of the convict endows him with a ball and chain.

Despite public acceptance of irons and the real need for them, they were unpleasant and sometimes dangerous to the wearer. Gaolers knew this well. Heavy fetters impeded movement, although prisoners managed to shuffle around with the chain held up by a string under their clothes. More important, if the irons were too tight or too heavy they could cut off circulation and cause severe swelling, "mortification" (gangrene), loss of a limb, and even death. At the end of the century, partly through the efforts of a liberal gaoler, John Higgin, the Castle became one of the first prisons in England to abandon the use of irons except as a combined punishment and safety measure for recaptured escapees. Higgin believed that ironing could produce "conduct which I could not effect by solitary confinement" among refractory prisoners, but he also went to some length and considerable risk to avoid fettering the insane.[32]

Little evidence has survived about the general health of prisoners in this period. In the late seventeenth century, when the gaols were crowded, times hard, and conditions poor, mention of sickness and epidemic disease is common. In the hard year of 1699, forty debtors who had been imprisoned for two years or more petitioned the Wigan Sessions. Many debtors, they claimed, had starved to death despite "the charities of many honourable persons," and many were now suffering from "a strange disease which immediately deprives them of theire reason amd sences, noe other reason whereoff can be given but theire unwholesome fare and bad lodging." Only the kindness of their gaoler, Henry Bracken, had prevented the "contagious distempers" from spreading even further. The parish register records an unusually high number of deaths among prisoners for that year.[33]

This is the last reference to epidemic disease in the Lancashire records until 1775, when the Lancaster Sessions ordered a special payment to a local apothecary who had saved the lives and restored the health of several prisoners.[34] Although there was some increase of disease in the 1720's, Lancaster apparently survived the first three-quarters of the eighteenth century without experiencing a serious epidemic. Though there were occasional and usually well-publicized epidemics in other eighteenth-century gaols, it seems likely that the picture of fever-ridden gaols beset with epidemic typhus has been overdrawn. It was at the end of the century, when serious overcrowding accompanied an increase in the number of long imprisonments and a fall in the value of allowances, that the problem became severe.* Prisoner deaths were usually noted in the register of the parish of St. Mary's, which included the Castle. Use of this source is open to technical objections, but it does provide a rough estimate of the absolute numbers dying during a period about which other information is lacking. The number of deaths is remarkably steady: in only eight years of the eighteenth century did more than five Castle prisoners die (not counting wives, children, and staff). Excluding 1715—when the Castle was filled with wounded "rebels," eleven of whom died—in only two years, 1728 and 1729, did more than ten prisoners die. According to the registers, an average of 2.36 prisoners died per year between 1690 and 1755, and an average of 1.88 between 1756 and 1820. A little more than three persons of all sorts residing in the Castle died annually between 1691 and 1755. This rate fell to a little more than two from 1756 to 1820.[35]

For those confined within its walls, life in the Castle bore a closer resemblance to that in an unreformed university than it did to a modern prison. The educational metaphor was frequently used for prisons, which were called "schools," "seminaries," and "colleges" of crime. The similarity did not lie only in the educational opportunities offered by each. Lancaster and many other gaols resembled colleges in physical layout, demography, controls on entry, and social customs. Lancaster was a residential building constructed around a central courtyard with a gatehouse, open at certain set hours, through which visitors had to pass. Its residents were largely young men, though a number of prisoners' families were permitted to live within the walls; of those listed in the parish registers as dying within the Castle, about one in six was not a prisoner. Gaols, of course, also contained female prisoners, whose numbers rose considerably toward the end of the eighteenth century; we do not know to what extent they were separated from the men before the Age of Reform.

---

*Joanna Innes has found evidence of several outbreaks of gaol fever in the eighteenth century in other provincial prisons, as have I. In many cases, however, these were due to exceptional circumstances, particularly to sudden overcrowding. There is no evidence that typhus epidemics were common. Mr. Sheehan has informed me that he has found a similar shortage of epidemics in the London prisons during most of the century (with the obvious exception of the notorious Newgate epidemic). Even a hundred documented instances of gaol fever in the eighteenth century would mean that any particular prison was likely to see only one outbreak in the course of the century. For the rising incidence after 1770, see below.

Some of the inhabitants acted as servitors for their wealthier companions. A small shop and a tap provided popular gathering-places for men whose social life was otherwise restricted, as well as a lucrative source of income for the gaoler. The prisoners dined together and shared common rooms, enlivening the monotony of viewing the same faces day after day by indulging in regular banquets and celebrations at night, and by playing games such as skittles, bowls, and draughts during the day. Some men took well to this institutional life while others hated it, but it had not been designed to be unpleasant.

Life in the eighteenth-century gaol, therefore, had many compensations lacking in the nineteenth-century prison—although debtors continued to enjoy great license long after the lives of other inmates had been more closely regulated. Nevertheless, the prison life of the period had its darker side. The Castle was always haunted by a handful of poor prisoners who had been convicted and sentenced to death, a penalty often commuted to transportation. While a rich felon could obtain a fair degree of comfort, those who could not afford extra fees slept on straw on the lower floors of the Dungeon and Well towers. Even the most optimistic account must note the description provided by one of Higgin's descendants, who wrote that the crowded Dungeon cells became so hot and were filled with "noxious exhalations so deadly" that the turnkeys each morning would leave the doors open for some time before they dared to enter.[36]

Though the communal nature of prison life offered important benefits to prisoners, it also had its drawbacks. The herding together of all sorts of prisoners without supervision was perhaps preferable to solitary confinement, but it created its own difficulties. By law, the gaoler had to provide debtors and criminals with separate sleeping quarters; though this provision seems to have been better enforced in the eighteenth century than it had been at the end of the seventeenth, felons and debtors continued to mix by day. Among them were the insane and the "weak-minded." Upon occasion these people could present a danger to their companions, and the more harmless ones were sometimes teased unmercifully.

Although drunken brawls were common in the Castle, evidence of systematic victimization is rare. In 1693 Thomas Fell complained that a prisoner acting as warder had maliciously beaten him "with un-Reasonabell bllowes," but the court rejected his complaint.[37] In 1703 another prisoner complained that his chambermates had pushed and threatened him for refusing to subscribe to an "unjust and unreasonable" information against the gaoler when the justices came to inquire into his conduct.[38] Life-threatening assaults seem to have been comparatively rare, but when a nineteenth-century parliamentary commission collected evidence on several prisons' experimental separation of prisoners, many witnesses testified that they were relieved to be protected from regular harassment by their fellows. The commission was biased, but there can be no question that constant, unavoidable, and unsupervised contact between prisoners was a mixed blessing.

The prison was not, or not always, a Hobbesian jungle, however. Ample evidence survives of strong and well-organized prisoner self-government in London; it seems likely that similar organizations existed in the larger provincial prisons, especially among the debtors. The earliest evidence of such a system in Lancashire appears in a rule book compiled shortly after 1772. Most of the rules themselves were, apparently, somewhat older. Ironically, the greatest part of the book is concerned with the establishment of an orderly mechanism for enabling debtors to collect debts owed to them by their fellows, including provisions for distraint and for the auction of belongings.[39]

According to this book, all the debtors met in a monthly "court" to hear cases and settle their accounts. Every three months the majority elected a constable and a judge. A sheriff, selected by "juniority," empaneled a jury who could hear cases of debt up to £5 and punish minor offenses. The court paid the constable either 2s. 6d. or 3s. a month, and also employed a person to fetch letters from town at 3s. a month. A "clerk" was permitted to charge fees for copying out "court" writs and for furnishing a copy of the orders that debtors needed the justices to sign in order to obtain allowances. Debtors could also hire court-approved counsel for 6d.

The court collected 7s. 2d. in "garnish" (a traditional entrance fee) from every new debtor. If the debtor refused to pay, it could collect the money by distraint. The 2d. went to the clerk, and 1s. went to ale. The rest of the money went to the court, which paid all its own expenses and salaries and distributed whatever remained equally to all the debtors except to any women, who paid half as much garnish and received a comparable proportion in return. The court also provided newspapers and a copy of Burn's *Justice of the Peace* for debtors to use. It punished infractions, including petty theft; fouling of the pump area, bowling green, or privy; drinking with Crown prisoners; emptying chamber pots out of windows; "abusing, aspersing or vilifying" another debtor; and swearing. Merchants from the town and Crown prisoners were allowed to plead cases by proxy. Finally, the court oversaw the organization of the chambers, ruling that members of each chamber were to subscribe jointly for fuel, that each chamber might collect a 1s. entrance fee after a trial period of three nights, and that the foreman of the jury and the constable were to examine each room for cleanliness once a month.

A petition of 1704, in a hand resembling that of Thomas Fell, suggests that this formal system of debtor self-government extended back at least to the beginning of the century. It complains that prison officers had appropriated the garnish money of 2s. 4d. a head and requests that it be returned to "such Constabell as the debtters in Lancaster Castell shall Apoynt According to the Ansshent Costoms."[40]

Prisoners also helped each other in informal ways. In 1737 the Quarter Sessions, apparently inadvertently, cut off the allowances of a number of "poor, necessitous" prisoners. According to a subsequent court order, these men "must inevitably have starved" without charity from the citizens of the town. Elizabeth Dickenson, the wife of one of the starving debtors, however, managed to find 2s. 3½d. to buy porridge, oatcakes, cheese, and small beer for Thomas Waring, a lunatic Crown prisoner whose allowance had been reduced. The justices later repaid her.[41] Another well-intentioned prisoner was Samuel Short, a gentleman debtor who, like the vicar of Wakefield, read the services of the *Book of Common Prayer* to his fellow prisoners on Sunday mornings and evenings. On two occasions Quarter Sessions noted its approval and voted him 40s. as a reward.[42]

It was not just the world within the walls that provided support for prisoners. The community outside was vital to their existence. Although most prisoners could not leave the gaol, a constant stream of townspeople wandered back and forth through its gates. The wives and children of debtors were free to come and go during the day. Debtors under mesne process also walked around the town or saw friends, creditors, and attorneys within the Castle. Many debtors worked in the gaol and were visited by employers, suppliers, and potential customers. Tradesmen came in seeking customers, delivering food and drink, and bringing supplies to the prison market, the tap, and the gaoler's house. Family and friends of the prisoners came, bringing with them small comforts.

The prison provided employment for the inhabitants of the town, while many prisoners relied on the town's charity. The Castle employed artisans such as masons, blacksmiths, glaziers, roofers, and carpenters as well as permanent staff such as night guards. It was the Castle that brought the Assizes to Lancaster, providing income for innkeepers, taverners, stablers, and anyone with a spare room to rent; for lawyers, solicitors, and clerks; and even for the tailors, dressmakers, milliners, and dealers in luxury goods who traded with the wives and daughters of gentlemen attracted by the festivities of Assize week. During the rest of the year townspeople could gain a small income by renting beds and furnishings to prisoners and by lodging and feeding their families and friends.*

In return, the townspeople gave charity to impoverished prisoners. Their help was particularly important when a financial emergency arose, since prisoners often had to wait until the next Quarter Session to remedy a mistake, enforce payment of overdue allowances, or gain consideration for special problems. Crown prisoners took turns begging in the town, while the charity box at the entrance to the Castle provided those permitted to beg at the grating with a fairly regular income. In addition there were charitable gifts and bequests; in 1770 debtors received £22 15s. annually from endowments.[43]

Under the act of 1670, debtors had the right to purchase food and drink from the town. This prevented the gaoler from enjoying a monopoly that would enable him to charge extortionate prices. Debtors knew their rights, valued them, and were quick to complain when they were infringed. In 1711 they complained to Quarter Sessions about a prisoner serving as turnkey who had interfered with their access to goods from the town and had charged fees to visitors, apparently against the gaoler's orders. When Quarter Sessions rejected their petition, they persevered and obtained a true bill at the Assizes; the final outcome is unknown. Debtors submitted a similar petition against a turnkey in 1748. Gaolers disliked the constant admission of goods, since the open gate was an obvious hazard to security, but they had little choice.[44]

The greatest advantage of this continuous coming and going from prison lay in the measure of protection it gave prisoners from systematic brutality or extortion. The justices of the peace, their clerk, and various officers of the court frequently visited the Castle on business, while most

---

*Joanna Innes has pointed out that the Assizes were not necessarily held in the same town as the county gaol. Nevertheless, this was by far the most common arrangement and in Lancashire was almost necessitated by rough terrain. When the south part of the county built a new prison in the nineteenth century, a new Assize soon followed.

inmates of the prison had family, friends, or associates in the town who could be counted on to protest any flagrant ill-treatment. That brutality occurred then as now there can be no question, but the openness of the prison made it more difficult for the gaoler to engage in actions of which the community disapproved.

Gaolers and Keepers

In the introduction to *State of the Prisons*, Howard wrote that he had originally begun visiting prisons in the hope of finding a precedent for paying gaolers salaries instead of permitting them to collect fees and profits from a prison tap. Following Howard's lead, prison historians have often emphasized the venality and corruption of the eighteenth-century gaoler and have suggested that the substitution of salaries for fees was one of the most important reforms of the late eighteenth century. The Webbs, for example, wrote that

So long as the keeper of the gaol was permitted to make a profit out of the prisoners committed to his charge, it was quite impracticable to secure conditions of health or decency, or even of common humanity. . . . The absence of an adequate salary and the opportunities for exaction had attracted to the office of gaoler, as was bitterly remarked, none but "low-bred, mercenary and oppressive, barbarous fellows, who think of nothing but enriching themselves by the most cruel extortion, and who have less regard for the life of a poor prisoner than for the life of a brute."[45]

This contention, however, is open to challenge. Wayne Joseph Sheehan's recent research on London gaols has shown that, though gaolers were very corrupt in the late seventeenth and early eighteenth centuries, a period of reform occurred between 1729 and 1732, and for the rest of the century the City aldermen succeeded in appointing gaolers who were generally honest, competent, and humane. "There are enough tributes to their good behavior and humanity," Sheehan comments, "to suggest that the popular stereotype of the cruel and oppressive gaoler no longer applied to the City keepers. Surely, the gaolers' improved conduct must rank as the most satisfying transformation in the City prison system during the eighteenth century."[46]

The Lancashire evidence also suggests that, though often venal, county gaolers were rarely cruel or barbarous. An examination of the differences between gaolers and keepers of county houses of correction suggests that the fee system did create serious inconveniences but that payment by salary was by no means the most critical factor in shaping the conduct of prison staff or in bringing about the changes associated with the Age of Reform.

Strictly speaking, the gaoler was the governor of the county gaol alone, while the keeper presided over the house of correction and other institutions such as lockups. In common speech the difference was often ignored. In some counties, the gaol and the house of correction were either under a single roof or near one another; in such places, particularly when the combined prison population was small, one man was often appointed to superintend both.

Even when held by a single man, however, the offices remained quite distinct. The houses of correction were governed entirely by the justices of the peace, who paid for the houses' erection, sentenced offenders to custody, and appointed keepers, fixed their salaries, and dismissed them at will. The justices thus exercised over keepers that complete control that reformers wished to place over gaolers at the end of the century. The county gaol, on the other hand, was still technically the province of the sheriff, who, even in Lancashire, retained the right to appoint its gaoler.

Whereas the keeper was legally entitled to a salary fixed by the justices and collected from the county rates, the gaoler usually maintained himself and his family by collecting fees. Sheriffs could and on occasion did provide salaries—in fact, between 1752 and 1770, sheriffs regularly paid £31 a year to Lancaster gaolers—but they had no power to collect money for that purpose from the ratepayers. Instead, they claimed their expenses directly from the Crown. Even when he received a salary, the gaoler relied on fees for the greater part of his income.

Though the difference in methods of remuneration was accidental, it nevertheless makes sense if the difference between the two prison populations is considered. There were always some gaol prisoners who could afford to pay for luxuries, but most of the inmates of the house of correction had been committed because of their destitution. Vagrants, vagabonds, men unable to support their bastards, and men who had left their families on the parish were almost by definition insolvent, while petty thieves and prostitutes had often turned to crime because of poverty. Moreover, most of the inhabitants of the gaol, in legal theory at least, were not undergoing punishment but merely being kept in a safe place until punishment could be enforced. Inmates of the house of correction were actually supposed to be undergoing "correction": they were not only to support themselves by hard labor but also to lead a spartan life.

Since the comforts that the gaoler supplied at a profit would have under-cut the purpose of the house of correction, the keeper was forbidden to provide them. For example, when the keeper of the Preston house was dismissed for misconduct in 1703, one of the articles against him was "that he does not set to worke Correct or punish such as have been Committed to him but entertains some at his owne table like boarders takeing . . . what he can get from every one."[47]

Since the keeper was expected to augment his income by acting as a taskmaster for his prisoners and since he sometimes continued to own a business, the salary attached to his post was only a part of his total income. At the beginning of the eighteenth century the keeper of Salford received only £14 10s. a year, which was raised in 1732 to £25. This, however, may have been considered a part-time job. The keeper of Preston, who was expected to live in, received £60 a year throughout the century—a relatively generous wage. The gaoler at the Castle, however, earned much more in fees; in 1783 John Higgin estimated his income from fees at £360 a year. During most of the century the gaolership was a very lucrative post.[48]

Because the post of keeper involved constant intimate contact with prisoners as a taskmaster, as well as commercial dealings, a lower level of earnings, and the supervision of a much humbler class of inmates, there was often a distinct difference between the status of the gaoler and that of the keepers. The gaoler of Lancaster was a very important man in the community. He was also, usually, a well-educated one. Bare literacy did not suffice for a position requiring a good deal of legal expertise; the gaoler had to decide whether a great variety of writs, warrants, and releases, particularly those involving actions for debt, were in order. Because of the seriousness of the crimes for which some prisoners were committed to the Castle, the post was a dangerous and responsible one; it was also financially hazardous.

In law, the sheriff, as custodian of the gaol, was responsible to the county for all prisoners within it. If a felon escaped, the sheriff could be fined, and if a debtor escaped, even if for only half an hour, the sheriff was liable to the creditor for the full amount of the debt. Sheriffs passed their responsibilities on to the gaolers by requiring them to sign a bond indemnifying the sheriff against any expenses caused by the gaoler's negligence. By the early nineteenth century, this bond was £10,000. Despair after the escape of a debtor who was being taken to London on a writ of habeas corpus allegedly caused one gaoler to commit suicide. Even before their appointment, therefore, gaolers needed to be, and usually were, well born, well connected, and reasonably well off. Though not aristocrats, they belonged to respectable landed and professional families, while keepers tended to be men of lower social status and to enjoy fewer opportunities for advancement and gain.*

William Tomlinson, the keeper of Preston from 1685 to 1696, had "little estate of his own" but married a widow with £40 a year. He had been a quartermaster in the militia and the deputy bailiff of the Earl of Derby before becoming keeper. His success as a bailiff in dealing with malefactors was one of the reasons for his appointment.[49] Thomas Whitlow, the keeper of Manchester from 1763 to 1790, was a chandler who employed the inmates in spinning wicks. Only one eighteenth-century gaoler (John Birdsworth) and one nineteenth-century keeper (William Liddell) are known to have been publicans, although in Bedfordshire men of this trade monopolized the office. Birdsworth was also the farmer of the vicarage lands. His son-in-law, Henry Bracken, who served briefly as gaoler, was a prominent local physician, educated at Leyden, who became mayor of Lancaster. One nineteenth-century keeper (Liddell) had been a sergeant in the army, while two gaolers (Higgin and Hansbrow) had been captains in the militia.[50] Three gaolers (John Ellitson and the two Higgins) were cousins of justices. Two gaolers founded gentry families, while the Higgins, father and son, inherited the estate of Wood Hey near Bury. John Junior's eldest son, William, became bishop of Limerick and Londonderry, while his third son, also called John, was a successful attorney and the town clerk of Lancaster. Another son, Thomas, who assisted his father but failed to replace him, was a cotton manufacturer and became mayor of Lancaster.[51]

One thing united the gaolers and the keepers. For both, keeping a prison was a family business. Edward and James Styth served as gaolers for most of the period between 1744 and 1771, while the father-and-son pairs of the Higgins and the Hansbrows governed Lancaster continuously from 1781 to 1867. At Manchester the Ouldhams and Walkers together governed the house of correction from before 1690 until 1755. William Dunstan and his two sons, Thomas and Richard, served as keepers from 1794 until 1841, while two more sons, George and Henry,

---

*John Higgin wrote that he had once held in custody two debtors whose joint debts totaled £59,000 and that two actions for recovery of debts had been brought against him (LCL, D 6351, no. 24). Cf. Eric Stockdale, *A Study of Bedford Prison, 1660-1877* (London, 1977), pp. 170-71.

served as deputy governors of the Salford New Bailey. The Stanleys at Preston seem to have been father, son, and grandson; with the Cowburnes they ran Preston from about 1703 until 1793, except for a single year. An undergaoler at Lancaster named James Birdsworth was probably a relative of the gaoler John, while John Higgin, Jr., employed two of his sons as assistants.

If such nepotism was an abuse, it was one that certainly continued unchanged into the nineteenth century. It also, however, reflected the value of experience in managing a prison. It was almost inevitable that the sons (and often the wives) of gaolers should assist them; the family lived in the prison, the gaoler was often away on business, and he had to have someone whom he could trust absolutely on the spot for twenty-four hours a day. Even the reformers emphasized the value of experience; they often recommended the hiring of army men, who had at least learned how to command others and how to administer. Essentially, therefore, both gaols and houses of correction tended to be family businesses with a fairly stable management. This continuity of management could make prisons resistant to major changes in penal philosophy.

Lancashire gaolers were frequently venal: happy to extend special privileges or to provide special goods for a price. John Higgin's recollections of his father's predecessor probably describe a typical eighteenth-century governor:

Mr. Dean was an intemperate Man, and encouraged drinking and Gambling in the Gaol, to benefit the Taps which were the perquisite of the governor[.] The two Miss Deans presided at the Wine Tap which was Kept in the Room now called the Snug. Beer was brewed in the Prison and sold in the Room still called "the Tap." The conducting of the Prison was a good deal left to the Head Turnkey, Robinson, who remitted punishment and granted favors to the Prisoners. One Gentleman paid as much as £20 for various indulgences he was committed for Forgery. [H]e wore no irons and in the end was allowed to sit in Miss Deans room.[52]

There is, however, only one case of habitual cruelty by a Lancashire gaoler: in the 1690's John Ellitson prompted a torrent of complaint from prisoners, who alleged that he extorted money from them, beat them without cause, chained them unreasonably, locked them up in disagreeable places, prevented free access to visitors, and engaged in various forms of corrupt behavior, including selling the lead off the roof and granting and receiving bribes.[53] Ellitson, however, both preceded and followed humane gaolers who were praised by their charges. His predecessor, James Melling, helped prisoners find room to work and lent them money to buy supplies, and his successor, Henry Bracken, sometimes forgave the fees owed him by poor prisoners and was credited by petitioners in 1699 with saving them from death by hunger and disease.[54]

Moreover, the prisoners' vigorous complaints against Ellitson's behavior suggests that they neither expected nor tolerated abusive or excessively corrupt behavior by gaolers. Scattered complaints in the course of the eighteenth century suggest that turnkeys—who were themselves often debtors—occasionally extorted money for admitting goods or prisoners to the debtors' side of the gaol. In one further case, a man held for sureties on charges of breaking and entering and attempted rape complained that the gaoler had confined him in the Condemned Hole. Because of this "intolerable" treatment, for which the gaoler had already been reproved by justices, the prisoner was discharged with a small fine.[55]

Little evidence about the conduct of keepers has survived. In the 1680's there were complaints about the failure of two successive keepers of Preston to live in the house. The choice of the next keeper, William Tomlinson, who had married the widow of a recusant, became a subject of a bitter political battle because of suspicions that he was a Jacobite. At one point a maidservant accused him of saying to some of his Irish prisoners, "I hate my very Christne name for the sake of the orringe pill," and then sitting down to drink with them.[56] Tomlinson's successor, John Bannister, proved even worse. Two towns preferred an indictment against him, and the Sheriff's Board dismissed him on charges of "extortion oppression neglect of duty wilfull and negligent escapes debauchery despiseing and affronting the Justices of the peace [and] contemning and disobeying their orders."[57] No evidence has been found of further complaints until the Cowburne affair in 1781. Howard observed that at one time the Preston keeper had become too old to manage his charges—a chronic problem throughout the period.

Though it remains sketchy, therefore, the Lancashire evidence tends to support Sheehan's contention that the conduct of prison officers improved after 1720 and provides no support for the widely held belief, repeated regularly in textbooks and histories, that eighteenth-century gaolers were cruel, oppressive, and barbaric. These contentions may be proved correct by further close investigation in other counties, but until they can be documented it is better to admit ignorance than to accept assumptions made without evidence.

It seems evident that the favorite panacea of the reformers and of later historians, conversion from fees to salaries, could by itself have had little effect on the penal system, since keepers were paid in this manner throughout the eighteenth century, with little effect on their conduct or on their responsiveness to the justices. If anything, the houses of correction were probably less well governed, less orderly, dirtier, more uncomfortable, and more licentious than the gaols, if only because their small size and powerless inmates aroused less interest among the justices and the public.

Furthermore, despite the Webbs' assertions, opportunities for improper profiteering did not occur only in institutions on a fee system. The gaoler made most of his profit by providing services that were, theoretically, in free competition with those available from the town. When he charged fees or provided drinks, prisoners knew what they were paying, and illegitimate exactions were difficult to conceal. The prohibition of alcohol and later of tobacco, like all such prohibitions, merely drove up the price of these goods and transferred the profits into even less reputable hands.

In fact, the adoption of a system of state provision of such commodities as food, furniture, and clothing offered the corrupt gaoler and his staff almost unlimited opportunities for peculation and for fraudulent dealings with contractors, at the expense both of prisoners (who received inferior goods) and of ratepayers. The justices had as much difficulty in preventing such activities as they had in eliminating direct extortion; William Liddell of Preston was accused of peculation in 1828, while the radical printer John Doherty, imprisoned for a few days in the New Bailey in 1832, claimed that its keeper was using the prisoners' bread to feed his horse, dogs, and pigs.[58] The question is not whether corruption was possible (it always is) but whether it was permitted; changes over the century in the standards by which men were chosen and by which they judged themselves were more important than an alteration in the method by which they were paid.

Nevertheless, the justices' anxiety to replace independent fee-collecting gaolers with salaried men who would be more firmly under their control is an important symbol of the justices' increased readiness to assume responsibility for prison administration and of their willingness to intervene directly if necessary. It was closely linked to other and far more important changes, of which the most important was, perhaps, the effort (often unsuccessful) to find "new men" to serve as gaolers and keepers,

men who displayed the humaneness tempered with firmness that the reformers valued. Other changes were intended to make prison government more professional, more consistent, and more directly answerable
to the justices and, as far as possible, to invest this newly responsible
government with many powers previously exercised by the prisoners.
The changes (sometimes unintended) in the role of the gaoler that these
efforts entailed were probably the most important single feature of the
prison reforms of the late eighteenth and early nineteenth centuries.

County Rates and Prison Allowances, 1690-1776

The amount that justices raised to build or repair prisons and to aid
prisoners could mean the difference between life and death for their
charges. On the other hand, since the maintenance of law and order in
general and of prisons in particular accounted for a significant part of a
rate that was both outmoded and inequitable, even well-intentioned justices had to balance the welfare of prisoners against the resentment of
ratepayers. The quality of their decisions was critical both to their prisoners and to their own standing in the countryside.

Lancashire's rating system descended from assessments made in 1334
for the "tenth and fifteenth," and continued in the same general form
until the nineteenth century. Rates were assessed from the top down
rather than from the bottom up. That is, instead of sending men around
to look at every piece of property in the county and then working out
what a given percentage of the total assessment would bring, the justices
started with the given amount they needed to raise from a new rate.
Then, meeting at the Sheriff's Board, they agreed among themselves
how the burden should be divided among the six hundreds. The amount
each hundred owed was then further divided among the parishes and
townships, often in the same proportions that they had originally paid to
the tenth and fifteenth. The constables of each township then collected
the money and paid it to the high constables for their hundreds.[59]

Fresh assessments were sometimes made within each township to distribute the burden more fairly among the ratepayers, but the town still
had to come up with its fixed amount. Despite the original intent of Parliament, assessments were made only on real estate, and once the assessment had been made for a particular rate the proportions by which the
hundreds contributed were never changed.

This system was relatively efficient and inexpensive to run, and it was
reasonably flexible in dealing with changes in the fortunes of individual

taxpayers. It was, however, ill adapted to absorb long-term changes in the prosperity of one region as compared with others, and it was extremely inefficient in tapping new or commercial wealth. The fact that each tax had its own assessment also meant that certain areas paid disproportionately more for certain projects and less for others.

Many other rates were collected from a smaller base than the whole county. Every parish paid for its own poor. Other responsibilities, such as highways and bridges, were paid for by a variety of authorities. Salford hundred alone paid for the Salford house of correction, while the other five hundreds jointly paid for Preston; for this reason, in Lancashire the costs of the houses of correction, although they were legally "county" houses, were not a part of the county budget as they were elsewhere. Even in the nineteenth century they always had separate accounts and separately appointed treasurers.

By the beginning of the seventeenth century, five taxes, or "leys," each with its own assessment, were regularly levied on the whole county: the subsidy, the [tenth and] fifteenth, the ox ley, the maimed soldiers and Marshalsea ley, and the soldiers' ley. The most important was the soldiers' ley, which was first assessed in 1588 to provide money for soldiers injured in the war with Spain.[60] This was a revision of the fifteenth, in which West Derby's liability was reduced and that of Leyland increased. In 1624 the Sheriff's Board decided that the fifteenth, which by then was three centuries old, had become too inequitable for regular use and agreed to make the soldiers' ley the basis for all general county rates.[61] It was this tax that usually paid for repairs to the Castle. The hundreds probably collected rates for the houses of correction on the same assessments. From the consolidation of the rates in 1739 until 1815, the soldiers' ley was used for all county expenditures, including ones previously financed from other leys.

By the late eighteenth century these rates completely failed to correspond with the actual wealth of the areas taxed. This is especially evident at the township level. Until 1815 Liverpool paid £4 9s. 5d. to a county roll of £1,000, while in the same hundred (West Derby), Ashton paid £7 11s. and Wigan £9 5s. 10d. Ulverston in Lonsdale paid £15 7s. 9d. for the same rate, although in 1801 Liverpool contained 5,322 taxed houses and Ulverston only 248.[62]

In 1637 a sixth rate was added. Called the prisoners' ley, it was levied in accordance with an act of 1572 that authorized justices to tax every parish up to 6d. or 8d. a week to provide support for the prisoners in the county gaols. The churchwardens were to collect the money each week and pay it to a special treasurer living near the gaol, who was to distribute it to the prisoners. The wording of the original statute is vague; the Webbs say that it was "originally in all cases confined to convicted felons," but the statute refers only to "prisoners."[63] Lancashire gave it to debtors as well. The prisoners' ley was always collected for a single fixed amount: £43 6s. 8d. (originally £43 15s. 4d.), which represented what the justices considered to be a reasonable weekly taxation of each parish as provided by the act. The money was paid to the high constables, who then paid the appointed joint treasurers, one of whom was always the mayor of Lancaster.[64]

By the late seventeenth century, Lancashire apparently collected the prisoners' ley between two and four times a year, spending between £80 and £180 annually. At a conservative estimate, spending at this level would provide allowances for about forty debtors at the usual rate of 1s. a week each, or for eighty felons at 6d. a week. The significance of such expenditures depends on what assumptions are made about the size and composition of the prison population, but it seems evident that a substantial proportion of all prisoners did receive county support.

In 1739 an act of Parliament consolidated the county rates, making it possible to collect them all together on the basis of a single assessment. In Lancashire the rate chosen was the soldiers' ley first established in 1588. A single treasurer for the county stock was also appointed, and the special prisoners' fund was merged with the others. Since the treasurer occasionally submitted his accounts to the Quarter Sessions, it is possible to gain some sense of the size and composition of the county budget and of the place of prisons within that budget, although the figures are only approximate. A five-year set of such budgets is shown in Table 1. The period from July 1745 to March of the following year is missing. Since the budgets cover the period of the '45, it is likely that certain expenditures, particularly that for troops, were unusually high.

"Vagrants" took over half of all expenditure. The main expense was probably the cost of removing vagrants to their place of settlement. Lancashire's expenditure on vagrants was disproportionately large because other counties often "passed" their Irish vagrants to Liverpool and left Lancashire to pay the fare for their voyage home. Lancaster Castle and its prisoners took about a fourth of the total (26 percent), with support for prisoners accounting for about a tenth. In less disturbed years, prisoners would probably have taken a slightly larger proportion of the

TABLE I
Lancashire's Treasurer's Accounts, 1743/4-1749

Period[a]	No. of months	Object of expenditure							Approx. avg. per month
		Vagrants	Troops	Bridges	Repairs to Lanc. Castle	Prisoners' support	Misc.	Total	
13 Mar 1743/4- 15 Jly 1745	16	£640.16.4	£30.9.2	£4.2.3½	£45.5.8	£187.15.9	—	£908.9.2½	£57
13 Mar 1745/6- 28 Apr 1747	13	1,011.0.5½	423.19.9	73.6.4	215.10.6	94.7.9	—	1,818.4.9½	140
28 Apr 1747- 23 Jly 1747	3	71.8.6	6.15.2	5.5.2	129.7.11½	31.4.0	—	244.0.9½	81
23 Jly 1747- 18 Apr 1748	9	410.6.0	68.10.3	60.3.0	31.14.8	82.18.5	£40.14.5[b]	694.6.9	77
20 Apr 1748- 4 Apr 1749	11	390.10.11	37.2.0	30.5.1	335.6.9	108.15.3	234.2.6[c]	1,136.2.6	103
TOTAL	52	£2,524.2.2½	£566.16.4	£173.1.10½	£757.5.6½	£505.1.2	£274.16.11	£4,801.4.½	£92
Percent of total		52%	12%	4%	16%	10%	6%	100%	

[a] Note that the financial and civil New Year began on March 25.
[b] For guarding bridges during cattle epidemic.
[c] Special work on bridges.

whole. Total county expenditure averaged a little under £100 a month or a little over £1,000 a year, a level at which it apparently remained until the last quarter of the century. Prisoners' allowances averaged a little under £10 a month, or £116 a year, an amount similar to that collected under the earlier ley.

In other counties, the costs of the house of correction would also appear in the budget. In order to estimate the total cost of county imprisonment, therefore, we must add at least £100 a year for the two houses at Preston and Manchester, since after 1732 the salaries of the two keepers alone amounted to £85. In other counties, where the houses were included in the budget and conveyance of vagrants was often less expensive, imprisonment would probably have accounted for a larger proportion of the whole, but even in Lancashire it was always significant. In England as a whole in 1792, maintenance of prison buildings took nearly one-third of the total county spending (29.2 percent), by far the largest single category of expenditure. Support for prisoners took an additional 14.5 percent. Together with prosecutions (10.8 percent), these costs of controlling crime took over half of the aggregate county expenditure.[65]

Many of the costs of law enforcement were not borne by the county but were distributed in an unpredictable way between the offender, his family, his prosecutor, and his parish. In theory, the offender paid his own conveyance fees, which could reach £4. The constable escorting him paid traveling expenses from his own pocket and then obtained an order for reimbursement from the offender. If the offender could not pay, his property was distrained. If that was insufficient, his parish had to pay. Constables often experienced a good deal of difficulty in gaining reimbursement, which did something to dampen their zeal. It also meant that it was more expensive for outlying areas to prosecute offenses than it was for those near Lancaster or the sessional towns. Conveyance to one of the five locations where the Quarter Sessions met was often expensive enough to discourage prosecution; conveyance to the Assizes was even more costly.[66]

Though constables "presented" and prosecuted petty offenses against public order, more serious crimes such as larceny, burglary, rape, or assault were usually prosecuted by the victim. Until 1752 all prosecutors and witnesses paid their own expenses, and for most prosecutors the process was both expensive and time-consuming. After 1752 poor prosecutors, and after 1754 poor witnesses in any felony prosecution, could receive compensation from the county rate if the offender was convicted of a felony. An act of 1770 authorized payment to prosecutors if the grand jury found a true bill, and to witnesses in any felony prosecution, but until Peel's Act (1826) this included only costs incurred after the indictment was drawn up and covered only felony prosecutions. Despite the limitations, these acts encouraged prosecution, while the repayments to prosecutors and their attorneys took a rapidly increasing proportion of county expenditure.[67]

Since Assize prosecutions were far more expensive than similar actions before petty or Quarter Sessions, many offenders apparently benefited from a reduction of charges to bring cases before lesser tribunals, as well as from a general reluctance to prosecute at all. On the other hand, prosecutions before the Assizes were usually for the more serious crimes, in which the costs of prosecution weighed less in the decision to press charges. It seems likely that the increasing compensation for felony prosecutions, therefore, led to disproportionate increases in the number of prosecutions for minor felonies (e.g., petty theft) as opposed to those for serious felonies (e.g., murder) or misdemeanors (e.g., assault). This factor, along with changes in sentencing laws, helps explain the rapid growth in the houses of correction toward the end of the eighteenth century.

One outlay not itemized in the treasurer's accounts is transportation of convicted offenders. It was an expensive undertaking. A standard minimum for one prisoner was £8 10s. 2d., but costs could rise to £12. Gaolers, who received a set fee per mile for each prisoner no matter how many convicts they took at a time, could make a good profit by conveying prisoners in groups. Because of the complexity of the transaction, the dependence of overseas voyages on good weather, and the financial advantages of delaying until there was a sizable group to be transported, felons often spent long periods in gaol after conviction. Women, and men in poor health, often never left at all, since the county did not transport those thought unable to support the rigors of the voyage or unlikely to find employment at its destination. Lancaster Castle thus contained a permanent population of convicts, although the county preferred to transport them.

There were always some prisoners, debtors and felons alike, who possessed the means to support themselves in comfort during their stay. Felons often managed to shelter their assets from the law. Debtors were not necessarily bankrupt. As long as a debtor remained in prison, his creditor could not recover from his estate. Debtors arrested on friendly process to clear other obligations and farmers, yeomen, or gentlemen who went to prison rather than sell their holdings probably began with enough to keep them in prison for some time. Many debtors were small businessmen caught in a temporary liquidity crisis, unable to collect from their creditors to pay their own debts. A long imprisonment, however, could reduce most prisoners to penury.

Many prisoners received financial help from their families and their friends. Families that could afford it were expected to support their black sheep; if they failed to do so, the justices would issue orders requiring them to provide adequate maintenance. For example, when a Lancaster apothecary, Thomas Whalley, had his wife, Priscilla, arrested in 1699—on the grounds that she had disturbed the peace, threatened his life, annoyed his tenants, drank, and was unfaithful—the Sessions ordered him to pay her the comparatively large allowance of 5s. per week.[68] Most families, however, would not have required a court order to persuade them to contribute to the needs of close relatives. The crucial factor was how far prisoners had come from home; in their petitions they sometimes pointed out that they were far from their friends, while Irish prisoners received special consideration because they had no local assistance.

Many prisoners could pursue their trade in gaol. In 1707 there was a short-lived attempt to establish a "Woollen Manufactory" in the Castle. Forty-seven debtors (including Thomas Fell) signed a petition to the Sessions saying that their allowances had been reduced because they were employed in the work but that since the scheme had fallen through, they were "ready to perrish for want of bread."[69] In 1722 a debtor named John Exton wrote that he had supported himself in prison for two years by weaving until prevented by the gaoler, John Birdsworth. There is little evidence about felons' work, but in 1767 their allowances were raised on the grounds that they were suffering from bad weather and unemployment.[70]

A few prison jobs were also available. Aside from those employed by the debtors' court or the individual rooms, one or more of the debtors always served as turnkey, a role that did not necessarily endear them to their companions, and others served as wardsmen or warders. A document of 1711 lists several prison workers, including three "bum bailiffs," a daily laborer, a turnkey at £12 a year, and a tapster at £10 a year. Two women were listed: one minded the prisoners' children and the other probably ran errands for a commission. All of these were also receiving the county allowance. Some casual work was occasionally available, particularly nursing for the women.[71]

Debtors who had demonstrated their insolvency at a hearing under one of the acts were in law entitled to an allowance of 4*d.* a day, or 2*s.* 4*d.* a week, from their creditors (this had been raised in 1728 from 18*d.* a week). Howard maintained that very few of the debtors he saw had actually succeeded in obtaining this money. This seems likely, since most debtors were released after insolvency hearings; few creditors were persistent enough to keep a demonstrably insolvent man in gaol at their own expense. Convicted felons awaiting transportation were in law entitled to the "king's allowance" of 2*s.* 6*d.* a week. Howard wrote that no felons were receiving this allowance at the time of his visits, although at least one sheriff recorded such payments to seven felons, in accounts submitted in 1773.[72]

The county allowance was intended to cover the needs of each prisoner alone. If his family was poor, it received relief from its parish. There are examples of family members imprisoned together receiving separate allowances. At the end of the seventeenth century, allowances varied greatly. On occasion, Quarter Sessions granted as much as 2*s.* 6*d.* a week. Other prisoners received much less; in 1695 a debtor named Richard Croser complained that his four small children were being maintained by their parish and that he himself was "liable to perish with hunger" on 6*d.* a week.[73]

The last five years of the seventeenth century saw a determined effort by the justices to regulate the system more closely. By this time the annual cost of the allowances far exceeded the amount the justices had originally provided, and the treasurer of the fund was making regular appeals for additional money. In 1695 the court forbade him to pay more than 1*s.* to any prisoner without an order from the Quarter Sessions. The justices had been issuing private orders, "3ˢ to some and 1ˢ 6ᵈ to others which is a great . . . oppresion to the County."[74] In the hard year of 1699, the court resolved that it would not allow any debtor more than 1*s.* unless he was sick. A petition by 49 debtors to the same session suggests that a "ratepayers' revolt" may have lain behind these efforts at retrenchment. The prisoners, "sore visited with strange diseases of long continuance," said that they were in danger of starving because the high constables had failed to pay the treasurer of their fund. The court ordered the constables to pay within two weeks or be fined £5 each.[75]

A further crisis arose in the 1720's, probably because of the sharp increase in the number of debtors. In the summer of 1721 the Sheriff's Board resolved that all debtors not under execution be cut off from their allowances. At Michaelmas the Lancaster Sessions accordingly ordered the treasurer to stop the allowances of 39 prisoners. That winter six prisoners wrote the Lancaster Sessions that the board had reduced them "to the greatest Extremity." They had appealed the board's order and been told to apply to their own Quarter Sessions for relief orders. Five more debtors signed a similar petition in the spring. At least four were reinstated, but the months of delay between the meetings must have reduced some at least to starvation. In 1724 the Manchester Sessions, without explanation, cut off thirteen debtors, and the Lancaster Sessions did the same to eight prisoners the next year.[76]

The greatest crisis came in 1737, when the Lancaster Michaelmas Sessions suddenly came to the conclusion that allowances for debtors were illegal and that the justices had no power to charge the inhabitants of the county with the cost. They ordered the treasurer to cease payment of allowances to debtors. The results were disastrous. Fourteen debtors nearly starved to death. The Epiphany Sessions, unable to tolerate this result, simply ignored the legal issue and ordered that the allowances be resumed, on the grounds that the prisoners were poor and necessitous. Thereafter, the justices continued the traditional practice and no further objection was raised until 1822, when an expenditure committee of the Annual General Session reported that the weekly shilling, now supplemented by ten pounds of potatoes, "may have proceeded from motives of humanity" but was not legally chargeable to the county rate.[77]

Although the justices had agreed to limit the allowances to 6*d.* a week for felons and 1*s.* a week for debtors, they had some difficulty in enforcing the limit, particularly in years of dearth and high prices. They also had difficulty in keeping people who did not need the allowances off the rolls. Orders on the treasurer could be made by single or "double" justices as well as by Quarter Sessions, and prisoners naturally sent to the most generous justice in their area. The Quarter Sessions, therefore, was engaged in a constant battle to restrain its more prodigal members. In 1733, for example, it reduced three orders and also dealt with a debtor who was receiving 2*s.* 4*d.* from his creditor but had repeatedly succeeded in obtaining allowance orders from single justices. In 1742 the court again ordered the treasurer to reduce excessive allowances. Six years later the Manchester Sessions ordered that all allowances be made by Quarter Sessions, but Lancaster amended the order to permit two justices to sign orders.[78] On the whole, the limits were fairly well maintained, but by the 1760's, as prices began to rise, it became increasingly evident that they were insufficient. In 1767 the Lancaster Sessions increased the allowances of felons to 1s. The order was meant to be temporary but it was repeated in 1768, 1769, and 1770. By the time of Howard's visits, 1s. was the standard rate. The shilling allowance, which provided less than two pennyworth of bread a day, also became increasingly inadequate and was gradually replaced by the provision of goods in kind, until in the nineteenth century a prison dietary was established.

It is difficult to assess the adequacy of these allowances for eighteenth-century prisoners. According to the Webbs, 1s. a week was common by the end of the century, although some prisons were lower and many higher. Lancashire, however, may have been unusual in giving any allowance to debtors. Furthermore, the cost of living varied from area to area and year to year. All that can be said is that Lancashire overseers offered similar sums to their poor and that debtors' allowances were actually somewhat higher per capita than those given to many poor families. The crucial question is, How much of their allowances did the prisoners have to pay in fees? Prisoners arrested on criminal process paid two sets of fees, at the beginning and end of their imprisonment (providing they were released). The fees at their entry paid the cost of their conveyance, admission, and "garnish," amounting to several shillings. At their release felons paid the gaoler's fees and a variety of legal fees—until 1774, when the court was permitted to order the county to pay as much as 13s. 4d. for every acquitted or discharged prisoner. Felons might pay other fees, to avoid irons, for example, or they might purchase extra comforts like washing, but in law they were not compelled to do so.

An extortionate gaoler could make felons so uncomfortable that they were forced to buy indulgence, but most felons were probably so poor that it was not worth his while to do so. Felons were not charged for their usual housing, in the worst cells in the prison, but wealthy felons sometimes rented more luxurious quarters. The county provided them with straw to sleep on, but some rented bedding. Once his entrance and exit fees were allowed for, a felon had nearly the whole of his allowance to spend on food, provided he was willing to endure the squalor that the justices considered good enough for criminals.

Debtors paid about 8s. for admission and discharge as well as a garnish of 7s. 2d. (Female debtors paid half as much garnish.) Theoretically, once in prison debtors could live as cheaply as felons if they lodged in the "common room" and either slept on straw or provided their own bedding. In practice, however, many debtors paid an initial fee and a weekly rent to inhabit one of the more comfortable rooms. Even the poorest debtors felt entitled to proper bedding rather than straw; if they lived too far away to transport their own, they rented a bed either from the gaoler or from townspeople. Debtors who claimed the utmost destitution sometimes mentioned that they had been reduced to selling their beds, while others included the cost of bedding in petitions asserting that their allowances were inadequate. The justices seem to have agreed that debtors, even when wholly supported by the county, were entitled to beds. By statute the gaoler could charge 7*d*. per person per week for a bed, whether single or shared, but many debtors paid 3*d*. to 4*d*. a week to townspeople for bedding and sometimes for washing as well.[79]

Although prisoners in receipt of a substantial income did not, by the middle of the eighteenth century, receive county allowances, the allowance was considered the bare minimum, to be supplemented by other means. It seems probable that nearly all poor debtors received occasional supplements to their weekly shillings. Although prisoners in the gaol were not required to work, they frequently did so without losing their allowances, and it seems likely that by mid-century they were expected to do so. In the rare cases of serious infirmity that kept prisoners in their cells, a supplement was offered; for example, in 1772 the court ordered an extra shilling a week for Sarah Shelfox, an aged transportee. Insane prisoners also received larger allowances. Prisoners who fell ill were provided with nursing, special food, and treatment by an apothecary at county expense. Though the gaoler probably earned more each year in fees and perquisites than all the prisoners together received in support from the county, after 1699 prisoners already on the allowance submitted very few petitions complaining of its inadequacy. This fact, together with evidence of the amounts paid in poor relief and the apparent absence of epidemic disease, suggests that the allowance was sufficient for most prisoners over most of the century, though it was by no means a liberal maintenance.

By the 1770's, however, inflation had made these allowances increasingly inadequate. Howard noted in 1777 that prisoners received about half as much bread as they had when the allowances were originally fixed, the penny loaf weighing about half a pound. As he wrote, "Many criminals are half-starved; such of them as at their commitment were in health, come out almost famished, scarce able to move, and for weeks incapable of any labour."[80] Fourteen years later, Jeremy Bentham was outraged on hearing that the dietary at Wymondham was 2*d*. worth of bread a day, along with some unspecified amounts of other foods. He commented that "under a regimen like this a prison must be a scene of perpetual famine. . . . I should speak honestly and call it *torture*."[81]

For poor prisoners, and particularly for poor debtors, the steadily decreasing value of the shilling allowance was probably the single most important factor affecting their welfare, and certainly helps to account for much of the misery and disease apparent in the prisons of Howard's day. Since Parliament failed to pass any insolvency acts between 1781 and 1793, debtors were unable to apply for their "groats" and were also spending longer terms in gaol, increasing their dependence on their allowances. Felons were also spending longer spells in gaol, after the disruption of transportation.

The justices were hampered in their ability to deal with these problems by legal restrictions and by the extremely antiquated and inefficient rating system. The rates had failed to keep pace with economic changes, and most of the judges, because they were rural landed proprietors, came from over-rated areas. Prison expenditure was a sufficiently large part of the budget to require careful control.

Under these conditions it is no wonder that the justices made every effort to keep the costs of prison administration to a minimum. The evidence shows, however, that a large proportion of all prisoners did receive assistance from the county and that this assistance was adequate if not generous through most of the eighteenth century. If the evidence does not support a very optimistic view of prison life, it also suggests that justices were not merely leaving prisoners to starve. Given the inadequate base of the county rates, the real question is not why the justices were anxious to control spending but how they managed to finance the enormous expenditures of the next age of reform.

The appalling conditions of mid-eighteenth-century English prisons have become a cliché, but one that so far lacks documentary support. The large London prisons, which usually furnish historians with their more sensational examples, were not necessarily typical; London evidence should not be extrapolated to the provinces, nor the rule of city corporations to that of rural justices. Even in the case of London, new research shows that the picture requires considerable modification and suggests that historians have been insensitive to major changes in prison life and governance that occurred before the Age of Reform.

The unreformed prison has its own history of reform. Over the centuries a marked pattern of change is apparent in every aspect of prison life. Prison conditions often mirror social stresses, and those periods when many factors interacted to cause a partial breakdown in prison conditions and administration have stood out particularly clearly. Such a period seems to have occurred during the hard years at the end of the sixteenth century. Similar difficulties arose during the political and religious controversies at the end of the seventeenth century, when hunger and disease reappeared together in prisons crowded with large numbers of prisoners of conscience. Signs of strain also accompanied a large increase in the numbers of gaoled debtors in the 1720's, at the time of the economic collapse that followed the South Sea Bubble.

Nevertheless, the mid-eighteenth century seems to have been a time of relative stability. Complaints from prisoners died down. The prison population remained stable or dropped. The problem of a corrupt, brutal, and extortionate prison staff had been dealt with in the early years of the century; following the departure of Lancaster gaoler John Ellitson in 1699 and of the keeper of the Preston house of correction in 1703 there were no further scandals for almost a century. The number of deaths dropped, though perhaps only because the population also dropped. Low, relatively stable prices meant that the fixed allowances were, if not ample, at least adequate. National legislation regulated prison fees. It is certainly still possible that many or most prisons in the mid-eighteenth century were places of terror and death, but if so, the onus of proof must rest on those who make the contention. Too many historians have relied on speculation, and it is as important to recognize what we do not know as to describe what we do. While this study cannot show conclusively that the horrors of eighteenth-century prison life have been exaggerated, it does reveal several factors that deserve consideration.

First, Lancashire's justices did intervene in prison affairs. They were attentive to the need to keep prison buildings in a tolerable state of repair and they were reasonably responsive to petitions from prisoners about this subject. They also provided a minimal level of financial support for insolvent prisoners. They occasionally investigated when prisoners complained of mistreatment. The eighteenth-century history of Lancashire's prisons suggests that the justices were usually well intentioned, although it also shows that they lacked energy and zeal, waited until they received petitions instead of initiating comprehensive changes on their own, and on occasion permitted errors and inefficiency to cause real hardship. Nevertheless, their general conduct compares favorably with that of many local governments today.

Second, prisoners, particularly debtors, knew their legal rights and were prepared to exercise them, either by petitioning the Quarter Sessions or by prosecuting delinquent prison officers—although it is true that most prison officers successfully escaped the criminal penalties attached to misconduct, at most suffering dismissal from office. In view of the notorious litigiousness of Englishmen, the prisoners' determination to defend their rights should not be surprising. The collections of signatures and marks at the bottom of petitions show that prisoners joined together to invoke the formal mechanisms of the national legal establishment that, in other ways, was being used against them. The riot and escape of 1755 shows that debtors who ordinarily accepted their lot were capable of a collective sense of grievance and concerted action when they believed they were being held illegally.

Third, though the prison death rate may well have been high, there is little evidence, before the last quarter of the century, that eighteenth-century Lancashire's gaols harbored the epidemic fevers that have become such a fixture of prison literature. Typhus is a disease of overcrowding as well as of dirt and hunger; there is no reason to believe that any of the three county prisons was frequently overcrowded in this period. When prisons did become crowded, at the end of the sixteenth, seventeenth, and eighteenth centuries, fevers apparently returned.

Fourth, prisoners received support from communities both within and outside the walls. The constant going and coming from the prison had a few disadvantages; it weakened security, enabled prisoners to consult with their partners in crime, and made it easy for prostitutes to ply their trade. On the whole, however, it was undoubtedly beneficial for the prisoners. Whether the community life within the walls was equally beneficial is a matter of opinion. It was certainly necessary; prisoners clubbed together to perform functions that no other authority was at that time prepared to fulfill, such as arranging for cooking, cleaning, and heating in their rooms. They administered justice and revenged misdeeds. They provided each other with entertainment, support in times of need, scribes and advisers, employers and servants. Though it was not exceptionally violent, however, the eighteenth-century prison community did not live in utopian peace. It contained bitterness, feuding, and intimidation. Some prisoners petitioned against the privileges of others. Prisoners who served as warders and turnkeys often behaved badly and were resented. Constant drunkenness and gambling created endless brawls. The justice of the prisoners' "kangaroo courts" was not necessarily either fairer or more lenient than that of the gaolers who would replace them. The gaolers themselves were often absent and, when present, apparently exercised little control over the behavior of either the prisoners or the turnkeys. Weak or unjustly treated prisoners had no recourse and no hope of protection from the relentless persecution of their fellows. Most obvious of all is the mixture of fear and contempt with which the debtors regarded the felons. Debtors not only approved of the separation between themselves and the felons, they demanded it.

In the absence of any adequate studies, it is difficult to date the onset of the next period of trouble with any precision, but it began perhaps as early as 1765. In that year prices rose, although they would rise more sharply later. In 1764 Lancaster Castle was presented at the Assizes for repairs; it was presented for a second time in 1775. In that same year, major rebuilding began at Manchester. In 1779 a gaoler committed suicide; four years later his successor died in the first major epidemic to sweep the Castle in the course of the century. By the time of John Howard's visits, Lancashire's prisons were undergoing what seemed to be yet another in a long series of periodic crises involving rising prison populations and prices. Lancashire was not unique in this regard. During his early visits, before the publication of *State of the Prisons*, Howard found several counties planning additions to their prisons or completely new buildings. What initially seemed merely one more episode in a long series of short-lived crises, however, began to take on an entirely different character as years passed and no relief came into sight. Instead of being a temporary aberration, the wretched state of England's penal institutions was becoming a permanent affront to an established tradition of rough but relatively humane administration. Moreover, prison crowding and hunger were beginning to threaten not only the sensibilities but also the lives of the county justices who administered them, as epidemics of typhus appeared. As the magnitude of the problem became evident, as new theories on crime and disease began to emerge, and as new resources became available, the response of the justices began to take on a completely new character. Under the guidance of a few energetic reformers, this response was to amount to a comprehensive attack on the communal life of the prison.

CHAPTER 2

Prison Populations

The Eighteenth-Century Stasis

Changes in the size and composition of the prison population are a vital key to the events of the Age of Reform, but the causal relationship is complex. The size of the prison population directly reflected the rate of prosecution (the crime rate), but this rate was not an independent variable. It reflected social and economic changes that may have actually increased the number of offenses, but it also reflected changes in the willingness of victims to prosecute, which in turn was conditioned by their fear that crime was increasing, by new government policies, and by their sense of the resources available for punishing offenders.

The changes in prison populations, moreover, did not merely reflect external events but themselves affected the nature and quality of prison life. A large institution cannot be run in the same way as a small one; incarceration in a room with twenty others is not the same as incarceration in solitude; a prison filled with short-term offenders is not the same as a prison filled with men serving life sentences; and populations that fluctuate or grow rapidly will not have the same effect as populations that reach the same levels over a longer period.

In sentencing, no clear distinction was made between the house of correction and the county gaol. Felons and misdemeanants went to both. The two institutions were not, however, completely interchangeable. Vagrants rarely went to the Castle (and then probably because they had originally been charged with another offense). Debtors never went to the houses of correction (except for a few who appeared at Preston in the nineteenth century). In general, since the Castle was by far the most secure prison and since the Assizes sat in Lancaster, prisoners charged with serious crimes, including nonclergyable felonies, went to the Castle, as did most prisoners held for failure to pay fines. The remaining prisoners went to whatever institution was most convenient at the time. The gaols, therefore, held only part of all prisoners, and punitive imprisonment in some penal institution was a common experience for offenders.

In the unreformed prison, fluctuations of prison population were common, and large changes could lead to serious crises. Over the years a complex of events recurred. Periods of rising population, rising prices, and social stresses are loosely coordinated with periods of new prison building and legislation. Common sense suggests how these factors might be linked, though the links are not necessarily direct. Research in a few counties has suggested that in early modern England, prosecutions, particularly prosecutions for property crimes, tended to rise in years of dearth.[1] Gaols that contained a large proportion of debtors were particularly vulnerable to periods of economic collapse.

Aside from the effect that rising prices and economic instability may have had on the crime rate and, hence, on the number of prisoners, they also had a direct effect on the conditions of prison life. Their impact was especially pronounced in the unreformed prison, because prisoners there depended on fixed monetary allowances. The substitution of provision in kind for money payments, though it had disadvantages, did at least provide a cushion against the total erosion of the value of support.

Though Lancashire enjoyed relative stability during most of the eighteenth century, in very bad years problems could interact to cause a vicious cycle. Dearth sent more debtors and possibly more criminals to the prisons, where they pressed on prison allowances at the very time that those who were already in prison needed more just to stay alive. Because the rating system was cumbersome and inequitable, it was difficult for the county to increase rates, especially at a moment when rate-payers themselves were suffering financial difficulties. Hunger and overcrowding raised the death rate. The timing of petitions and the evidence of mortality statistics suggest that the most serious suffering among prisoners was caused by these sudden crises and not by chronic neglect.

The Rising Numbers

Prison populations seem to have been relatively stable during the mid-eighteenth century, but at the end of the eighteenth century a new pattern emerged. Though it seemed initially that the prisons were experiencing yet another short-lived surge in numbers, that surge was, in fact, part of a much more extensive and rapidly accelerating trend. Beginning at some point in the late eighteenth century, prison populations rapidly reached crisis levels and then continued to rise throughout the first half of the nineteenth century. There is no question that this rise occurred. The difficulty is to determine its causes and to explain the effect it had on prison life and organization.

Traditional histories have limited their discussion of prison populations largely to the immediate Howardian period—that is, to the last two decades of the eighteenth century following publication of *The State of the Prisons* in 1777. The historians have attributed the sudden and dramatic increase in new prison construction (42 new penal institutions were begun in 1789 alone) to two factors: the revulsion aroused by Howard's revelations and a sharp increase in prison populations resulting from the disruption of overseas transportation of convicts during the American Revolution.

Howard was certainly interested in encouraging new building; he published several plans and was a close friend of the prison architect William Blackburn. Nevertheless, there is no evidence that Howard's efforts were decisive. For one thing, enormous sums were spent; it is incredible that one man's influence, however great, could have persuaded the frugal justices and the notoriously tight-fisted corporations to make such commitments. For another, given a stable prison population, many of Howard's suggestions could have been adopted without such large-scale building. Occasionally he commented that the "situation" of a prison was unhealthy and should be changed, but most magistrates could have brought their prisons to an acceptable level of cleanliness and comfort without tearing them down entirely. About Lancaster Castle, for example, he wrote that it would "be a good gaol" if a new infirmary were built.[2] Instead of basking in Howard's approval, however, the Lancaster justices embarked on a massive program of building and repair that involved presenting the Castle for the second time in ten years and the construction of new courts, a new gaoler's house, new debtors' rooms, and a whole new felons' prison, all before 1794. Just about the only thing they did not build was a new infirmary.

It seems likely that such massive building was related to major changes in the size and composition of the prison population, but the rise caused by the disruption of transportation overseas was probably smaller and more gradual than many historians have realized. First, even at the best of times there were often delays in transporting convicts. Second, some felons had never been transported. Third, although the national total of convicted felons may have seemed large, there were not very many in any given provincial gaol. In 1779, after transportation had ended, London held nearly 200 felons, but Howard found only 16 felons in York, England's largest provincial gaol, and only 11 in Lancaster. Finally, what the war gave with one hand it took away with another; less serious criminals could now be impressed into the armed services. The immediate effect of the American war, therefore, was as much a change in quality as in quantity. As Michael Ignatieff has recently pointed out, it was the return of peace in the early 1780's that marked the real crisis, as the number of convicts began to mount and the Home Office became more and more dilatory in arranging for their removal.[3]

Factors other than the disruption of transportation contributed to the rising number of felons. As Sir Leon Radzinowicz has shown, the number of offenses designated as felonies grew rapidly in the eighteenth century, at the same time as the percentage of convicted felons executed for their crimes dropped.[4] In most provincial prisons the absolute numbers of convicted felons remained relatively small in the 1780's: in 1783 Stafford gaol had 15 convicts out of a total prison population of 90, and Warwick only 7 out of a total of 91. The lack of facilities for keeping felons, however, and their relatively long stays made the problem a serious one; the fears expressed by county sheriffs and gaolers about mutinies and outbreaks of epidemic disease proved well justified.[5] Moreover, the problem accelerated at the end of the century. The number of criminals who remained at Lancaster from an earlier Assize had reached 72 by the March Assize of 1801. This increase probably resulted from the use of imprisonment as a substitute for execution or removal, since the number of prisoners for trial apparently remained relatively steady between 1767 and 1806, with a spike in 1801. Between 1806 and 1817, however, the number of prisoners for trial at the Assize also increased rapidly. After 1806, not only were fewer felons removed but more were prosecuted as well, and the two trends together raised the number of criminals in the Castle who were serving sentences or awaiting transportation from 33 in 1806 to 232 in 1817. The number dipped again briefly after the peace (see Table 2).[6]

Felons were only a part of the increasing prison population. Toward the end of the eighteenth century, the number of prisoners in all cate-

TABLE 2

Prisoners Listed in Lancaster Assize Calendars,
Selected Years, 1767-1822

Year	March		August	
	No. in calendar	No. up for trial	No. in calendar	No. up for trial
1767	—	—	—	28
1775	—	25	—	—
1776	—	21	—	—
1782	—	31	—	—
1783	—	25	—	—
1792	—	27	—	—
1793	—	—	—	14
1794	—	21	—	—
1801	173	101	177	71
1802	130	39	118	41
1803	110	32	127	36
1804	115	39	101	39
1805	97	33	58	18
1806	60	27	112	59
1807	115	62	106	37
1808	115	38	115	53
1809	117	46	126	58
1810	130	55	124	63
1811	130	53	126	49
1812[a]	129	55	182	90
1813	154	75	137	53
1814	134	57	137	67
1815	184	91	161	21
1816	216	74	265	94
1817	352	120	348	101
1818	328	128	270	47
1819	256	112	183	75
1820	227	123	246	85
1821	258	105	221	56
1822	221	77	—	—

[a]In May 67 prisoners were up for trial in special Luddite Assizes.

gories, including debtors, began a steady rise that would last until the mid-nineteenth century. At the moment, we cannot pinpoint the starting point of this trend; in some counties it might have been under way as early as 1760. In Lancashire, it was evident by the 1780's. Though eighteenth-century figures on debtor populations are poor, a count of the number of debtors filing insolvency papers reveals a slight rise in the 1770's and a more sustained increase beginning in the 1790's. What hap-

TABLE 3
Debtors Committed to Lancaster Castle, 1798-1818

Year	Number committed	Discharged as insolvent		Year	Number committed	Discharged as insolvent	
		No.	Pct.			No.	Pct.
1798	162	22	14%	1809	309	52	17%
1799	175	33	19	1810	306	75	24
1800	190	51	27	1811	366	107	29
1801	247	59	24	1812	303	115	38
1802	206	38	18	1813	343	141	41
1803	207	54	26	1814	272	122	45
1804	202	31	15	1815	282	128	45
1805	203	62	30	1816	441	181	41
1806	266	41	15	1817	576	250	43
1807	267	47	18	1818	526	221	42
1808	319	59	18				

SOURCE: *Parliamentary Papers.*
    NOTE: A letter of John Higgin gives the following total numbers of debtors committed to Lancaster Castle: 1815, 238; 1820, 546; 1826, 734; 1828, 551; 1829, 590; 1830, 643.

pened in the 1780's is unclear, because between 1781 and 1794 Parliament failed to pass any insolvency acts, but it seems likely that this inaction increased the number of debtors remaining in prison for long periods.[7]

Figures collected by Parliament reveal that the number of debtors committed to Lancaster Castle continued to rise rapidly in the first two decades of the nineteenth century (see Table 3); other sources show that their numbers reached a peak in 1827 and then remained at a high but relatively stable level.[8] Total committals of debtors rose from 162 in 1798 to about 734 in 1826. Parliament tried to reduce the severe overcrowding among debtors by easing their release under the insolvency acts and making these acts permanent, but even these measures were not enough to compensate for the increasing flood of committals. Indeed, they may have made the problem worse, since they led debtors to seek committal on friendly process in order to clear their debts. Increasing crowding among the debtors drove Lancaster's gaoler, John Higgin, almost to desperation and led to several outbreaks of unrest on the debtors' side of the gaol.

The population rise in the houses of correction was equally dramatic. Evidence from calendars suggests that in the mid-eighteenth century two or three dozen offenders came before the Preston and Salford ses-

TABLE 4

Prisoners Listed in Calendars, Preston and Manchester Houses of Correction,
Selected Years, 1756-1790

| | | | | | Manchester | |
| | | | | | | No. in |
Year	Preston	Manchester	Year	Preston	Total	custody
1756	3	10	1778	39	43	—
1759	8(Ep)	16(Ep)	1779	24	54	—
1760	4	26(E)	1780	23	49	17
1765	34	13	1781	32	55	23
1766	—	30(Ep)	1782	39	49	17
1770	22	39	1783	39	72	31
1771	24	39	1784	65	84	26
1772	20	30	1785	56	82	26
1773	—	38	1786	72	88	44
1774	35(E)	—	1787	57	88	38
1775	29	30(T)	1788	70	112	42
1776	25	49	1789	58	111	44
1777	31	48	1790	106	175	—

NOTE: Ep indicates Epiphany Sessions, E Easter Sessions, T Summer Sessions. All others are Michaelmas Sessions.

sions. The Preston and Salford houses probably held between five and twenty offenders each between sessions; Howard found as few as six and as many as 21 in Manchester. In the mid-1780's, however, the numbers listed for trial at both houses approximately doubled (Table 4). By 1790, 175 prisoners appeared in the calendar for a single Manchester Session. Committal statistics collected by Henry Fielding, the Salford chaplain, show that there were 685 committals in 1801. This figure would rise to a high of 4,034 in 1827. By 1801 there were already 243 felons committed to Manchester and the number continued to rise steadily, nearly quadrupling by 1826. Equally important, however, was the number of misdemeanants. Starting at 360 in 1801, the committal rate had risen to 1,365 in 1825 and 1,772 in 1827, nearly five times its level at the beginning of the century. The number of petty offenders, such as vagrants, also rose sharply (see Table 5).[9]

For the period between 1820 and 1842, we at last have both total criminal committals and daily average populations for all Lancashire's prisons, including the new house of correction at Kirkdale, near Liverpool, which opened in 1820. Though the pattern varied slightly from prison to prison, total committals at the four institutions combined continued

TABLE 5

Total Committals to the Salford New Bailey, 1801 and 1811-1827

Year	Vagrants	Nonpay-ment of bastardy orders	Uttering base coin	Lewd women	Offenses against game laws	Mis-demeanors	Felons	Total
1801	24	46	6	5	1	360	243	685
1811	49	136	14	9	2	324	219	753
1812	87	172	20	8	4	328	257	876
1813	69	144	13	8	7	456	306	1,003
1814	98	109	4	16	6	480	327	1,040
1815	210	168	5	23	4	631	425	1,466
1816	253	330	10	28	16	888	454	1,979
1817	485	516	21	33	13	1,034	792	2,894
1818	329	331	16	23	9	875	746	2,329
1819	725	431	19	30	22	1,077	737	3,041
1820	961	403	14	18	18	1,070	853	3,337
1821	783	336	9	27	8	1,136	706	3,005
1822	374	271	13	19	6	1,204	725	2,612
1823	289	344	10	19	6	1,110	712	2,490
1824	405	318	7	15	7	1,321	893	2,966
1825	220	320	10	21	10	1,365	933	2,879
1826	369	610	32	20	37	1,161	937	3,166[a]
1827	780	532	16	24	21	1,772	889	4,034

SOURCE: Manchester Central Library, Henry Fielding, "Tables Showing the Total Number of Prisoners Committed to the New Bailey, Salford, under the Several Charges Specified . . ." (paper read to the Manchester Statistical Society, 1834-35).

[a]Corrected from the original.

to climb until 1842.[10] The daily average population, however, began to fall after 1834, suggesting a drop in the length of sentences. The combined daily average population rose by 600 prisoners, from about 1,440 in 1820 to 2,040 in 1834, before falling briefly to its earlier level in 1837. The number of prisoners in individual prisons continued to fluctuate throughout the middle of the century, but the worst strain seems to have come in the period between the 1780's and the 1830's, whose unprecedented problems took administrators by surprise (see Table 6).[11]

This trend may explain why the steady efforts at prison reform throughout the period from Howard to the accession of Victoria seemed to have borne so little fruit. Reform did take place, but it was often overwhelmed by the increasing numbers of bodies. This steady and rapid increase in prison populations is the single most important fact underlying all the changes in early-nineteenth-century prison administration.

TABLE 6
Daily Average Population, Lancashire
Prisons, 1823-1842

Year	Lancaster	Preston	Kirkdale	Salford	Total
1823	271	143	507	517	1,438
1824	280	148	529	603	1,560
1825	313	125	489	601	1,528
1826	368	166	580	609	1,723
1827	457	251	613	674	1,995
1828	427	191	560	529	1,707
1829	358	183	533	469	1,543
1830	406	211	539	504	1,660
1831	437	204	522	480	1,643
1832	424	206	588	543	1,761
1833	408	226	574	524	1,732
1834	427	528	573	512	2,040
1835	450	160	627	552	1,789
1836	437	175	615	530	1,757
1837	341	174	337	572	1,424
1838	455	183	368	653	1,659
1839	451	174	315	586	1,526
1840	460	214	344	641	1,659
1841	516	216	417	685	1,834
1842	515	234	494	719	1,962

Some Causes of the Rise

Though the rising tide of inmates both caused and complicated efforts at prison reform, it would be a mistake to simplify the relationship between these factors. The increase in prisoners may have led to prison reform, but prison reform may also have contributed to the increase in prisoners. The rising number of petty offenders in penal institutions suggests not only a higher crime rate but also a greater willingness to take formal legal action over conflicts previously solved less formally. Enlarged prison capacity made this decision possible in cases where it had not been so before. The Manchester house of correction, for example, was rebuilt in 1774 and again in the late 1780's, opening on a new site in 1790. Preston reopened on a new site in 1789. In all three cases, the number of names in prison calendars rose sharply immediately *after* the new prison opened.

In a sense, therefore, the prison reformers who built larger prisons may have helped to create the problem they wished to solve. Some reformers of the time understood this dilemma. Sir George Onesiphorus Paul, for example, was very concerned about the increased readiness of Gloucester justices to commit previously tolerated offenders to the new prison built by his efforts.[12] This discretionary element in the system of justice affected petty offenders to a much greater extent than it did those who had committed graver crimes; murderers were always prosecuted, but lewd women were not. The knowledge that felons were likely to be imprisoned rather than executed may also have encouraged the upgrading of certain offenses to felonies and made convictions easier to obtain.

Michael Ignatieff and others have argued that the economic and social strains of the late eighteenth century encouraged those in authority to send more and more offenders to gaol. Along with recent historians of crime, they have pointed to specific new laws related to the needs of a market economy: laws designed to increase the control that masters exercised over their workers. Other laws, such as those permitting summary committals, encouraging prosecution of certain offenders, and allowing manipulation of the powers to condemn and reprieve, more generally enhanced both the actual and the symbolic power of a class that felt itself threatened by social change. The effect of these changes was to increase the number of those imprisoned not only for felonies but for petty offenses as well.

These scholars have also pointed out that the rising number of prisoners in the late eighteenth century was only part of an increasing resort to institutionalization. For example, Andrew Scull has claimed that in this period the English abandoned their traditional family-centered response to insanity and, indeed, to all forms of deviance. He attributes this change to the development of a mature market economy and to an increasing commercialization that made the "ruling class" receptive to the idea of institutionalization for "problem populations." Another factor was that the proportion of the population directly dependent on poor relief had increased "at precisely the point in time when the growing power of the bourgeoisie and their increasing dominance of intellectual life was reducing the inclination to tolerate such a state of affairs." Simultaneously, new theories were portraying insanity, for the first time, as "a condition existing more pervasively among the lower classes of the community—a distinct species of pathology which could not be considered as just one more case of poverty and dependency."[13]

As an explanation of the rise of institutions, this emphasis on broad social changes is more satisfying than the traditional emphasis on political events such as the disruption of transportation. Nevertheless, such models often conflate the "bourgeoisie" with the "ruling classes" and assume that though social changes might take place at the bottom of the pyramid, intellectual changes occurred only at the top. It was the "ruling class" that changed its "receptivity" and the "bourgeoisie"—which has somehow replaced the aristocracy—that lost its "tolerance." Ignatieff is more careful in identifying the reformers he has in mind as a group associated by politics and religion as well as by class, but he too writes as if the decision to resort to institutional solutions for social problems was made wholly by a small elite group of "Whig" reformers, with the rest of the nation merely reacting to their lead.

At no time during the Age of Reform did the bourgeoisie play a significant part in county prison administration, though its role began to grow toward the middle of the nineteenth century. It is true that some members of the traditional professions, particularly doctors and clergymen, and some gentlemen who had inherited mercantile wealth did participate in the administrative decisions of this period, but in Lancashire, at least, the traditional landed gentry remained firmly in control of county administration. It was they who raised the rates, ran the prisons, and presided over the courts.

Both the landed gentry and the bourgeoisie certainly exercised an important influence over the rate of prosecution. Each group could and did initiate prosecution. Gentlemen could prosecute in their own right and, acting as justices, could put pressure on constables to enforce the laws against alehouse keepers, prostitutes, and similar petty offenders. Masters could prosecute their workers, tradesmen could imprison debtors, and members of the trading classes could and did form societies to finance and encourage prosecutions.

There is no reason, however, to assume out of hand that the upper classes—however defined—were the only group to respond positively to the social changes of this period or to the accompanying growth of institutions. Many other groups participated in the expansion of the system of justice. Petty juries could veto the sentences of those charged with indictable crimes by finding them "not guilty" or by committing "pious perjury" if they felt the legal penalty was too severe, and they did not hesitate to use this power. The minimum property qualification to sit on such a jury was a £10 freehold or copyhold, a lifetime leasehold of £20, or the possession of £20 worth of property.

Furthermore, most crimes in England were prosecuted by the victim;

though government officers and gentlemen initiated some prosecutions, there was also a growing stream of complaints, informations, depositions, and prosecutions from workmen whose pockets were picked in public houses, women whose linen was stolen from clotheslines, husbandmen who had lost their poultry, wives beaten by their husbands, drinkers assaulted in alehouses, and quarreling neighbors, as well as from those who simply objected to nuisances or to immoral activities in their neighborhood. For such people, the expansion of local institutions offering justice, and the growing concentration of population in areas near these institutions, presented a new opportunity as well as a new form of oppression. In the English system of justice, which depended on citizen participation for prosecution, the power to decide to prosecute was diffused throughout the population and was much less amenable to deliberate policy decisions than it was in Europe or the United States.

It seems likely that the enormous social and political changes under way by the end of the eighteenth century would have affected the willingness of the lower social groups as well as of the "ruling classes" to prosecute. Increases in the mobility of the population and the growing size of towns did not have to amount to actual urbanization before the delicate links binding village communities could be strained. The behavior of villagers was finely balanced between their desire to maintain "neighborliness" and the need to control the behavior of their more aggressive or obstreperous members; as towns became bigger and their citizens began to encounter more and more strangers, neighborliness ceased to exercise such a strong claim on their patience. At the same time, other traditional mediating institutions, such as the church, lost much of their power.

The destruction of these links also compelled Englishmen to turn to different, more formal and institutional modes of punishment. Methods intended to invoke community censure and eventual reconciliation, such as pillories, processions, and public confessions, began to lose meaning. There was little point in issuing a stern warning or binding a misdemeanant to keep the peace when the offender was a stranger who could easily melt away to commit further offenses elsewhere. The rich were not the only ones to be disturbed by the way that economic disruption and the growing market economy had undermined traditional communal controls over behavior; the poor, though they often committed offenses, were also far more vulnerable to the dangers and losses caused by a breakdown of order.

Even apparently simple reforms could acquire a momentum of their own and contribute to the rising numbers of inmates. Such reforms affected members of different groups in ways that were completely unintended, and often unanticipated, by their original proponents. For example, one important contributor to rising prison populations was the steady effort of the central government to compel counties to assist with a wide range of legal costs. Parliament passed a long series of acts to this end, beginning in 1752 and culminating in Peel's Criminal Justice Act of 1826. The first of these acts permitted courts to award compensation for expenses to poor prosecutors, and later poor witnesses, in a gradually increasing number of cases. Other acts repaid constables for conveyance and paid the clerk's fees of acquitted felons.[14] These acts were particularly important in counties such as Lancashire, where the high cost of conveyance and of travel to trials acted as a significant brake on prosecutions.

These acts extended the protection of the law more fully and fairly to the poor—particularly to the working poor, who under the old system were frequently unable to prosecute crimes committed against them because of the cost and the loss of time involved. Reimbursement for time and out-of-pocket expenses made it possible for the poor as well as the rich to use the process of law to redress personal injuries and, in that sense, made the law more egalitarian. These acts also helped correct the serious inequities experienced by poor people accused of crimes. Their estates were no longer subject to distraint for conveyance and, if found not guilty, they were less likely to be held in prison for legal fees.

Indivisible from the increasing equality of access to the law was the increased encouragement to prosecute. Indeed, these amount to the same thing. An increasing reliance on the courts, however, caused unprecedented and unanticipated changes in local administration. The new acts, which greatly benefited some poor people and liberated others, sent ever more offenders—a disproportionate number of whom were also poor—to gaol. The rapidly increasing populations of convicted offenders in local prisons eventually contributed to national intervention in prison administration, which altered the balance of relations between the prisons and the communities that surrounded them. That change, in turn, often disconcerted the local justices who had encouraged prosecution in the first place. Equally disconcerting to the justices was the fact that the rising demand for judicial services, which were often needed most in urban areas that had few suitable landed gentlemen, eventually compelled them to accept some changes in the social composition of the county bench.

Moreover, these acts imposed new and extremely heavy financial burdens on the counties, which now had to pay most of the cost of what had previously been private prosecutions. These costs rapidly became the single largest item in county budgets, and the counties demanded that the national government assume some of the burden. When it did, however, the inevitable result was a partial loss of local autonomy and the increasing integration of localities into a more uniform national network. Counties began to lose control over their own rates and expenditures, which again caused changes in the role of local government.

Finally, an inability to quantify the "actual" increase in the incidence of crime does not constitute proof that no increase occurred at all. Indeed, it seems reasonable to assume, with earlier historians, that the intense political, social, and economic turmoil of the years of war and Industrial Revolution did increase the incidence of "real" crime. There is also some merit in the eighteenth-century argument that more trade led to more opportunities for criminals. Finally, demographic change may have increased the number of youths "at risk." The balance of the evidence still suggests that eighteenth-century fears had some foundation in fact, even if the reaction was sometimes excessive: increasing prosecution accompanied rather than counterfeited an increased rate of crime.

However complex the causes, the result was unambiguous: a rising tide of prisoners. Their unprecedented numbers posed a formidable challenge to a society that had tried to maintain a tradition of relatively humane administration. In Lancashire the rise in prison populations was especially dramatic, and the social stresses particularly acute. Even if social anxiety lay behind both the increased committal rate and the demand for a more vigorous prison discipline, these two results to some extent canceled each other out. It was simply not possible for Lancashire's prisons to cope in any coherent way with the constant and constantly increasing flood of humanity. Moreover, the increasing reliance on imprisonment to punish petty offenses eventually led to extremely short average terms of confinement. These short terms made nonsense of the reformers' ambitious plans. The growth of large institutions contained within itself enough contradictory tendencies to frustrate most systematic attempts at change and to ensure that those changes that were made would have unexpected results.

CHAPTER 3

The Decision to Reform

Changing Attitudes: Thomas Butterworth Bayley and the Salford Bench

The surge of prison populations at the end of the eighteenth century and the growing misery of long-term prisoners as a result of rising prices would probably have evoked some response from the justices.* Two critical factors ensured that the solution chosen was the incarceration of substantial numbers of offenders in large institutions built on a plan that encouraged classification (or at the extreme, separation) of prisoners—institutions governed by a new sort of staff and guided by a new system of discipline. The first factor was the threat of gaol fever. The second was the appearance of a small but influential group of leaders among the county gentry dedicated to an active policy of reform: men like Sir George Paul in Gloucestershire, Samuel Whitbread in Bedfordshire, the Duke of Richmond in Sussex, and Thomas Butterworth Bayley in Lancashire. Bayley's character and convictions left an indelible stamp on Lancashire's prison system.

Bayley was born in 1744 of a respectable Nonconformist Manchester

---

*The mention of long-term prisoners may surprise some readers, since average prison terms were very short in the nineteenth century. In the late eighteenth century, however, gaols held two groups for longer terms than was common during the mid-eighteenth century: debtors, because there were no insolvency acts, and felons, because there was no transportation and there were fewer executions. These long-staying groups were especially vulnerable to worsening conditions. It is true that as the nineteenth century progressed, the *average* term became shorter because of the increasing percentage of petty offenders. This average, however, conceals changing proportions at both extremes, as imprisonment replaced both whippings and executions.

family. His father, Daniel, was a deputy lieutenant for the county. Both Daniel and his father-in-law, Thomas Butterworth, were trustees of the Cross Street Chapel in Manchester. Thomas also became a trustee, while another of his colleagues on the bench, Dorning Rasbotham, was the son of a trustee. As with Howard, it is difficult to gauge the extent of Bayley's religious conviction; the Webbs describe him as an occasional conformist, while one of his sons was to become an archdeacon of Stow and a canon of Westminster.[1] Like so many of England's legal reformers, Bayley was educated at Edinburgh. In accordance with his Presbyterian/Unitarian upbringing, he seems to have been a rather radical young man; he corresponded with Wilkes and joined the Society of the Supporters of the Bill of Rights. In fact, he even offered to marry Wilkes's daughter. He was also a founding member of the Whig Club.[2]

Throughout his life, Bayley remained faithful to the Wilkite principles of his youth. John Brewer has recently written that the Wilkite views of the law rested on four main principles: first, that public officials should be accountable to the people for their actions; second, that justice should be impartial, providing equal access to the law for everyone, giving no special protection to those in high places, and preventing the abuse of the law for gain by corrupt officials (including prison officers); third, that every accused offender should receive due process without intervention by the Crown or by those in power; and finally, that all officials should govern by the consent of the governed, without relying on military sanctions.[3] Along with Beccaria, the Wilkites believed that the law must be clear and unambiguous, publicly known, and consistently applied in order to maintain both justice and deterrence. They also held strong views on the duties of the magistrate. They loathed "trading justices," and when they themselves obtained office, they tried to set a high—and highly public—example of good conduct. Brewer concludes that although Wilkites wished to improve the lot of the poor and expose abuses, they did not accept the "paternalism of the moral economy," since several of their leaders advocated a free market economy.[4]

Bayley's career exemplifies these preoccupations and ambivalences. A devoted reader of Adam Smith, he believed that the problem of hunger in the countryside could only be solved by improved methods of tillage, including the enclosure of common lands—not by the enactment of Corn Laws.[5] (His agricultural experiments, conducted on his own estate, Hope, led to his becoming an F.R.S.) He applied similar beliefs to the industrial world that was growing up around him, writing in 1802 that the weavers who were petitioning for regulation of their trade were "deluded by cunning Democrats to solicit what they cannot obtain, or which if obtained would materially injure themselves."[6] Yet his attitude was not completely unsympathetic; in 1798 he had urged Pitt to adopt a minimum wage bill "to keep quiet the lower Orders and conciliate their good Will."[7] He is said to have personally dispersed at least one riot. Moreover, he was one of the chief influences behind the 1802 bill to regulate children's work in factories.[8]

As a judge, Bayley adamantly refused to seek pardons for those whom he had convicted (since justice should be consistent and determinate), but he showed continuing concern for the welfare of convicts, frequently writing to the Home Office to protest conditions in the prisons and the Hulks. A strong opponent of trading justices, he was ready to resign over an obnoxious appointment to the Salford bench but remained in the hope of furthering plans for a police "which I have endeavoured to establish for 25 years of laborious service."[9] Like Howard, he bitterly opposed the fee system in prisons.

Bayley soon became a leading member of the Unitarian "establishment" in Manchester and also an important figure in its scientific community. He served as a trustee of the Warrington Academy. Together with Thomas Percival, his closest friend, he founded the Manchester Literary and Philosophical Society. With Percival and the Society's secretary, John Ferriar, he founded Manchester's Board of Health in 1796. Like many Manchester Nonconformists, he emphasized the importance of education. He was a founder of Manchester's unsuccessful College of Arts and Sciences, and encouraged the establishment of Sunday schools, "to counteract the causes of increasing vice and misery, by promoting the moral and religious instruction of the rising generation amongst the poor." Such activities reveal his consistent adherence to the principles of his youth.[10]

This Unitarian "Whig of the old school" succeeded not only in the liberal city but in the Tory county. He joined the Salford bench shortly after leaving Edinburgh and became perpetual chairman of the Quarter Sessions. During the war with France he joined the militia and became lieutenant-colonel-commander of the Manchester Volunteer Corps. He was one of Lord Liverpool's chief local advisers and recommended to him (as chancellor of the duchy) suitable candidates for the bench. He also became receiver-general of the duchy quitrents and served as high sheriff and constable of Lancaster Castle.[11]

Bayley was, therefore, peculiarly well placed. To local projects he could lend his power and prestige as a justice, at a time when very few of Manchester's ablest men could attain that office, while to his work on the bench he brought a Nonconformist zeal for good works combined with a knowledge (as a friend of Percival's and a member of the scientific community) of the latest developments in public health and social thought. He was an extremely active justice at a time when Salford, as a result of Lancashire's custom of banning manufacturers from the bench and of Lord Liverpool's distaste for Nonconformists, was chronically short of magistrates. Manchester, which was still governed by a court leet, had no Quarter Sessions of its own, so the Salford justices determined all the city's criminal cases.

It is difficult to measure the extent of Bayley's influence on the Salford bench. Dorning Rasbotham was clearly a strong ally, as was Samuel Clowes, who joined with Bayley to report on the Salford house of correction, but the attitude of the other justices remains obscure. Bayley, however, was undoubtedly the strongest force on the bench, and he probably framed most of its decisions. For whatever reasons, the Salford bench in these years displayed a distinctive style and showed a particular preoccupation with the maintenance of godliness and public order.

For example, when the Lord's Day Proclamation appeared in 1781, it was entered in the order books of the different sessions, with a list of signatory justices. Five justices signed in Lancaster, two in Preston, six in Ormskirk, and thirteen of the relatively small Manchester bench. When the proclamation "for preventing Vice, Profaneness and Immorality" appeared in 1787, the Salford Sessions, including Rasbotham, Bayley, and Clowes, was the only one to take special notice of the event, "being convinced of the propriety and Necessity of a strict Compliance with it." It was the Manchester justices who alone repeatedly emphasized the need for "humane confinement" in the prisons.[12]

These conflicting impulses shaped the new prisons: a traditional hatred of disorder and particularly of license; a new severity and rigor of enforcement, resting on the hope that the consistent application of the law would increase deterrence and reduce offenses; an emphasis on individual moral regeneration; and a concern for the welfare of the disadvantaged as well as a more fundamental concern with the protection of the public and the maintenance of order. The same impulse that imprisoned drunkards abolished the prison taps. The knowledge that the taps had been abolished increased the readiness to imprison. The increasing disarray of England's prisons and the anxiety to reform them were indivisible from an increasing anxiety to restore order to the outside world.

County Institutions on the Eve of Reform

Lancashire had already begun to rebuild its penal institutions before Howard's visits and before the end of transportation to America. The Salford house of correction was presented by a grand jury and rebuilt between 1770 and 1775 at a cost of £1,671. Lancaster Castle had been presented in 1764 but apparently only for the purpose of carrying out repairs.[13]

Meanwhile, Parliament passed several important acts governing prisons. In 1759 it authorized justices to make rules for the governance of prisons, which would be hung up and displayed to the prisoners. In 1773 it ordered the justices to appoint chaplains for the gaols; although the Webbs maintain that this act was neglected, Lancaster complied with it, appointing a regular chaplain in 1774. In the same year (1774), Alexander Popham successfully sponsored two parliamentary bills. One of them ordered the release of acquitted prisoners in open court so that they could not be held for nonpayment of fees. The other, known as the Gaol Fever Bill, required regular cleaning, annual whitewashing, ventilation, the appointment of a regular doctor, and the provision of separate sickrooms.[14]

The Hulk Act of 1776 permitted the use of the Hulks for prisoners originally sentenced to transportation (or sentenced to death and pardoned on condition of transportation), while William Eden and William Blackstone attempted to find a more permanent solution to the problem by drawing up regulations for national penitentiaries to hold convicts. Their plan, passed as the Penitentiary Act in 1779, was greatly admired by Bayley, who lamented the government's dilatoriness in establishing "the most effectual Mode of Punishment, both to *prevent* Offences, and to *reform Criminals*."[15] Another act of the same year attempted to reduce the number of imprisoned debtors by forbidding imprisonment for debts less than £10.

Although Lancashire apparently complied with all these acts, they affected prison life only indirectly, by causing a slight reduction in the total number of inmates. Because the Castle was already relatively clean, for example, the main effect of the Gaol Fever Act was to cause the justices to set aside two rooms in the Dungeon Tower for the sick and to give a new title to the man who already served as apothecary to the prisoners.

Acts passed in the following years were to have a more profound effect. The first of these resulted from the efforts of Thomas Gilbert, who reverted to the seventeenth-century vision of the houses of correction as institutions for disciplining the idle poor. (This act passed in the same session as another with the same author. "Gilbert's Act" provided for the union of parishes to build workhouses and to improve the relief of the poor; its passage encouraged justices to intervene more actively in the parochial administration of poor relief.) Gilbert pointed out that few bridewell prisoners actually performed useful labor. His act of 1782 required the separation of bridewell prisoners by age and sex, the banning of alcohol, the provision of workrooms, and the enforcement of productive labor (up to twelve hours a day). Its embargoes on contact between the sexes and its requirement for classification according to crime to avoid the "contamination" of the less guilty meant that many houses of correction had to add extra rooms. Again, both Manchester and Preston had already anticipated some of these provisions; both already separated the sexes and encouraged their inmates to work. The act did finally compel Preston to raise its keeper's salary to £80 and to abandon its tap, something Manchester had done in 1777.[16]

The final, and most important, acts concerning prisons were passed in 1784. These established committees of justices to authorize expenditures. For the first time Parliament explicitly permitted the complete destruction, removal, and rebuilding of county gaols, and authorized justices to borrow for this purpose on the security of the county rates, a device developed by Paul in Gloucestershire. The acts prohibited the use of dungeons (i.e., below-ground cells) for imprisonment. They extended to the county gaols the provisions for classification followed in the houses of correction (under Gilbert's Act) and to the houses of correction the provisions for cleanliness previously applied to gaols. It was after passage of these acts that Lancaster, Preston, and Manchester gaols were all rebuilt.[17]

Though Lancashire complied with these acts relatively promptly, they really permitted change more than they caused it. Parliament passed such acts because the members, themselves country gentlemen, wanted the power to carry out reforms in their own counties. The justices of the more liberal counties waited for new laws that would entitle them to take action that cost the ratepayers money; they were not reluctantly forced into activity by a powerful Parliament. Less liberal counties could and did simply ignore these acts. That many justices wished to rebuild their gaols is shown by the large number of private acts passed to expedite the process. Prison acts to some extent governed the chronology of certain reforms, since the justices waited for their passage, but it was other, underlying changes that really forced reconstruction.

Manchester, with its reform-minded bench, perhaps provides the clearest example of this process. In 1777, only two years after they had finished rebuilding the house of correction, the Salford Sessions resolved to inquire into the condition and management of the prison.[18] Immediately after the passage of Gilbert's 1782 act, the Sessions nominated Clowes and Bayley to inspect the house in accordance with that act's provisions. Their report, which appeared in 1783, showed that even in new prisons traditional problems remained and that the rising population was already causing crowding, filth, and indiscipline. Their recommendations epitomized the goals of the eighteenth-century reform movement.

Clowes and Bayley had found the prison in the charge of the turnkey's wife. Although the prisoners had no complaints about the keeper, the rooms and the inmates were crowded, dirty, and offensive. Most of the prisoners were idle, others were spinning wicks for candles—"a very unprofitable sort of labour." There was no tap and no fees, and the surgeon visited regularly, but there was no chaplain, no religious instruction, and no allowance for food or clothing. Because of the rising population of "this trading County," the practice of confining felons for trial at the Sessions in Salford rather than at Lancaster, and the substitution of imprisonment for transportation, the prison was crowded "beyond what was possible to be conceived" when it opened in 1774.[19]

Clowes and Bayley recommended that the hundred buy additional land and erect a new courthouse, offices, chapel, workrooms, and a separate court to divide petty offenders from felons. "For want of *such Separation*," they pointed out, "most Gaols are wretched *Schools* of Wickedness, where many Persons, (especially of tender Years, as yet not hardened or profligate,) are *nominally* sent for Correction for trifling Crimes, but in *fact* are doomed to *Destruction*."

Second, they urged that the prisoners should be set to work. "It is reasonable," they wrote, "that Prisoners should labour for their own Subsistence; this will tend to preserve their Health and Chearfulness, and it is well known that constant and laborious Employment is most friendly to the Principles and Habits of Virtue." Moreover, they added in a note, "Hard Labour and Confinement are admirable Punishments also for many Sorts of Crimes, which are the offspring of *Idleness* and *Dissipation*." The main object of work, therefore, was to make the prisoners into better men and women; earnings were a secondary consideration. Nevertheless, like so many others, the two justices believed that prisoners, if industrious, could earn enough to offset nearly the whole expense of the prison. Even in Lancashire, this hope was to prove overly optimistic.

Finally, Clowes and Bayley urged that the whole prison be swept and washed regularly and that the windows of every room be opened daily. Two rooms were to be set aside for an infirmary. Each room was to have clean towels twice a week and every prisoner a clean shirt once a week. Iron bedsteads were to be provided, along with straw and blankets, in order that each prisoner might sleep in a separate bed in the night rooms—except the felons and the refractory, who were to be confined in cells but change partners nightly. All prisoners were to wash their hands and face every day before receiving their food. The inspectors established a fixed diet and ordered that irons, which they considered to be unnecessary because of the strength of the building, be removed from all prisoners. They also recommended that any new night rooms be small enough to allow prisoners to sleep alone and suggested a corridor plan. All of these regulations closely accorded with Howard's proposals in the preface to the *State of the Prisons*.

The report suggests that the reason for rebuilding was a large increase in population. The form recommended for the new building, however, was determined by a combination of moral and sanitary considerations. The prisoners were to be separated by sex and crime for moral reasons, but the cellular plan, the separation by night (particularly the rule that prisoners could not share beds), and the goal of having one prisoner in each night cell all seem to have been prompted by a desire to avoid physical as much as moral contamination. Similarly, they promoted work, first, because it improved health, second, because it was ethically desirable, and finally, because it saved money—in that order. Acts of Parliament seem to have been only an auxiliary reason for making changes that were desirable on other grounds.

In Bayley's eyes, Preston's problems were even more pressing than those of Manchester, because Preston, unlike Manchester, still maintained the traditional fee system and prison tap. In 1781 he suggested to a Preston justice that the persistence of these practices had created a corrupt and brutal regime. He said that he had recently examined a Preston prisoner named Ellen Gregson about a felony committed by William Collier. In the course of her examination, Gregson alleged that Edward Cowburne, the keeper, had loaded her with heavy clogs and irons, which had caused dangerous wounds in her legs, that he often locked her in a dungeon and beat her, that he made the prisoners work for him at low wages, that he took one ounce of every pound of flour brought into the prison, that he supplied prisoners with necessities at high prices, that he punished complainants by striking them with a clog, and that he had extorted 7s. 6d. as a fee from departing prisoners.[20]

As proof of these charges, Bayley included a letter found on William Collier in which he asked his wife to send him 7s. 6d. for his discharge fee, along with a "dasent pare of Brichas to put on and Somthing to ty A Bout my Neack and a Hat to put on for you No that I have none to Cover my Hed." "It appears to me shocking," commented Bayley, "that 7s. should be demanded from a *naked* Man. . . . Mr. Howard has some noble Observations on this Subject of extorting Fees from poor Prisoners: I doubt not you have his excellent Book."

Bayley felt obliged to offer a little advice to the Preston justices:

I will just hint to you, That the Justices here very frequently visit and examine our House of Correction without the Gaoler; That he has a fixed Salary of £60 per annum, and is not allowed on any Pretence to take Fees . . . nor to sell Ale, Beer—or any other Thing to the Prisoners. He is a Chandler and employs many of them in Spinning *Wick*, but We take care That He gives the usual Prices for it. Since We discontinued the Tap in the Prison—The Change in the Regularity of it is amazingly great, And I would rather double our Governors Salary, Than suffer him again to sell Liquors in it.

This is a rather different picture of the Manchester prison from the one Bayley was to provide two years later; the latter leaves the reader with the impression that the prison had been neglected by the justices and that many of the prisoners were left idle.

When the Preston justices examined Cowburne, he denied all the charges. His deposition reveals a half-reformed institution, run in a benevolent way but lacking Manchester's rectitude. He stated that Gregson arrived at Preston with sores on her legs, attributed variously by the doctors attending her (whom he paid) to venereal disease and scrofula. He denied locking her in the dungeon but admitted that he had put her in a "dark box" (probably one of the sleeping cells seen by Howard) to punish her after she had disrupted the prison by declaring that "whilst there was a man in the House she would have him." She had broken down part of the prison to get to Collier, costing the county £16 in repairs, and had torn the prison blankets and bedding. Her "Allurements and Enticements" had forced him to discharge a turnkey.[21]

Cowburne absolutely denied the charges relating to provisions, a denial confirmed by the woman who fetched goods for the prisoners. He admitted that he employed some of the prisoners but said that Gregson had worked for other prisoners, reeling worsted. Twice he had given her 9s. 3d. when she was sick and he had given 5s. 11d. to Collier, from a bequest augmented from his own pocket. He also provided poor prisoners with meat from his own table "to prevent them from absolutely being starved." He conceded that he charged fees and kept a tap but pointed out that both were perfectly legal and that Manchester was the only prison in the country without a tap. He denied holding any prisoner for failure to pay fees. To support his contentions, he called a servant and the surgeon, who had unsuccessfully treated Gregson for scrofula and was paid two guineas by Cowburne.

Cowburne's testimony shows that Preston was by no means a model prison. The walls could be broken down. Turnkeys slept with prisoners. Prisoners hired one another. Sick prisoners depended on the charity of the keeper to avoid starvation. If Cowburne did not actually detain prisoners for his fees, he probably gave them the impression that he would. To men like Bayley, such a regime seemed corrupt and licentious. Nevertheless, if this testimony is to be believed, Preston was run in accordance with old-fashioned standards of management and with a certain benevolence. Prisoners chose their employers and their work; they were paid directly in money and could send a servant down to purchase whatever they wished with their earnings. Prisoners were by now receiving blankets and bedding. Charitable funds were distributed to the sick, who also received prompt medical attendance. The prison was still very small, but the justices kept an eye on its affairs. By midcentury standards, Preston was quite acceptable, and gaolers were sometimes slow to adjust to the expectations of reformers. Nor was the Preston bench filled with reformers. Despite Bayley's urgings, they failed to abolish the tap or to take further action. Lancaster also made no major changes until after the great epidemic of 1783.

The Decision to Rebuild

Clowes and Bayley submitted their report on Salford in May of 1783. In July a special adjournment of the Manchester Sessions approved the report but postponed consideration until the next sessions. It also approved the recommendation made by a grand jury at the Assizes that a special adjournment of the Preston Sessions be held to consider the state of the Castle and of the houses of correction.

That summer, gaol fever struck Lancashire. Already endemic in Liverpool, it had spread to Manchester and Preston. A prisoner from Manchester brought it to Lancaster Castle, where it killed several people, including the gaoler. At Michaelmas, fear of fever drove the justices out of Preston to Chorley. There a bench that included Bayley, Rasbotham, and Clowes from Salford resolved that Preston also needed a new house of correction and that Lancaster needed a house for the gaoler, rooms for debtors, and separate rooms and courts for the male and female felons.

At Epiphany, with fever still raging, the Lancaster Sessions proposed a spring meeting of the Sheriff's Board to discuss the problem. The Manchester Sessions, considering that the houses of correction were "crowded with very great numbers of unhappy Wretches, many of whom are dangerously Sick of a putrid fever," concurred, adding in its own didactic style that the prisons should provide "Humane confinement, wise correction and exemplary Punishment and that they may be constructed so as to prevent the dreadful public Calamities which may be occasioned by the Increase of the said distemper among the poor Prisoners and from them spreading itself [*sic*] abroad."

Preston was presented in the summer of 1785. In the fall, the Lancaster Sessions appointed a committee to report on improvements to the Castle. Howard's friend William Blackburn provided the initial plans. The Michaelmas Sessions of 1786 chose Thomas Harrison of Chester, a distinguished local architect, to produce the final design. In the winter of 1785 Manchester again resolved to rebuild its own house of correction in order to add workrooms and allow prisoners to be classified and housed in separate cells, as well as to gain enough space for a total of 100 prisoners. Blackburn (who died at Preston in 1790) was again the architect. Construction began at Manchester in 1787 and at Preston in 1788. Liverpool borough also rebuilt its gaol, on a radial plan of Blackburn's, and its house of correction in 1786.[22]

The timing of the decision to rebuild suggests that neither Howard nor parliamentary legislation played a decisive role. Lancaster and Manchester had already taken some steps toward reform before Howard's first visit, although these measures later proved inadequate. The initial moves in the second and much more important wave of reform in the 1780's, at both Manchester and Lancaster, again antedated the important legislation of 1782 and 1784. In 1784, in fact, the county was eagerly awaiting new legislation.

Though certain local leaders constantly agitated for reform, the immediate precipitant of the decision to rebuild the gaols was the fear of fever. The rising prison population, which helped breed fever, would probably have compelled rebuilding eventually, but the close correlation between the arrival of the epidemic and the universal decision to go ahead with massive reconstruction suggests that the threat of fever won the more cautious justices over to the recommendations of the activists. Without that threat, the justices might have been less willing to give men such as Bayley a free hand to rebuild entirely instead of making a few judicious alterations. The content of the reforms—the design of the buildings, the supervision of officers, the rules, dietary, and so on—was determined by the reformers, because no one else had much interest in the subject. But had it not been for crowding and disease, they might have agitated indefinitely. Bayley himself wrote in 1785 that "many of the Judges, and the greater part of the Magistrates—have had no *other* Object in view—than to prevent the Contagion of the *Gaol* Fever; Fear, and the selfish ideas of personal Safety carry them so far; the other great Points of Policy and Humanity in the plan of the Penitentiary House, Solitary Imprisonment etc. have been treated as chimerical—and expensive *Experiments*."[23] This argument gains further strength from the fact that the Hulks, which were almost certainly far worse than the unreformed gaols and which had been intended only as a temporary expedient, survived eighty years of continuous and bitter criticism from men such as Howard himself. The final decision to abandon them was attributed by at least one contemporary observer to the cholera epidemic of 1849.[24]

Historians have failed to appreciate the role of typhus for two reasons.* First, they have always assumed, following the Webbs, that epidemics of gaol fever were so common in the eighteenth century as to be unremarkable. Thus they neglected to realize the significance of the epidemic of the 1780's. Though gaol fever may have been endemic, however, it seems unlikely that epidemics were frequent. Even in London such events were not taken lightly. Moreover, the renewed emphasis that

---

*Robin Evans and Michael Ignatieff are exceptions. Evans lists two major causes for prison rebuilding, the American war and gaol fever. He discusses the analogy between fear of contagion from fever and fear of contagion from vice and points out that prisons were rebuilt in courtyards on airy sites to prevent fever.

physicians such as Percival placed, in the 1780's, on the efficacy of environmental "public health" measures led to a new willingness to turn to rebuilding and increased separation as a cure.

Second, because of their reliance on national sources such as debates on bills, historians have failed to stress the fact that Howard's visits came at the beginning, not the end, of a period of accelerating crisis. The smooth progress of parliamentary legislation should not conceal this fact. Writers frequently suggest that after Howard's visits, the cessation of transportation in 1775, and the publication of *State of the Prisons* in 1777, new ideas gathered momentum and conditions grew steadily better. In fact, however, in the 1780's many prisoners were still dependent on fixed money allowances, which were being severely eroded by rising prices. Not only untransported felons but also many more misdemeanants and offenders judged under summary process crammed the gaols.

To make these points is not to take a materialistic view of reform. Gaol fever frightened the justices, but they would not have chosen rebuilding as a remedy unless doctors had begun to suggest that this was the best preventative. If the reformers were beginning to speak of an equation between physical contagion and moral contamination, it was the physicians who supplied them with the idea of separation as a preventative for disease.

The Challenge of Gaol Fever

Bayley's background enabled him to act as a bridge between the conservative bench and a more radical group of Manchester thinkers who were interested in a new approach to social problems. It was this group that set the agenda for the coming age of social reform in the north of England. Most of them were physicians, and the reappearance of epidemic typhus gave them the leverage they needed to press for a comprehensive program of reform. In turn, this program depended on changes in the traditional models of disease transmission. These changes were to have a profound effect on all of Lancashire's social institutions, including its prisons, which were for the first time explicitly designed to prevent both physical and moral contagion.

These doctors formed part of a closely knit circle of friends who were linked by political and religious sympathies as well as by a general interest in scientific progress and social reform. In general they were Nonconformists (usually Unitarians who called themselves Presbyterians) who had received their education in provincial dissenting academies before proceeding to Edinburgh. With little prospect of advancement in London, many chose to remain in the provinces, where they established a network of provincial scientific societies. Among those who remained in the north were Dr. John Heysham of Carlisle, developer of the "Carlisle Life Table" and author of a book on typhus; Dr. John Heygarth of Chester and later Bath, a close adviser of Howard's and the inventor of fever hospitals; Dr. John Aikin, son of the head of the Warrington Academy and biographer of Howard; and Drs. Matthew Dobson and James Currie of Liverpool.[25]

The Manchester members, who were all closely associated with Bayley in the founding of the Literary and Philosophical Society and other city institutions, included Thomas Percival, John Ferriar, and Charles White, a prominent local obstetrician, son-in-law of a local justice and sheriff. They shared a strong interest in public health stemming from personal experience, a belief that public health problems were closely linked to other social problems, and the hope that they could develop statistical methods that could guide a rational policy to control and reduce the incidence of disease. They were closely connected to French reformers such as d'Alembert, Voltaire, Lavoisier, Diderot, and Pinel and to the Americans Thomas Jefferson, Benjamin Franklin, and Benjamin Rush, as well as to Joseph Priestley, who had taught at the Warrington Academy. Howard himself stayed at Warrington while publishing *State of the Prisons* at the press of William Eyres and formed close friendships with the circle around the Academy.[26]

To understand the role these men played in the creation of Lancashire's social institutions, one must first understand the development of disease theory in the eighteenth century. As the century opened, two equally plausible and apparently incompatible models of disease transmission held sway: contagionism and anticontagionism, or miasmatism. In practice, nearly all physicians adopted a compromise, but the different formulations of that compromise resulted in bitter divisions within the medical community. They also proved critical in determining the direction taken by reformers late in the century.

Though contagionism had a long history, it could not account for some of the most puzzling features of the epidemic diseases. It could not explain why they *were* epidemic—that is, why their incidence varied so dramatically from year to year and also from season to season. Moreover, observation proved clearly that many who had frequent and direct contact with sufferers nevertheless escaped infection themselves. For this reason, medical writers from Hippocrates on had recourse to atmospheric explanations, based on the "epidemic constitution" of the atmosphere, that is, on the specific combination of temperature, moisture, season, elevation, and local peculiarities.[27]

In the mid-eighteenth century attention began to shift from the temperature or moisture of the air to the role of filth as a cause of air pollution and, therefore, of disease. According to this theory, decay or putrefaction, generated in organic materials such as excrement or marshy bogs or even produced as a result of ordinary breathing, released poisonous particles into the air. When these reached a certain concentration disease resulted. The revival of miasmatism, or the "filth theory of disease," in the early nineteenth century by men like Chadwick fueled the first national public health movement.

Contagionists, on the other hand, believed that though filth contributed to the spread of disease, epidemic diseases could not arise spontaneously out of conditions in the environment. Rather, these diseases were brought into a community by infected persons or goods and could spread only by direct contact with others. This contact did not have to be by touch; clothing or air, particularly polluted air, could carry particles of disease emitted by a sick person, but only across a few feet at most. Thus, isolation of the victim, particularly in a well-ventilated room, and efforts by the attendants to avoid contact and to cleanse themselves of any lingering particles on their bodies or clothing could prevent the spread of disease.

Contagionism and miasmatism stood at opposite ends of a spectrum that permitted many shades of opinion in between, but the extent to which doctors emphasized one or the other had a crucial effect on their choice of preventive measures. If the natural conclusion of miasmatists was that health rested on the control of sources of atmospheric pollution, such as open sewers, the natural conclusion of contagionists was that the first line of defense against epidemics must be quarantine. Both groups believed in cleanliness, but the contagionist cleansed from the inside out—first the person, then the room, then the street—while the miasmatist cleansed from the outside in—first public spaces, then private.[28]

The emphasis that contagionists placed on direct contact also led them to stress the discrete nature of epidemic diseases and thus to classify the wide array of symptoms seen by the physician into syndromes characteristic of specific diseases. They relied on an analogy with smallpox: inoculation could exactly reproduce one case of smallpox in a second subject.

The first bundle of symptoms exactly resembled the next. Miasmatists, on the other hand, believing that diffused atmospheric conditions caused disease, were less interested in sorting symptoms into groups of specific diseases. A particular state of the atmosphere affected everyone and caused symptoms that should appear in all victims. Many miasmatists believed that though there were different diseases, in any particular season sufferers from all diseases would exhibit certain common tendencies. Thus, when conditions favored digestive diseases, victims of both influenza and scarlet fever would exhibit symptoms of digestive disease.[29]

By the early eighteenth century these two "scientific" views of disease had prevailed over the earlier models, which had been based on divine intervention, astrology, or the humors. Over the next two centuries the emphasis kept swinging between the two views, while each was progressively refined. The first landmark was the publication of Richard Mead's *A Short Discourse Concerning Pestilential Contagion and the Methods to Be Used to Prevent It* in 1720. Mead was largely concerned with the plague, which had appeared in France and was menacing England, but his remarks applied to all contagious fevers. He admitted the theory of humors enough to argue that a body in which they were not properly balanced was more susceptible to infection. He therefore recommended a healthy life, free of depression or passion, a good diet, and "cooling" or "acid" foods such as citrus fruit and vinegar, to "keep the blood from inflaming."

The main part of this short book, however, was devoted to the assertion that contagion was actually spread by three agents: air, diseased persons, and goods transported from infected places. To control the first, Mead recommended greater cleanliness, including street cleaning. He suggested that houses be strewn with "cooling herbs" and washed with water and vinegar: "As *Nastiness* is a great Source of *Infection*, so *Cleanliness* is the greatest Preservative."[30] To control the other two agents he suggested that goods and persons entering the country from abroad be quarantined and that the attendants of the sick be careful not to inhale near them.

Mead specifically mentioned prisons in his book, pointing out that gaol fever was "always attended with a Degree of Malignity in proportion to the *Closeness* and *Stench* of the Place: and it would certainly very well become the Wisdom of the Government, as well with Regard to the health of the *Town*, as in Compassion to the *Prisoners* to take Care, that all Houses of Confinement should be kept as Airy and Clean, as is consistent with the Use, to which they are designed."[31]

Mead carefully evaluated the relative usefulness of contagionist and miasmatic models. He concluded that "a corrupted state of Air is without doubt necessary to give these Contagious Atoms their full Force," but "it is evident that *Infection* is not received from the Air itself, however predisposed, without the Concurrence of something emitted from Infected persons."[32] Mead, therefore, accepted the contagionists' emphasis on the specificity of epidemic diseases but also the miasmatists' argument that disease could be transmitted over a distance by corrupted air. It should be remembered that Mead was writing about plague, which, since it is carried by rats, has an incidence that cannot be explained by direct physical contact between victims.

The generation of physicians who flourished at mid-century was able to make important contributions to public health based on Mead's compromise. Nevertheless, their interpretations of his work often seriously circumscribed their efforts. Doctors never entirely lost sight of the need for cleanliness—which, if pursued single-mindedly, could have helped reduce the incidence of disease—but, presented with a multicausal theory of disease, they tried to achieve prevention by concentrating on the most easily controlled causes. Though they accepted elements of both explanations, they thus tended to lean toward miasmatism. For example, Sir John Pringle, president of the Royal Society and the leading expert on prison medicine of his time, developed an elaborate causal theory dependent on the climate, the air, and the humors. It led him to recommend, among other things, that fever patients be scattered in many small hospitals with those ill of other diseases or injuries, instead of being isolated in a single place.[33]

The best example of the drawbacks of this approach is the famous outbreak of gaol fever at Newgate in 1750, when the terrified authorities brought in the best available consultants, Pringle and Stephen Hales, a specialist in disease in the navy. Discovering that Newgate was very dirty and unbearably offensive, the two concluded that the solution lay in an enormous ventilator (Hales's own invention) that could expel the noxious miasma. The prison was first cleaned by the sheriff and some assistants, but there is no evidence that they washed any of the prisoners.[34] Belief in the efficacy of the ventilator may have led the authorities to overlook more traditional remedies, such as whitewashing and the burning of clothing and bedding. When the epidemic appeared at Bedford, the justices there also erected a large ventilator.[35] Miasmatism, as it was practiced in the middle of the eighteenth century, therefore, encouraged a reliance on palliatives that removed or masked unpleasant odors without destroying the causes of disease.

By the late eighteenth century, medical thinkers had developed a third approach to disease. This view, which has been called sensualism or Hartleian materialism, rested on Locke's contention that all knowledge depended on sense impressions. Because the physician also attained knowledge through his direct experience of his patients, the first state of sensualism encouraged empiricism: a reliance on clinical experience rather than on medical theory, on symptoms rather than on causes, and on the symptomatic classification of disease. It thus assisted the development of both statistical and clinical medicine.[36]

The second stage of materialism, however, had a more complex effect, because it stressed the divorce between the outside world and the sensate individual, dependent on his sense impressions and his physical integrity for all his information. Where traditional philosophy had assumed a split between a faulty body and an eternal immaterial spirit, materialists emphasized the unity of body and spirit and hence the close identification between psychic and somatic health. Because the spirit was part of the brain and the brain was merely a physical organ, a part of the body, anything that disrupted the body might affect the brain and its perceptions, and an injury to the brain could cause a disorder of the intellect or even of the conscience. It followed that moral failures, such as crime, and mental failures, such as madness, might result from physical diseases. Healing the body might cure the spirit. Medicine, therefore, might be considered a "moral science." Conversely, if the sense impressions of the victim mediated all knowledge of disease, perhaps what seemed to be objective diseases were merely the products of a disordered nervous system.[37]

Michael Ignatieff has recently suggested that the rise of materialism led doctors to espouse the curative value of institutional care for the poor and, thus, encouraged the development of large social institutions. He argues that the identification between body and mind fostered by "Hartleian materialism" led Lancashire physicians such as Thomas Percival to emphasize the role of mental problems, such as depression and remorse, in causing illness. Disproportionate illness among the poor, therefore, could signify moral failures such as lack of discipline. This theory could easily lead medical thinkers to use "the language of social and moral condemnation veiled as the language of medicine."[38] In this way, the use of "Hartleian categories provided 'scientific' legitimacy . . . for medical condemnation of the indiscipline of the poor" and "led doctors to be confident that once the bodies of the poor were subjected to regulation, their minds would acquire a taste for order." For this reason, medical reformers such as Percival "insisted that institutional confinement was the sole way to change the poor. The sick could not be cured in their homes; they had to be given moral therapy in the hygienic asceticism of an institutional quarantine."[39] Early prison reformers like Hanway merely borrowed this conceptual framework in arguing that crime was also a disease.

Unfortunately for this argument, the Lancashire physicians who were especially fertile in creating medical institutions, such as Percival and Ferriar, were contagionists who explicitly rejected materialism.[40] They did, however, accept the materialists' view of the importance of direct clinical experience and also their interest in, although not their explanation for, the connection between psychic and somatic disorders. They founded insane asylums, wrote extensively on insanity, hypochondria, and hysteria, and maintained close connections with lunacy reformers such as Rush and Pinel.

In general, although they, unlike the materialists, held that diseases were objective entities that came from outside the sufferer and were transmitted by contact, the Lancashire doctors also believed that the resistance any individual could offer to invasion by a disease was affected by his or her general physical and mental health. Thus, Howard explained the susceptibility of robust young convicts to gaol fever by the sudden shock to their spirits caused by their being ironed and thrust into close, offensive dungeons. Ferriar argued that the general debility among the poor caused by inadequate diet and night work rendered them especially vulnerable to epidemics. Both the physical and the mental debilitation of the poor increased their liability to disease.[41]

Though this approach sometimes led physicians into class-based moral strictures, it also left them in a rather ambivalent position with regard to society as a whole. It suggested that the first line of defense against disease might be quarantine but that prevention of widespread debility would involve fundamental changes in society. It also suggested that the sudden resurgence of fever might be the result of social failure. This line of thought helps to explain the generally radical political views held by this generation of physicians and their uneasy attitude toward the rise of the factory. Bayley, Percival, and Ferriar were leading advocates of factory reform, and several medical reformers were widely suspected of Jacobinism.[42]

These reformers were by no means unhesitating proponents of institutional confinement for the poor. In general, they preferred to treat the poor at home. The new dispensaries that appeared in this period were specifically designed to enable the poor to receive medical aid without being admitted to hospitals, and some institutions, such as the Manchester Infirmary, also experimented with "home patient" schemes. White, his protégé Aikin, and Percival all wrote extensively on hospital management. They warned doctors to ensure that hospitals did not spread disease instead of curing it and to take great care to avoid admitting unsuitable cases. Percival, for example, urged that hospitals keep complete records of their patients so that doctors could compare the outcome of institutional cases with those they saw at home in order to avoid admitting patients who would have a lower risk at home. "The discretionary power of the physician or surgeon, in the admission of patients," he wrote, "could not be exerted with more justice or humanity than in refusing to consign to lingering suffering, and almost certain death, a numerous class of patients, inadvertently recommended as objects of these charitable institutions."[43]

Their disease theory led these doctors to believe that all large buildings in which many people were gathered—particularly those whose inmates were debilitated—posed a serious threat to public health, whether these buildings were hospitals, factories, or lodging houses. Percival warned that "no precautions relative to the reception of patients, who labour under maladies incapable of relief, contagious in their nature, or liable to be aggravated by confinement in an impure atmosphere, can obviate the evils, arising from *close wards* and the false economy of crowding a number of persons into the least possible space."[44]

Because disease resulted from contact or close proximity and not merely from poisoned air, however, contagionist physicians believed it was possible to design buildings that could reduce or eliminate the dangers of cross-infection and institutional epidemics. Moreover, they believed that the use of such structures to quarantine the sick could prevent epidemic fevers from spreading among the population at large. This goal, however, could be achieved only with close attention to the institutions' design and administration.

Like prisons, hospitals face a dilemma: how to ensure close supervision of patients and, simultaneously, provide patients with privacy and separation? The two are at odds: if patients are placed in single rooms, nurses cannot observe all of them constantly. Moreover, single rooms are more difficult to keep clean and demand more space, requiring nurses to walk long distances. They are also more difficult to ventilate effectively.

The theory of disease transmission that any particular writer espoused helped determine his choice of plan. Miasmatists urged that all fever hospitals be removed to the country, where the air was purer and there was less danger that the miasma emanating from the hospital would infect surrounding communities. If people spread contagion, their ingress and egress could be controlled, but if contagion was spread in the air, no one could prevent it from escaping. Moreover, in the country, buildings could be scattered over a site, thus providing free ventilation and avoiding the dangerous buildup of poisons in the air. If this plan was not followed, patients could not be grouped together by disease because the increased concentration of poison in the air would increase the severity and contagiousness of their disease. Miasmatists such as Florence Nightingale campaigned for long wards that could be constantly supervised by a single nurse, that could be thoroughly and easily cleansed, and, most important, that could be thoroughly and constantly ventilated.[45]

The contagionists, on the other hand, argued that patients should be separated from each other as far as possible, preferably in small single rooms but if necessary in rooms holding only two or three patients. As with the prisons, this plan proved impossible to implement. The contagionists next urged that all patients suffering from similar ailments be grouped together in separate areas or institutions. They also encouraged hygienic controls on traffic in and out of the hospital; the hospital, they felt, should be quarantined from the surrounding community. The poor were discouraged from visiting sick friends, patients' clothing and possessions were to be purified on entry, and nurses were to take precautionary measures on entering and leaving. Measures designed to prevent people from transmitting disease by direct contract were more important than the removal of the hospital to an isolated site; indeed, these reformers preferred urban sites as both more accessible and less threatening to the poor.[46]

There was a strong resemblance between these new hospitals and the new prisons. Percival, in fact, when asked about the design of a new county hospital and later the new House of Recovery, recommended the plan of the New Bailey.[47] This resemblance was not due merely to an unconscious or metaphoric association between moral and physical contagion but also to the fact that in the late eighteenth century the need to control physical contagion was paramount in both institutions. With a partial remedy at hand, the threat of disease, and particularly of typhus, was increasing rapidly.

Typhus, or gaol fever, is caused by a microorganism called *Rickettsia prowazeki*, which is carried by body lice. It is traditionally known as a hardship disease, because to take hold it requires a combination of dirt (to support the lice) and malnutrition or stress (to lower resistance). Since lice do not fly and since they die rapidly once infected with typhus, they cannot carry the disease very far; close contact, therefore, is necessary to spread the disease and overcrowding is necessary to support a large epidemic. A certain degree of dirt and privation in the population at large provides the reservoir of lice and endemic disease that enable epidemics to break out in crowded institutions. Small gaols could foster endemic or occasional cases of typhus, but it seems unlikely that most of them could have experienced frequent epidemics in the relatively uncrowded conditions of the early eighteenth century. The most notorious cases in early modern England were the "black Assizes," when the disease spread in packed courtrooms; similarly, the great Newgate epidemic of 1750 followed overcrowding resulting from postwar demobilization.[48]

At the end of the century, at about the time of Howard's visits, there was a resurgence of the disease. Howard himself found some record of gaol fever within the past decade or so at about 20 of the 105 prisons he visited. Liverpool borough gaol suffered in 1775, and in the same year some sort of illness affected the Castle. The epidemic of 1783 hit Lancaster, Liverpool, Manchester, and many other local prisons along with towns throughout England. It was followed by further epidemics in the succeeding decades.[49]

These prison epidemics had two main causes. The first was a growing incidence of typhus among the population at large. This was the natural result of all the changes associated with urbanization: a rising population, domestic crowding, and filth. The war may also have helped generate these outbreaks; armies and navies, like gaols and hospitals, were always particularly susceptible to typhus, and soldiers and sailors had enough contact with the general population to spread it. Though it is probably true that prisoners infected others with typhus, it is also true that new prisoners had carried it into the gaols from infected towns.

Gaolers and justices perennially claimed—along with generals, captains, and corporations—that the disease had not originated in their prisons but had been brought from somewhere else. Their protestations held some truth, for conditions in some of the northern towns were far worse than they were in the houses of correction. Even Carlisle, which was, comparatively speaking, a model of cleanliness, suffered from an epidemic in 1781. Liverpool suffered from an estimated 3,000 cases of typhus annually in the years between 1787 and 1796.[50] Endemic and epidemic typhus was also common in Manchester. Engels, writing in 1844, stated that it had never been wholly stamped out in Manchester's worst slums. Between 1846 and 1848 there were still more than a million cases of typhus and typhoid in England as a whole.[51]

The second reason for the rising incidence of typhus was that the gaols themselves were becoming more crowded, especially with felons who—because they often came from the poorer parts of the population, because they were the worst-treated class in the prisons, and because they tended to spend longer periods in confinement—were especially susceptible to disease. Under such conditions, no matter how clean the gaol was usually kept, typhus often broke out. Even today, it is difficult to control lice when large numbers of people live together in a single area, although we know how typhus is transmitted and have more effective disinfectants. Not even conscientious cleaning could have eradicated the disease. Dirty conditions among the felons probably promoted the Lancaster Castle epidemic of 1783, but we know that John Higgin, who succeeded his father in that year, was always extremely anxious to keep the prison clean. Everyone who visited it (except Henry Hunt) commented on its cleanliness. Yet Higgin himself wrote that it was impossible to prevent disease when the prison was crowded. Nor was he the only gaoler who noted the connection between typhus and overcrowding. The Home Office papers from 1783 to 1786 are full of urgent pleas from local authorities for the removal of the growing number of long-stay transportees because their presence increased the chances of disease.[52]

The rise of typhus in the late eighteenth century contributed to the rise of contagionism, and contagionist theory led doctors to understand that typhus was a specific disease and thus to identify the group of symptoms that characterized it. Because of its emphasis on discrete diseases, contagionism encouraged the effort to sort different "fevers" into distinct diseases. In turn, the prevalence of typhus led to the adoption of contagionist models, because the model of disease transmission suggested by contagionism applies well to the way typhus actually spreads; although it is an insect-vector disease it can only spread in close proximity. The incidence of other insect-borne diseases, such as plague and yellow fever, and of such water-borne diseases as cholera is much harder to explain by direct personal contact between victims. Thus other disease models prevailed in America, where yellow fever was the greatest threat, and in nineteenth-century England, which was obsessed with the fear of cholera.

Typhus was a frightening, dramatic, and dangerous disease, and the new understanding of its transmission and spread was likely to cause both fear and guilt among local administrators. As doctors accumulated evidence, they were able to show that the disease flourished in conditions of overcrowding and squalor, often in places such as army barracks, ships, hospitals, gaols, factories, and the new urban slums. The revival of typhus in these areas suggested that certain social failures were responsible for the miserable conditions that bred it. Though comprehensive social reform was desirable to eliminate the underlying cause, however, contagionist theory suggested that the first and most immediate line of defense against typhus was the establishment of institutional quarantine in buildings that not only isolated sufferers from the outside world but also circumscribed their contact with each other.

The fear of fever prodded men into action, and the new insights of medical theory determined the direction of that action. Justices felt that the existing state of affairs directly threatened their own well-being and that of the general public. They believed that they could avert the danger by constructing new prisons. Having accepted this reasoning, they saw many additional advantages to better-located buildings laid out in small rooms rather than open wards. The prisoners themselves could now be protected (it was hoped) from epidemics of gaol fever by the rigorous imposition of cleanliness and by the construction of their own lazarettos in the form of separate infirmaries. Moreover, the use of plans like those recommended for the new hospitals would bring greater security and reformation as well as better control of disease. If the majority of justices were interested only in preserving their personal safety, the few reformers such as Bayley who played an active role in planning and administering the gaols were prepared to take a longer view and to ensure that the new buildings were designed to promote moral and spiritual as well as physical integrity. The new prisons owed their existence to overcrowding and disease, but they owed their design and their discipline to a small group of dedicated reformers who were determined to exploit this opportunity to fashion a new model of correction.

It was the growing fear of typhus that was the decisive factor in determining the timing of new prison construction. It was the Gloucester epidemic that enabled Sir George Onesiphorus Paul to persuade his reluctant fellow-justices to construct a new gaol at enormous expense. The chronology of the rebuilding in Lancashire shows a similar conjunction of a great man and a great fear.

CHAPTER 4

The New Discipline

The Establishment of Fixed Rules

Lancaster Castle was the first prison in the county to have fixed rules; a committee consisting of Bayley, Rasbotham, and four other justices drew up a suggested code for the criminal prisoners in 1785. Rules were drawn up for Preston in 1792 and for Salford in 1794, after the new buildings had opened. A second set of rules, applicable only to Crown prisoners, was established for Lancaster in 1795 and approved by the Assize judge.[1]

It was natural that as the prisons grew bigger and more complex, administration would have to become more formal, but as Michael Ignatieff has pointed out, the establishment of written rules was also a deliberate measure intended to increase the rationality and accountability of the system. Prisoners would know what was expected of them and where they stood. They would know how they must behave and also how the gaoler ought to behave toward them. Prisoners would be accountable to the gaoler for their behavior and the gaoler would be accountable to the justices for his. The mere existence of this rational environment was supposed to aid in the reform of the deviant.[2] English reformers, from the Levellers to the Wilkites and Benthamites, had urged the creation of a fixed, rational, comprehensible, and written code of law, believing that good laws in themselves might help make good men. It is perhaps ironic that their dreams came to fruition only in the world of the prison—a world that in other ways represented the antithesis of that society of consenting, independent, and free citizens that so many of them had envisioned—and that these very rules helped strip prisoners of the last vestiges of self-government by mutual consent.

Although they controlled the behavior of both the prisoners and the gaoler, the written codes had a more radical effect on the prisoners than on their keepers. Gaolers had already been subject to a long list of regulations in common and statute law; the new rules simply added the further requirements of recent legislation. Although measures were taken to make gaolers more accountable for their adherence to the new rules, such as the appointment of visitors and the requirement that books be kept, no new sanctions were added. If a gaoler persistently misbehaved or broke the rules, the justices could in most cases do nothing but attempt to have the sheriff dismiss him. The only criminal sanctions were those provided by much older laws.

For the prisoners, however, these rules marked a distinct change. Although Puritans had attempted to enforce a "reformation of manners" in certain city prisons at the beginning of the seventeenth century, these efforts had had little permanent effect. In every area except escape, laws concerning gaol prisoners had been permissive rather than restrictive; they had established rights such as free access but said nothing about prisoners' behavior. Bridewell prisoners seem to have been similarly unrestricted in practice, although in law they were supposed to work. With the establishment of fixed rules, however, came a specific set of punishments for their infringement, to be enforced either by the gaoler himself or, if the breach was serious, by the justices. The mere establishment of written rules, therefore, marked a transition from an informal justice administered in many cases by the prisoners themselves to a formal justice administered by the gaoler and magistrates.

What the gaolers lost in autonomy, they gained in authority and responsibility. This development may have been unpopular with lazy gaolers who wished to be left in peace to neglect their charges, but reform-minded gaolers welcomed their increasing power to interfere in the daily lives of their prisoners. The difference such a code could make is clear in Lancaster Castle, where, because of problems in obtaining the approval of the Assize judges, the debtors were still without rules in 1812, although rules had governed the Crown prisoners since 1795. Even allowing for the greater license always permitted to debtors, the difference this disparity created in their respective positions was enormous. John Higgin had little power to prevent drunkenness, theft, quarreling, or even violence among the debtors. Unless they appealed to the usual processes of law (e.g., having an assailant bound over to keep the peace), all that he could do was persuade the justices to withdraw the offenders' allowances. The formal rules cost the prisoners a good deal of freedom, particularly at Manchester, where the zealous magistrates expected repentance and reform, not merely the good behavior accepted at Preston and Lancaster. On the other hand, the prisoners did gain a measure of protection both from each other and from the exactions of mercenary gaolers. This same process is apparent in many other areas of reform.

Accountability

The reformers were extremely anxious to increase the accountability of the entire prison staff. This was to be achieved in three ways. First, the gaoler's income was to come from the justices rather than the prisoners. His financial interest in the conduct of the prison was consistently and steadily reduced. This movement began very early: the prevention of extortion was one of the first objects of prison law. Prohibitions on the sale of office, for example, were enacted in 1421 and 1623 as well as 1718. An act of 1729 had required that a table of fees be fixed and publicly displayed and had set up a machinery for hearing complaints of extortion. Beginning with the abolition of prison taps so strongly urged by Bayley, a series of steps substituted a fixed salary for a variety of fees; the final act came in 1815.[3] Some gaolers supported this change; at Lancaster John Higgin took the initiative in persuading the justices to replace his fees with a salary.[4]

More important in controlling corruption was the use of paid professional subordinate officers in jobs traditionally held by prisoners. The new turnkeys were strictly forbidden to accept any payment from prisoners, although in many gaols, including Lancaster, they could still accept gratuities for showing visitors around. At the beginning of the nineteenth century, Lancaster turnkeys still collected money from prisoners to purchase goods in the town and to convey mailed parcels from the station to the prison, but Higgin eventually put a stop to this service, although he still allowed them to traffic in bread. By 1812 it was a very serious thing to accuse a turnkey of accepting bribes or gratuities.[5]

A second way of gaining oversight over prison staff was the requirement that they keep a full set of written records, open to inspection by the local magistrates. This meant a journal for both the chaplain and the surgeon. The gaoler, aside from his own journal, was expected to keep separate registers recording admissions and releases, punishments, financial transactions, and prisoners' daily conduct. Apparently, this rule was frequently neglected; in 1812 none of the Castle officers kept a journal although financial accounts, a punishment book, and a register of prisoners did exist.[6] Following the strong recommendation of the commission of 1812, compliance became more regular. Such record keeping, as the commission pointed out, not only made officers more accountable but also offered them some protection against malicious accusations by prisoners.

Finally, there was the increased supervision of the justices. Visiting justices were first authorized by an act of 1785. Lancashire lost no time in appointing them, but they varied in their zeal. Bayley, inevitably, seems to have been very active, not only in visiting Salford and later the New Bailey but also as a member of the building and finance committee for Lancaster. James Fenton, the recorder of Lancaster, whom Howard praised for his humanity, was probably another conscientious appointee. After the deaths of the reformers, however, and the ebbing of the initial excitement, the justices became more lax.

Boards of visitors, often including all the justices in the division, continued to be regularly appointed, but they did not take a very active interest in the good government of the prisons. Justices were quite ready to attend when the gaoler asked them to strengthen his discipline by ordering additional punishment or by binding disputants over to keep the peace. Their main effect, therefore, was to increase control over the behavior of the prisoners, not to correct excesses by the gaoler. Any improvement in the gaolers' conduct, therefore, probably came from greater care in making the original appointment, or a different moral climate, rather than extensive on-the-job supervision.

Chapel

Lancaster Castle had no professional clergyman until one was required by an act of 1773. Having appointed the chaplain and agreed to pay £36 toward his salary of £50, the local justices naturally wished to see his services utilized, but chapel services were not popular with the prisoners. In 1777 John Dane complained to the Sessions that some prisoners were avoiding chapel or misbehaving during services. The justices immediately ruled that all Anglican prisoners were to attend services and to behave themselves or lose their allowance. Dane could simply give the county treasurer a list of miscreants and their names would be removed from his list of recipients.[7]

This is another example of the way in which a "reform" undoubtedly beneficial in intention became a means of greater control over prisoners. Originally, the intention was to provide a service, but the justices, having paid for the service and being increasingly worried about the spiritual welfare of their charges, decided to compel them to use it.

Furthermore, the actual decision was made on the initiative of the gaoler, not the justices. John Dane, who later hanged himself and whose administration was deplored by the Higgins, hardly qualifies as a reformer, but even he, in one way, was seeking greater order in the gaol. Instead of seeing the period as one in which zealous and high-minded justices gradually imposed their vision on callous, brutal, and ignorant gaolers, one might equally well see the position as reversed, with gaolers asking largely uninterested magistrates for greater power to regulate their charges.

Several of these themes reappear in a petition John Higgin sent to the Preston bench in the summer of 1785. Higgin complained that since the abolition of the prison tap prisoners were sending for liquor from the town at unreasonable hours. He added that persons from the town were causing inconvenience by attending the Sunday services at the Castle and requested the direction of the court for his future conduct. The court resolved that he had "a right and ought in the faithful discharge of his Duty to Exercise his Authority Discretionary in all matters that may tend to the good and better Regulation of the said gaol and prevent Intemperance." It also affirmed his right to ban visitors from chapel.[8]

Again, in this case, it was the gaoler who initiated the action by asking for advice from the bench. (In 1786, when the rules had been established, the committee had recorded that Higgin approved of the regulations, being "above all things desirous to have as little as possible left to his Will or discretion in the management of his prisoners.")[9] The decision of the bench, however, was to confirm his own regulatory powers. Instead of being a mere security officer, paid to keep inmates from escaping, the gaoler was becoming an active pastor—a governor rather than a keeper. Moreover, the net result of the decision was to restrict the access of outsiders to the prison, whether they were publicans, whose hours were to be limited, or would-be chapelgoers.

A subsequent entry in Higgin's journal, made more than thirty years after his original request, sheds some light on his motives for seeking to exclude outsiders from the chapel. On April 18, 1817, a Mr. Ripley of Lancaster presented himself at the Castle gate, armed with a letter of admission from R. Atkinson, Jr., a local justice. The previous week, Thomas Higgin had refused to let him in. Atkinson, John Higgin wrote angrily, "I would gladly suppose, must have been imposed upon otherwise he would not have thought his Interference necessary. —If he had given himself time to Reflect, I presume he would not have given an order for the admission of a Drunkard, who is become Bankrupt . . . to gratify his Curiosity in gazing at the unhappy Men under sentence of Death."[10]

Higgin combined a moral disapproval of Ripley with a humanitarian distaste for the idea that condemned men should be regarded as interesting exhibits. Such voyeurism was a popular eighteenth-century recreation. Higgin, whom his chaplain believed to have "feelings of humanity too great for the situation he holds" because he found public executions so distressing, was clearly revolted by this custom.[11]

After so many years of autocratic power, however, and because he disliked the justice in question, Higgin also bitterly resented such interference with his authority. In his journal, which the justices were supposed to read, he wrote:

This is not the first time of the improper interference of this young Magistrate. . . . After 35 years Service in a very arduous and responsible situation I ought to be able to judge as to the propriety of admitting persons into the prison. The manner in which this Note was sent bespeaks the Hostility and Enmity of this Gentleman. . . . However willing I may be to accompany Mr. Atkinson Junior, or any other Magistrate,through the Gaol, yet I must say, that it is not decorous to grant orders of this Nature which can only be done to annoy me in the Execution of my Duty.

By this time, instead of pleading for greater regulation of the prison by the justices, being "desirous to have as little as possible left to his Will," Higgin had come to feel that they were interfering with his authority to run the gaol along reforming lines. This evolution is partly due to the changes of time; Higgin himself was growing older and more crotchety, while the justices with whom he had cooperated were dying and being replaced by lesser men. It was also, however, part of a real transition in the role of the gaoler.

Prison Clothing

Originally, there were two humanitarian reasons for providing prisoners with clothing. First, many prisoners either arrived in rags or were soon reduced to raggedness. Not only was this state uncomfortable and unhealthy, but it made it more difficult for the prisoner to find work after his release. Second, dirty clothing was well known to cause infection. Filthy clothes harbored parasites, encouraging typhus and skin ailments. Reformers soon realized that a complete change of clothes had other advantages, including increased security. If the county provided clothing it was almost inevitable that buying in bulk would result in a uniform, which also guaranteed fair distribution and made it possible to clean and return clothing without complicated sorting. Uniforms, in turn, made criminals easily recognizable at a time when fetters, the traditional means of distinguishing them, were falling into disuse. Recognizable clothing at least complicated escapes. Bentham, always ingenious, went so far as to suggest that prison uniforms be made with one sleeve long and one short; prisoners would then acquire a distinctive tan that would brand them even without their clothes.

An additional advantage of a prison uniform was the humiliation it imposed on the wearer. Fetters had also served this purpose; their abandonment perhaps made reformers more conscious of this effect. The adoption of uniforms addressed the "lesser eligibility" problem confronting reformers; as they increased the physical comforts of prisons they had to find compensatory psychological discomforts in order to discourage criminals. Uniforms did both at once; they were cleaner, better, and more comfortable than the prisoners' own clothing and yet were still humiliating to wear.

Exactly the same process went on inside the prison: different classes of prisoner were distinguished from each other by different clothing or badges, making it easier for prison officers to tell at once where they belonged and painting the felon with a deeper dye (at least in official eyes) than the misdemeanant. Uniforms were, therefore, part of the process of institutionalization, which marked prisoners as members of a community apart. They were also part of the process of classification, which sought to segregate different groups of prisoners from each other to protect women, the young, and the relatively innocent from "hardened felons." (The ultimate conclusion of this process was solitary confinement.)

This argument can be carried too far, however. Most magistrates, more concerned with bricks and mortar than with "chimerical" ideas about transforming prisoners' minds, were not particularly anxious to introduce uniforms, provided that other measures could be taken to safeguard health. The Lancaster rules called for cheap and useful uniforms, "so contrived as to prevent escapes," the Preston rules included the provision of white flannel clothes suitable for the season, and the Manchester rules, as usual the most ideological, mentioned a uniform and, for the worst felons, shaven heads and "Certain Marks or Badges of Disgrace . . . as well to humiliate the Wearer, as facilitate Discovery ,in case of Escape." Nevertheless, we have no evidence that any of these prisons actually adopted uniforms at the time. Lancaster was still without uniforms 26 years later, when John Higgin explained to the commission of 1812 that the justices had balked at the expense. Instead, the clothes of incoming prisoners were baked in an oven, thus satisfying the concern for health if not for moral suasion.[12]

Again, Higgin himself seems to have been the chief supporter of the proposed reform, arguing that the cost of providing clothing for the most ragged was taking a large proportion of the Charity Fund. In 1816 his son was finally able to report that he had clothed fourteen condemned men for the first time in the new uniform of blue and yellow. In 1820 Gurney wrote that the Castle prisoners were manufacturing all their own clothing.[13] Preston, meanwhile, seems to have bought clothing piecemeal for such prisoners as needed it.

On the whole, although the eventual introduction of prison clothing contributed greatly to the health and comfort of the poorer prisoners, it to some extent restricted their freedom and certainly branded them as members of an outcast tribe. In this area as in many others, what seemed initially to be a humanitarian measure and a real benefit to many extremely ragged prisoners was to prove a mixed blessing.

Prison Labor

Prisoners in the houses of correction had always been expected to work. Stuart legislation had required the counties to provide the necessary implements. Eighteenth-century writers frequently complained that the bridewells had completely failed to comply with this requirement, but it seems likely that Lancashire had a relatively good record in this respect. Occasional inventories and bills mention such implements as cards and looms, while other sources suggest that prisoners usually depended on the proceeds of their labor. Many prisoners in Lancaster Castle also worked for their keep, although the gaolers were occasionally hostile to the practice and the prisoners had to find their own materials and tools.

During this period two changes took place in the nature of prison labor. First, it became more strictly regulated. Originally, prisoners were paid directly in money for what they did, on a piecework basis. Though the master of the house of correction was supposed to "set the prisoners to work," the real constraint, in the bridewells as in the gaol, was economic. Just as in the world outside, in prison one could work or starve. Prisoners with means apparently were not otherwise compelled to work in either institution, nor, apparently, were the hours, sort, or amount of work specified.

The many improvements in the prisons essentially achieved a more democratic provision of goods in kind rather than money. The state undertook to guarantee a minimum supply of food, staff income, accommodation, heat, cleaning, and (eventually) clothing. In order to repay itself for these benefits in at least a symbolic manner, the state confiscated the profits from prisoners' labor, leaving them only a very small percentage of the wages they had earned, and controlling the use of even that remnant.

Since the prisoners no longer received a full reward for their labor, and since their necessities would be supplied whether or not they actually applied themselves to their tasks, the authorities had to substitute indirect compulsion, that is, statutory punishment, for the earlier direct economic compulsion. At the same time, the county, rather than the prisoners, became the judge of what they should do, what they should produce, how long they should work, and what they should consume. The keeper, from being one employer among several, became the person authorized to punish prisoners if they refused to work for the county, and the gaoler, for the first time, enforced labor in return for prison allowances. This development in some ways paralleled the development of the factory system outside, where the need for machines to work constantly, the difficulty in controlling quality, and the impossibility of estimating each person's production on a piecework basis led employers to regulate the hours their employees worked, to punish lapses or misbehavior, and to establish regulations for conduct.

The second change was the transformation of prison labor from a primarily reformative activity to a more punitive one. The increasing benefits of imprisonment had created, in the minds of reformers at least, a problem of "lesser eligibility," of making the prisons disagreeable enough to deter crime. Among those now confined in the bridewells were convicted felons, who deserved severer treatment than petty offenders, but prisoners could not simply be made to work more than people outside. Many laborers already worked to the limits of their strength and beyond, while legislators would not force inmates to work to the point of damaging their health. Moreover, hours had to suit the capacities of the weakest, not the strongest. The act of 1782, therefore, established a maximum of twelve hours' labor, of which two hours were allowed for meals, bringing the total down to ten. The need to allow the prisoners air and exercise, as well as security considerations, brought the average down even further, since the prisoners were most safely locked up, unlocked, and counted by daylight. The winter workday was only about eight hours in all, with time out for meals, exercise, and other routines. In fact, the net result of the new regulations was, probably, that many prisoners worked less than they had when left alone to earn their own keep.

For petty offenders such a regime might be acceptable, but legislators felt it was inadequate for the increasing number of felons. For this reason the Hulk Act of 1776 ordered that convicts be set to hard labor, presumably something more arduous than common prison work. There was a fundamental conflict between the attempt to provide particularly odious labor for felons and the desire to encourage reformation. By making work itself a punishment, hard labor was unlikely to establish a positive attitude among inmates. In fact, however, prisons found it difficult to provide unpleasant labor. Tasks such as stone breaking posed obvious security problems, although some gaols did introduce stone sawing. The workhouse occupation of oakum picking was sometimes used, and Lancaster Castle punished rule breakers by setting them to wind bobbins for the weavers, but these were hardly the laborious, physically demanding occupations Parliament had in mind. Sexual bias relegated the most arduous job, the laundry, to women. Eventually, therefore, either the prisoners sentenced to hard labor ended up doing the same work as everyone else, which was the most profitable arrangement, or the justices and gaolers exercised their ingenuity in developing completely useless tasks merely to "torment" the prisoners. (The word is Bentham's; he bitterly opposed the practice.)

Cubitt's treadmill, introduced in the 1820's, was the logical result of this process, but "shot-drill" also proved popular. The latter required men to carry heavy balls of shot from one pile to another and back again. Such Sisyphean labors had certainly not been envisaged by the more progressive reformers; Bayley had urged, with Howard, that the primary purpose of prison labor was to make prisoners better men and to preserve their health and "cheerfulness." Punitive labor was, however, the inevitable concomitant of improving prison conditions to the point that administrators feared imprisonment was becoming attractive.

Although many reformers of this period saw the imposition of labor as the sine qua non of their schemes, it was rarely carried off with success. This failure stemmed partly from the reformers' own fatal ambivalence about whether prisons were reformative or deterrent, but still more from their inability to create institutions that could be penal while providing labor with substantial rewards. In the end, labor was split into two parts. One part was purely punitive. Though it may have done something to keep inmates healthy, hard labor produced little of value and made no pretense of redeeming the mind. The other part became something close to occupational therapy. Only in rare cases were prisoners productive. The new rules made it difficult to avoid work entirely, but since the prisoners had little real incentive, it took a herculean effort to persuade them to work very hard. Despite all the reformers' hopes, few inmates can have found prison labor either satisfying or reformative.

Drink

Throughout most of the eighteenth century, Lancashire prisoners, whether debtors or felons, bridewell or Castle inmates, received their allowances and earnings in money and purchased their own food and drink (with the exception of spirits, which were prohibited by an act of 1750). For such prisoners, a prison shop and tap was an obvious convenience, provided it did not become an instrument of extortion. Legally guaranteed access to similar goods in the town provided an automatic control over the price and quality of the goods offered. John Higgin mentioned that he had made a large profit from the Lancaster tap, selling good wine at a reasonable price.[14]

Zealous magistrates would have liked to abolish all alehouses and prison taps. Not only did the latter offer opportunities for extortion and bad conduct by the gaoler but they also led to tippling, drunkenness, and rowdiness. Aldermen in seventeenth-century London attempted to ban strong beer and ale, and in 1729 a parliamentary committee reminded members of the numerous inconveniences of prison taps.[15]

Beer, however, if not vital to life, was at least important to it. Poor felons could be left to drink water from the Castle well. Debtors, however, were legally entitled to beer and considered having to drink water instead a severe hardship. Many houses of correction did not have an adequate supply of drinking water; Howard wrote that at Preston the prisoners had no water all all. Beer, therefore, along with internal taps, remained a feature of all three Lancashire institutions for most of the century.

The attack on drink in the 1770's and early 1780's was at least expedited by the fact that the improvements of buildings and the measures necessary to improve health greatly increased the amount of water regularly available and used in the prisons. The new buildings included pumps, cisterns, baths, and sewers. Obedience to the provisions of the Gaol Fever Act required a fairly large and regular supply of water for filling baths and washing the rooms. The towns themselves were slowly improving their water supplies, though they lagged far behind the needs of their growing populations.

Although much of the prison water came either from wells or rainwater, it was still a health hazard, as the frequent epidemics of bowel disease show. By forcing prisoners to abandon beer for water, the reformers may have unintentionally done something to counteract the other benefits of greater cleanliness. One advantage of using old castles for gaols was their deep and separate wells.

Thomas Butterworth Bayley's energetic campaign to abolish taps made Manchester one of the first dry prisons in the country. The Salford justices saw all alehouses as breeding grounds of crime and disorder, but it was easier to impose their distaste on institutions they controlled. Their hostility also implied a hardening attitude toward criminals: while providing for the prisoners' necessities, they also demanded greater discipline and the abolition of all unnecessary comfort or cheer. The justices, being virtuous, certainly thought that prisoners should have no more cakes and ale. For this reason, they did not merely forbid the keeper to sell alcohol, they forbade prisoners to have it at all unless ordered by a surgeon. At Lancaster, where the bench was less zealous but still reformist and influenced by Bayley, the prison tap remained until abolished by law in 1783. Although the 1786 rules allowed all prisoners to bring in three pints of ale a day, this was forbidden to criminals by the 1795 rules. At Preston, where Bayley had little influence, the justices also permitted Cowburne to keep his tap until 1783. Moreover, the Preston rules of 1792 specifically permitted prisoners to have both milk and small beer occasionally, presumably at county expense since no one was allowed to bring it in or sell it.[16]

Although Higgin had persuaded the justices in 1785 to allow him to limit the purchasing times of liquor for the debtors, no one ever succeeded in controlling their alcoholic consumption. Poor debtors would order their permitted ration of three pints of beer and then sell it to the wealthy. Stronger liquor was regularly smuggled in. The records of the early nineteenth century are full of the resulting drunken brawls, which make it easy to understand why the authorities were so anxious to control drinking.

Aside from a simple dislike of drinking and drunkenness, reformers abolished taps because they wanted to end the gaoler's dependence on the prisoners for his income, with its tendency to encourage extortion and improper favoritism. The reformers were concerned not merely to improve the lot of the poor prisoners but also to increase the severity meted out to the better-off. The abolition of the gaoler's chief source of income, moreover, and its replacement by a salary controlled by the justices increased (at least in theory) their ability to make the gaoler answerable to them. Howard made many of these points in *The State of the Prisons*; the Manchester bench merely echoed him when they explained in 1777 that "it is Highly requisite that no Gaoler or other Servant be suffered to hold the Tap. . . . Gaolers who hold or let the Tap, find their Account in not only Conniving at but promoting Drunkenness, besides the Gaolers Interest in the Sale of Liquors, may prompt him to be partial in his behavior to his prisoners, and to treat at least with neglect those who are poor and have nothing to Spend."[17]

The abolition of the tap and other measures drove such transactions underground but did not by any means eliminate them. It removed one important source of favoritism, corruption, and violence, but there were many others. All three houses of correction suffered from abuses that were ignored or disregarded by the justices. Without continuous and energetic action by the prison governors it was impossible to control corruption and bribery among the turnkeys, and without continuous superintendence by the justices many governors continued to make corrupt profits and to play favorites among the prisoners. Though the abolition of the prison taps was a definite step forward in the battle against corruption, it was by no means the end of the war.

Diet

In the 1770's both debtors and felons at Lancaster received a shilling a week, most of which they spent on food, while bridewell prisoners pur-

TABLE 7

Approximate Weekly Dietaries of Lancashire Prisons from Rules

Lancaster Castle (1786)	*Salford (1794)*
Felons:	10½ lbs. bread
10½ lbs. bread	4 lbs. potatoes
7d. worth of cheese, butter,	1 lb. beef
peas, potatoes, turnips, etc.	3¼ oz. salt
½ lb. beef	1 pt. peas
1 qt. broth	12 oz. oatmeal
4 oz. salt (1812)	3 oz. cheese
(Approximate cost, 2s. 7d.)	1½ oz. rice
Debtors:	
1s. worth of bread	
10 lbs. potatoes	
Preston (1792)	
10½ lbs. bread	
10½d. worth of	
peas, potatoes, etc.	
½ lb. beef	
1 qt. broth	

chased food with their earnings. As inflation ate into the value of the fixed county allowances, reformers urged that food be provided in kind, both to guarantee prisoners a minimum level of support and to prevent them from spending an undue proportion of their county money on drink or other nonessentials. Manchester, however, was the only prison that decided to specify the entire diet in weight rather than value; both Preston and Lancaster established a weight for bread but set a money value for accompanying vegetables and dairy food. Debtors received ten pounds of potatoes each week along with a shilling's worth of bread.

The establishment of fixed dietaries, like all the other reforms we have examined, had the double purpose of providing a reliable minimum level of maintenance, which was desperately needed by the poorer prisoners, and at the same time of making imprisonment more severe by reducing freedom of choice, imposing a bland diet, and outlawing small luxuries. For the prisoners who, lacking friends, family, money, or work, had occasionally been in danger of starvation in years of dearth and high prices, the new dietary offered a real advantage. This advantage was achieved, however, at a severe cost for everyone else, since the fixed diets were inadequate (see Table 7).[18]

There are two standards against which this diet can be judged. By a

modern standard, it was seriously deficient in calories and many nu-
trients, although the Lancashire habit of substituting potatoes for bread
or gruel explains why scurvy was a less serious problem there than in the
south. To judge it by the standard of the times, two questions must be
answered. How did the prisoner's diet compare with that of some comparable person outside? And, given a certain per capita allowance of
money, was its content a reasonable choice? It is hazardous to make any
firm statements about the diet of the free poor, but Drummond and Wilbraham have collected some useful evidence. Among other things, they
estimated the cost of some of the budgets from Frederic Eden's *State of
the Poor*. For example, a laborer, his wife, and three children living in
Kendal in Westmoreland spent, according to their estimates, about £20
2*s.* out of a total income of just under £30. Counting the three children
as two adults, this represents an annual per capita expenditure of £5, or
about 2*s.* per week. In 1786 the cost of a similar diet at Lancaster was 2*s.*
7*d.*[19]

Prison diets can also be compared to those of other large institutions,
such as the army and navy. The military diets, like those of the prisons,
made little allowance for fresh fruit or vegetables (except potatoes), but
they provided much more protein and were more expensive, although
still inadequate calorically. The army allowed a pound of bread and a
pound of meat per soldier per day. The navy spent 9*s.* 2¼*d.* per sailor
per week in 1811. Even by contemporary standards, therefore, prison
diets were at a low level, although probably somewhat better than those
of the worst-paid urban workers or country dwellers in years of dearth.*

Most important, however, is the question of what sorts of change these
dietaries imposed on prison standards. The mere drawing up of the dietaries did not result in their enforcement. It took a long time to establish these dietaries as the unalterable and single sources of food. The
evidence from this period shows that given the choice, prisoners spent
the same allowances on a greater variety of food and strongly resisted the
imposition of the high-starch diet.

---

*Sir Noel Curtis-Bennet, *The Food of the People* (London, 1946), pp. 179-80. See also
J. C. Drummond and Anne Wilbraham, *The Englishman's Food: Five Centuries of English
Diet* (London, 1958), appendix, p. 563, which includes a rough estimate of the nutritional
value of this and other dietaries. The Poor Law Commission, however, published diets
purporting to show that the independent agricultural laborer was the worst fed and the
convicted or transported thief the best off. See W. E. Passey, "Houses of Correction in
England and Wales" (M.A. thesis, University of Liverpool, 1936), appendix 1, pp. 116-
17.

In the beginning, although food was now provided in kind, it was easily converted back into cash. Prisoners received their entire daily allotment every morning. They could then sell or barter unwanted items (especially bread) to local traders, who came up to the Castle with food, for items they preferred. By 1812 there was a common kitchen for the felons, but it does not seem to have been much used, and the debtors always did their own cooking at the fireplace in their rooms. At some point before 1812, John Higgin stopped the direct trade between criminals and townspeople because "some remarks had been made in Lancaster, that the prisoners in the Castle had more bread than they could eat." He therefore ordered that the criminals were to sell their bread only to the debtors, through the medium of the turnkeys (since the criminals and debtors were not allowed to communicate); but the criminals were still free to spend money they gained in this way on other food. A little later Higgin forbade the women to buy coffee and tea because they were injuring their health by selling too much bread in exchange for these "innutritious" beverages.

When the commission of 1812 asked Higgin why he did not prohibit the sale of bread rather than the purchase of tea, he explained that the women substituted cheaper oatmeal and potato cakes for their bread and used the extra money to buy "milk, vegetables, and other nutritive food . . . and I considered the cakes . . . as wholesome as bread, and therefore not improper to be substituted . . . if the women liked it better."[20] This is evidence that when left to themselves, prisoners sometimes chose a more nutritious diet than that offered at the same cost by a fixed dietary. Even the despised coffee and tea were not wholly useless beverages since they were safer than water and were usually taken with sugar and milk, supplying badly needed protein and calories. The commission, however, unmoved by Higgin's arguments, urged that the sale of bread be prohibited.

Four years later, the twin problems of increasing population and the resulting disorder led Thomas Higgin, then acting as his father's deputy, to impose further controls on food. This action aroused the hostility of the prisoners and led to a bitter confrontation. The porridge war began on August 30, 1816, when Thomas recorded in his journal that "owing to the very crowded state of the Gaol, the prisoners have some difficulty in cooking their victuals. I observe that this is a source of frequent quarrelling amongst them—and this added to the difficulty of their paying Rooms Money—are the causes of almost endless dispute and inconvenience—so much so—that I think of putting the prisoners upon a dietary system—this will certainly deprive them of many little comforts, but upon the whole will I trust be productive of much good."[21]

On November 25 Thomas began making porridge in the kitchen boilers. That night the prisoners in the first yard sent a message to all the others, telling them to reject the porridge and refuse to go to work in the morning. Higgin also made a tactical error: fearing that it would take too long to cook the porridge in the morning, he ordered it to be made in the evening and reheated the next day. "Altho the Porridge was excellent last Evening," he wrote, "yet I find it impoverished by standing all night and not so well flavoured." Understandably, prisoners in two yards rejected their gruel in the morning and refused to work. Higgin took their food away, locked them in their cells, and told them they would have nothing else. He commented angrily that "it is lamentable to see such insolence within the walls of a prison, when thousands of the industrious and labouring poor, cannot get bread." There were further disturbances that afternoon and the next day, providing Thomas with "proof of the Spirit of insurrection . . . that prevails in the Gaol." At one point he and his father were attacked by a group of prisoners, forcing him to draw his pistol, but he eventually prevailed, putting the ringleaders in solitary and rewarding the well-behaved with a quart of soup paid for from the Charity Fund.

Although Thomas's imperious temperament, so different from that of his father, doubtless exacerbated the situation, it is easy to understand why the prisoners resisted a change that deprived them of "many little comforts." Not only had they to some extent lost the privilege of preparing their own food, but the porridge itself was unappetizing and unsalable. The change, therefore, meant a reduction in both the variety and the quality of their diet. Though nineteenth-century gaolers continued to substitute gruel or potatoes in times of dearth, bread remained a staple of the prison diet. In the middle of the century, prisoners still "trafficked" in bread despite the gaoler's best efforts to prevent the practice. By now, however, criminals could not obtain food from outside and bartered or sold their rations to their fellows, at some cost to their health.

The gradual introduction of fixed dietaries lessened the prisoners' freedom of choice and, while saving a few from hunger or starvation, caused malnutrition for many. Here again it was the gaoler, not the justices, who made many of the decisions about when and to what extent a reform would be introduced.

*

Many writers have maintained that the new prison discipline resulted from the disruption of transportation during the war with America, which caused an intellectual revolution by forcing reformers to develop a "punitive" rather than a merely custodial institution in order to deal with all the convicted felons who had previously been shipped out. Though this argument does contain an element of truth, it is still a serious overstatement. First, the increasing number of felons who could not be transported represented only a part of the changing size and composition of the prison population. Far from being central to the new prisons, the most serious class of "transportees" was treated in the local prisons as an embarrassing appendage.

Second, this argument is too narrow because it looks only at England. The problem of maintaining offenders at home had existed for a long time on the Continent, where transportation was uncommon, though not unknown. Most educated Englishmen must have known something about penal policies in Europe, particularly in Holland, France, and Germany. Even the Hulks were by no means an English innovation; French convicts had for many years done "galley service" in stationary old ships, working at the same sort of dredging and dockwork ashore that the English were later to introduce. Moreover, many continental countries (including Russia) were at this time reconsidering the uses of imprisonment and prison discipline, as the campaign by Beccaria and others forced them to develop alternatives to the death penalty. The United States also developed a new and highly experimental prison discipline during this period. The disruption of transportation was a uniquely British problem, but the changes that followed it appeared, for one reason or another, in many other countries as well.

What seems to have underlain these changes in both population and regime throughout Europe was an increasingly severe and "legalistic" or formal attitude toward offenses, which combined with a rising population and economic hardship to increase both formal prosecutions and total convictions. Meanwhile, a growing respect for the value of human life inspired measures to reduce prisoner mortality, both directly (by reducing the number of executions) and indirectly (by reducing hardship and disease). People were valued more highly and judged by a higher standard. Both this new severity and this new benevolence affected not only the total numbers of prisoners (more were going in and fewer leaving) but also the quality of the discipline imposed on the small world within the walls. Population growth alone would have necessitated many of the changes—such as new buildings, improved measures for public health, increasingly formal regulation, and more responsible officers— but this influence was undeniably accompanied by changes in attitudes and, in fact, partly caused by them.

Another way in which the established argument is too narrow is that it tends to ignore the houses of correction, the traditional penal institutions. This period did not so much foster a new idea of punitive imprisonment as simply mark a final stage in the gradual but steady assimilation between the gaols and the bridewells. County gaols already provided secure custody for dangerous offenders and were accustomed to hold long-stay inmates. Houses of correction were accustomed to provide penal imprisonment, though usually for relatively short terms—up to about three years. In this period the houses of correction expanded rapidly and, in the process, adopted the greater security and more formal regulation of the gaols, while the gaols kept their increasing numbers of sentenced offenders busy by imposing the labor previously required by the houses of correction. Lancaster Castle, in fact, began officially to accept "bridewell prisoners" from Manchester, while Manchester held nearly all its own felons. In a sense, we can say that prisoners began to be classified on a regional basis, rather than by the gravity of their crime. Exactly the same process has taken place in England since the Radzinowicz report of 1968 and the development of "dispersal prisons" to deal with a similar problem of rising population, and it appears to have resulted in similar changes in discipline.*

If these are the possible underlying explanations of the reforms, what was the nature of the reforms themselves? Looking at them in one way, we could say that these reforms created an embryonic welfare state incorporating many advances that would be introduced only haltingly in the world outside. Prisons guaranteed subsistence, housing, and medical care, provided water, cleaning, and lighting, and offered free social services such as schooling and counseling. This gain, however, was achieved only at the cost of introducing many more regulations and petty restrictions and by virtually confiscating wages. Seen in another way, the reforms represented the systematic imposition of a puritanical code that was hostile to even the most innocent pleasures and that tried to impose continuous penitential drudgery in place of drinking, smoking, playing,

---

*See Roy D. King and Kenneth W. Elliott, *Albany: Birth of a Prison, End of an Era* (London, 1978). The "dispersal" policy and the arrival of serious offenders at Albany forced an increasingly rigid and formal regime onto an initially informal prison.

free speech, and good cheer. All the senses were "mortified"; cells were even designed to prevent the prisoner from seeing out the window. Food was deliberately made bland, clothing ugly, and beds hard.

Perhaps the fairest summary of the reforms would be to say that they systematically sacrificed liberty to equity and security. Many basic needs were supplied, but at the expense of freedom of choice and self-determination. In some cases, such as diet, this loss was so great that it actually undermined the ostensible purpose of the reform, which was to improve the inmates' health. In other cases, such as the imposition of cleanliness, the benefits far outweighed the cost.

In most of these cases, the reformers knew what they were doing; the effects were intended. They wanted to humiliate prisoners and to compensate for greater physical comfort with increased mental distress. They also wanted to reduce the power of the prison community. Equally important, however, was an unintended and paradoxical result of their efforts. The reformers had meant to protect the prisoners and to increase the supervision and accountability of the gaoler. In fact, the day-to-day administration of the reforms created a bureaucracy far more powerful than anything that had gone before. Everything the reformers did increased the presence, the responsibility, and the power of the gaoler. It is not surprising, therefore, that many reforms were actually made on his initiative. It was the gaoler who chose the diet, found the uniforms, and classified the prisoners. It was the gaoler who gained the legal right to administer formal justice and to enforce with a wide range of penalties the increasing number of prison rules. His greater powers were almost entirely gained at the expense of prisoners' rights or by the forfeiture of their responsibilities. An anarchic democracy became an autocracy.

The loss of prisoners' rights in turn brought the growing isolation of the prison community, impeding the effectiveness of magisterial supervision. As the institution began to provide basic commodities such as food and clothing, as the gaoler gained the legal right to punish prisoners and the power to control what they said and did, he exerted more control over what outsiders, including his nominal supervisors, could discover about the prison. Most gaolers did not seriously abuse the power they were given, while the increase in their responsibilities encouraged the development of a professional attitude and attracted many able administrators. Nevertheless, this development does explain why the very worst prison scandals (cases not of neglect and indifference but of positive and systematic brutality—of deliberate starvation, whippings, beatings, and other tortures) occur after, not before, this period of reform, which enabled gaolers to clamp the lid down on simmering gaols until they exploded.

This increase in the gaoler's power, however, like all the other reforms we have discussed, took place very slowly; it was barely beginning in the late eighteenth century. Although most of the reforms had already been required by the prison rules, many were not actually adopted for decades. In the next chapter we will examine the position of John Higgin in the early nineteenth century to see how this gradual change affected life in Lancaster Castle.

CHAPTER 5

The Reforming Gaoler

Was It Murder? The Commission of 1812

After Howard's death in 1790, his work was taken up by James Neild, treasurer of the Society for the Relief and Discharge of Persons Imprisoned for Small Debts. By the turn of the century, Neild was becoming concerned about the lagging pace of reform; legislation had been passed but was not enforced and the prisons were in many cases as bad as they had been before Howard. In order to publicize the problem he made a second survey of English penal institutions, visiting Lancaster at least three times—in 1802, 1805, and 1809. Neild had nothing but praise for Higgin's general method of administration:

In the excellent management of this Prison . . . there is the most clear and demonstrative proof of how much more *Humanity* and *Firmness* operate to produce penitence and reformation, than *Harshness* and *Severity*; which . . . tend rather to harden the heart than reform the manners. . . . They were all usefully and peaceably at work; . . . no Criminal was ever fettered at any time when I have been here. . . . Such is the force of well-tempered authority, the influence of example, and the impressive weight of steady, calm, and active attention to duty.[1]

Nevertheless, signs of strain were just below the surface. The prison's population was rising rapidly. In 1802 Neild found a total of 166 prisoners. By 1809 the total was 218; most of the increase was due to an additional 40 debtors. Neild commented that the debtors' wards were overcrowded. When there were no more than seventy or eighty debtors, many could have their own beds, but on his last visit there were only three single beds in the whole debtors' wing. From January to August of 1812, the average number of prisoners was 291, and on August 12 the total was 340. Political tension was also evident. "A spirit of restlessness" had led the debtors to form a "committee of *Association*, or *Secrecy*," and "by correspondence with others, equally misadvised, . . . they were led to believe that a Gaoler had no controul, and might even be set at defiance." For this essay in independence they were disciplined by the county.[2]

Neild expressed particular disquiet over the treatment of the handful of lunatics in the Castle. Lunatics could be sent to Lancaster under the vagrancy laws, but usually they had committed a serious crime (often murder) and had been declared insane by a jury. They thus tended to be violent and intractable. Legislation passed in 1809 provided for the establishment of county lunatic asylums, but these could not be built immediately, and it was not until 1816 that most lunatics were removed from the Castle.

In many regards, the lunatics in the Castle were better off than their counterparts in asylums. They were kept separate in a new tower that had a kitchen, a dayroom with a fireplace, pump, and privy, and sleeping cells above. They were fettered and chained only as a last resort, although sometimes this restraint extended to chaining them to their beds or seats. Thomas Higgin had visited the Manchester Asylum to study methods of treating the insane, and later entries in the gaoler's journal suggest that the Higgins gave these inmates a good deal of compassionate attention.

Frequently violent, often dangerous, and always enigmatic, the lunatics posed a serious threat to prison order. Neild strongly recommended that a special "recess" be set aside for them, saying that he had found "*five Maniacs*, two of whom were furiously frantick" in 1805. He warned that the lack of proper facilities personally endangered the gaoler and the staff, and suggested that the lunatics be removed to a hospital or "some retired seclusion."*

Neild's warning went unheeded, but his fear was justified. Seven years later the treatment of a lunatic, combined with the other tensions Neild

---

*James Neild, *State of the Prisons in England, Scotland and Wales* (London, 1812), p. 329. Though lunatics had occasionally been committed to the Castle in the eighteenth century, the problem really dated from the act of 39 and 40 Geo. III, c. 94 (1799). Passed in a panic after an assassination attempt on the king, this act provided for the detention of criminals acquitted of serious crimes because of insanity.

had seen in the prison, were to produce the greatest storm in the Castle's history and lead to a full-scale investigation of Higgin's administration by a parliamentary commission. Its report shows how the room system of self-government among the debtors functioned under the stress caused by political divisions, overcrowding, and aggressive or drunken members. It also shows how a reforming gaoler exercised his authority.

On May 4, 1812, a Lancaster debtor named John Unthank wrote a letter to Sir Francis Burdett, asking him to say something in the House of Commons about the confinement of lunatics in county gaols. He suggested that if lunatics could not be removed entirely, they should at least be in the care of a civilian. As it was, not only the lunatics suffered but also the debtors, who, being nearby, were "subject . . . to the *Screams of the unfortunate People which is really excruciating* to the feelings to hear."[3]

As Unthank wrote, the screams of one of the lunatics were echoing through the prison. James Rawlinson had been convicted at the 1809 March Assizes of killing a man "in a fit of frenzy," and was found insane by a jury. He had once attempted to hang himself in prison, but was cut down just in time. In late April 1812 he became very violent and agitated and began screaming "Murder! Kill me! Kill me!" On the morning of Friday, May 1, he was, with some effort, put into a separate cell.[4] On Saturday night, May 2, Thomas Birch, an elderly turnkey in charge of the lunatics, took his grandson, Thomas Wright, and a Crown prisoner, Thomas Lee, up to Rawlinson's cell to give him his dinner. Birch was afraid of Rawlinson, who had often torn his clothes and assaulted him. As they opened the door, Rawlinson rushed out of the cell and grabbed Birch. Birch managed to push him back into his cell and then sent for John Cooper, another turnkey.

What happened after that was a matter of some controversy. Everyone agreed that there were blows. Cooper stated that when they opened the cell to remove Rawlinson's heavy clogs, Rawlinson rushed out, grabbed at Lee's genitals and got his trousers, and kicked violently. Cooper then hit him a few strokes with a light switch to make him loose his hold. Rawlinson was wearing heavy fustian trousers and all four testified that the blows were only as hard as were needed to loosen his hold and had done no damage.

Seven debtors—Jacob Wilson Wardell, George Tengatt, George Collier, James and William Mallalieu, Joseph Dickinson, and William Goulden—later testified that they heard shouts and the sound of blows. A Crown prisoner named Thomas Griffith said that Lee had told him he had kicked Rawlinson in the ribs with his clogs, and that Birch and Cooper had beaten Rawlinson with "the bull's pizzle . . . at one end as big as my fist."⁵ Lee, however, who had since been discharged, vehemently denied most of these statements. The whip in question was a gentleman's light riding switch, "about the thickness of my finger." The beating was not violent and he had not told Griffith it was. Elijah Major, a Crown prisoner named by Griffith as present at this conversation, denied it ever took place.⁶

The beating may have been more severe than any of the four participants was willing to admit, but Rawlinson's subsequent conduct suggests that he cannot have been seriously injured. The next day another turnkey, John Clark, went with Birch and a Crown prisoner named John Dewsnip to give Rawlinson his breakfast. They discovered that he had managed to break his figure-of-eight handcuffs. When they opened the door, Rawlinson rushed out screaming, spat in Clark's face, and said, "I wish I had my bloody knife." Dewsnip, who had had no part in the events of the previous day, testified that Rawlinson was in good health. Clark said that Rawlinson had no breeches on. He saw his body up to the hips and there was no mark on it. The men decided to put a stronger pair of handcuffs on the lunatic: two bracelets joined by a short chain. On Wednesday, May 5, Rawlinson's screams ceased. When Birch, Wright, and Lee came up to his cell with breakfast, they found him dead. They stated that he had managed to take his stockings off, twist them into a rope, and wind them around his neck in such a way as to strangle himself.

In the meantime, Unthank was having troubles of his own. In the autumn of 1811 he had engaged in a series of drunken brawls with two debtors named Spencer and Drummond. When Higgin heard that Spencer had broken his leg fighting Unthank, he had written to the justices, declaring both men guilty of riotous and disorderly conduct. The justices had promptly suspended Spencer's and Unthank's county allowances. When Unthank received Burdett's answer to his letter on May 15, he began to gloat in a manner that several of his fellows found offensive. One of them heard him say, "We have laid a scheme for the old villain, we'll teach him for taking my bread and potatoes away, blast him." Drummond took exception to Unthank's words and got into another altercation with him.⁷

The next day Drummond sued the articles of the peace against Unthank before James Stainbank, a Lancaster justice. Stainbank ordered

Unthank to find sureties to keep the peace, but the Lancaster tradesmen refused to provide bonds, "on account of Mr. Higgin." Unthank was, therefore, imprisoned on the Crown side of the gaol from May 16 to May 18, when he was able to find mitigated bail. On his release, his old room-mates threw him out and he had to find a new room.[8]

Shortly thereafter, Unthank was involved in yet another dispute, this time with turnkey John Clark, and was again bound to keep the peace. When he could not find bail, Higgin interceded to have his bail excused, saving him from further confinement. Unthank complained, however, that Higgin had refused to send for his friend, Jacob Wilson Wardell, as a witness on his behalf. Wardell consoled him by agreeing that it was very bad conduct toward him but that they "should set all to rights by and by."[9]

Wardell then took up the correspondence with Burdett himself. Unthank, he wrote, "seems funked from an Idea that he shall be further persecuted by the Gaoler," but Wardell was prepared to continue the correspondence for him. "My Motto is nec cupio, nec metuo," he wrote. Wardell briefly sketched his own character—"I am perfectly independent in my principles; . . . *intentionally* it is not in my Nature to exaggerate anything"—and went on to inform Burdett of Rawlinson's death. He hinted that Rawlinson had been murdered after "an unmerciful flogging." The coroner's inquest had been extremely perfunctory and he, Wardell, had heard two Crown prisoners, Richard Smith and Thomas Lee, say that when they laid out Rawlinson's body it was "a Mass of congealed Blood and disfiguration." He warned that Smith and Lee might not tell the truth until their discharge because they were in Higgin's custody, adding that many debtors were afraid of Higgin because he had two brothers-in-law on the bench and could prevent their discharge.[*]

Wardell wrote several more letters to Burdett but made little progress in his attempt to have Rawlinson's death discussed in Parliament. Although he complained that the scandal could not be considered fairly in Lancashire because the justices were biased, he did succeed in gaining a local inquiry into other possible abuses. On May 26 he wrote to the sheriff of the county charging that Higgin had failed to remove ordure from the Castle, that he refused to open the prison gates for shipments of coal

---

[*]PRO, HO 42/125, May 24, 1812. The sister of a third justice, Col. Bradshaw, was married to another of Higgin's brothers-in-law.

weighing less than ten hundredweight, that he failed to visit debtors' rooms, and that he had prevented two poor debtors named Hayes and Goulden from receiving charitable funds for their legal expenses because they had not hired Higgin's son John, a local attorney.*

Within two weeks the justices held a special hearing on Wardell's charges. Nothing in Wardell's letter or the recorded testimony before the magistrates referred to Rawlinson, although the justices seem to have looked into the matter privately later that summer. Meanwhile, another group of Castle debtors set up a committee to defend Higgin. One hundred fourteen debtors out of an approximate total of 146 then in the Castle signed a petition to the justices expressing indignation at the "dark, silent, insidious and assassin-like" behavior of Wardell.[10]

The hearing first considered the matter of the ordure. It turned out that it came from the twice-yearly emptying of the Castle cesspool and had remained for a day or two longer than usual because the carters were celebrating the Whitsun holidays. Higgin admitted that he restricted small coal deliveries but explained that this applied only to deliveries by horse and cart, since they required that the entire gate be opened, endangering security at a time of serious overcrowding. Several debtors testified that they customarily demanded a load of coals as room-money from new entrants and that the ten hundredweight then supplied was usually adequate. If it was not, they made a collective subscription for a new load. A debtor whom Higgin paid to keep the passages clean testified that Higgin himself often provided coals for prisoners who could not afford them. The only complainant for this charge was William Mallalieu; since he and his son had successfully prevented between twelve and twenty debtors from entering their room they may have had more difficulty than most in procuring coal.

Higgin admitted that he did not visit the debtors' rooms daily, but the debtors wrote that they preferred the existing arrangements. He denied absolutely the charge that he was involved in improper dealings with Hayes and Goulden. His son John stated that he had obtained the release of Hayes and of another debtor named Chapman gratis but had refused

---

*PRO, HO 42/125, May 31, 1812. See also *PP* 1812-13 V, Report of the Commissioners on the State of Lancaster Prison, and the Treatment of Prisoners Therein, pp. 82-83. Thomas Higgin described Goulden as "a bad character," with some justification. Goulden himself admitted to the commission that the members of his room had expelled him twice within the past year for being drunk and disorderly. At the time the commission met he was reduced to living in a cell.

to act for Goulden because his brother Thomas Higgin gave him a bad character. He was able to submit the letter he had sent his agents saying that Hayes and Chapman were very poor, requesting them to obtain their release "as an act of charity," and offering to pay their stamp duties from his own pocket. It is difficult to disentangle what happened in Goulden's case because Goulden was illiterate (Higgin wrote his letters for him), but apparently his plaintiff refused the £5 offered by the Thatched House Society to compound for his debt. Later, when he became supersedable (eligible for release by the courts rather than his creditor), Higgin told him that he himself would have to find the money for his legal fees.

At the end of the hearing, the five justices decided that the charges were "wicked, malicious and without foundation." As a punishment for bringing malicious charges they withdrew the allowances of seven debtors: Wardell, the Mallalieus, Goulden, John Hankin, William Rideal, and George Tengatt. With a single trivial exception, this list comprised all those who had given any evidence, however unimportant, for the complainants. Five of those seven were later to be among the seven who testified to hearing blows on the night of May 2. The Annual General Session, meeting two weeks later, seconded the justices' conclusions. The prisoners in the Castle celebrated Higgin's discharge by wearing oak leaves in their hats; Wardell was later to charge Thomas Higgin with distributing these and so encouraging a spirit of "party."

Wardell remained determined to press his case. On June 17 he sent four petitions to Burdett: one each from Tengatt, Hankin, and Goulden, and the fourth from a newcomer named Samuel Scuffum, a former actor. Wardell ended a long account of the hearing with a bitter attack on the conduct of the justices who were trying to "impress a *Terror amongst* the *Debtors* . . . to frustrate the possibility of any future Accusation. . . . The Gaoler has much Reason to *dread* future Evidence . . . by the Criminality of Conduct of his Turnkeys in flogging the Felon to Death I wrote to you some time ago."[11] Three days later he anxiously wrote again, accusing Higgin of bribing his witnesses, by giving "12 of the greatest Blackguards 5 *Shillings each* which he said was the *benefaction* of some Person. . . . I cannot but disbelieve that any one would give a benefaction under such restrictions."[12]

It seems strange that Wardell should profess ignorance of the source of this money, since both Howard and Neild refer to a list of benefactions at Lancaster that included one of £3 from Henrietta Rigby's estate to provide 5s. each to "twelve of the most necessitous and well-behaved prisoners."[13] It is only fair to Wardell to add that two of the recipients of the benefaction testified in Higgin's favor at the hearing and that two served on the committee that produced the petition of the 114 debtors against Wardell. Three of the twelve were also among the six debtors who sat on the coroner's inquest over Rawlinson. Another three had, along with Goulden, recently lost their allowances for being party to the sale of beer, but the three former were restored after making an apology that Goulden failed to second. Because of overlaps, seven of the Rigby beneficiaries had nothing to do with subsequent events. Although there is no evidence that Higgin did anything but distribute the money to those he found most "deserving," Wardell's complaint does light up a certain moral ambiguity in the role of the reforming gaoler, who had simultaneously to act as impartial arbiter and selective benefactor for those he lived among, in order to encourage "reformation" and "good behavior." When to this dual role was added laxness on the part of the superintending authorities and bitter political divisions within both gaol and county, it was almost inevitable that some prisoners would feel aggrieved.

On July 3 Burdett presented the four petitions to the House of Commons. The three from Goulden, Tengatt, and Hankin complained that they had lost their allowances after giving evidence at the magistrates' hearing and that such action must tend to discourage complaints in the future. The fourth, from the actor Scuffum, alleged that he had been unjustly confined in a punishment cell without a bed, fire, candles, pen, ink, paper, or clean linen, and that the laundress and a Mr. Stanton, a "comedian," were refused access to him.[14]

None of the petitions referred to Rawlinson, but in the course of the debate Burdett read one of Wardell's letters suggesting that Rawlinson had come to his death by foul means. He also read a letter from John Spencer complaining that when "by mere accident I slipped off a Stone in the yard and most unfortunately broke my leg," his surgeon had not been allowed in to set it properly, as a result of which he was still lame.[15] Burdett, though dubious about the charges because he had so often heard Higgin praised, felt the debtors' petitions should be pursued. It seems likely that the petitions would have received little attention if the suspicious circumstances surrounding Rawlinson's death had not loomed in the background. The Commons finally decided against a parliamentary inquiry (which would have been limited to the charges in the petitions) after Castlereigh promised that the government would make its own investigation into the conduct of the gaol. Meanwhile, Higgin and the justices collected their evidence and assumed a united front.

The government's investigation took the form of a royal commission of three men: Benjamin Hobhouse, Thomas Macdonald, and William Roberts. It was empowered to hear all complaints and charges, written and spoken, not merely those that had been the subject of the petitions to Parliament. The commission's report began by dismissing the complaints made before the justices in June, using the depositions made then as proof that they were unfounded. It also dismissed three further complaints from Wardell but found that Thomas Higgin had in fact told Wardell that he had been "horsewhipped and horseponded at York" and had later threatened to pull his nose if they ever met outside the prison. Higgin claimed provocation and escaped with a reprimand.[16]

The commission then commented with some asperity on the characters of Wardell, Unthank, and the Mallalieus. Wardell had revealed his "temper of mind" in a letter to the justices' clerk boasting of the fortune he had spent, including estates worth £30,000—"a history," wrote the commission, "which, it is evident, he considered as calculated to give impressions the direct reverse of those to which they seem to be entitled."[17] The report went on to speak of evidence showing that Wardell had sworn revenge on the gaoler with the Mallalieus' support, and that Unthank and Wardell had "laid a scheme" against Higgin. Unthank himself, from his own evidence, was frequently drunk and quarrelsome, while James Mallalieu "showed the spirit of his character, by declaring, when asked if they had requested to have it [their allowance] back, that they could not 'cringe' to the magistrates who had decided against them."[18]

Next, the commission considered the four petitions one by one. Several witnesses testified that Samuel Scuffum had sworn to escape, and that his confinement was thus a fair punishment. Moreover, Scuffum's own statements before the commission directly contradicted many of the complaints in the petition. Most important was his testimony about the conduct of Cooper, the turnkey who had locked him up, since Cooper was also the man accused of beating Rawlinson. Scuffum said that Cooper had behaved "very politely," and his account suggested that

Cooper had displayed considerable patience.[19] Scuffum also related how Higgin had interceded for him after his fellow debtors had "hooted" him out of his room for petitioning Parliament and had accused him of theft. The commission thus dismissed his petition.

The commission dismissed the other three petitioners as well, pointing out that there was evidence that they had conspired against Higgin and that in any case they could have regained their allowances by writing an apology in the customary manner. The commission then considered a more serious charge made by John Spencer in a letter to Burdett. Spencer was the debtor whose leg had been broken when Unthank knocked him down. He was treated by the prison surgeon's apprentice, who turned out to be Robert Higgin, yet another son. Higgin did not splint the leg but only bandaged it. Spencer suspected that the leg was not properly set, but when the surgeon, Mr. Baxendale, came, he left it as it was. Spencer then sent his wife to John Higgin to ask for another doctor, but the gaoler said, "He has had Mr. Baxendale, has not he; what does he want?" and turned away.[20] After trying for nearly a week to obtain a second visit from Baxendale, Spencer decided to hire a private surgeon, a Mr. Howitt, but he arrived late in the day and was turned away at the gates.

More than a week after the accident, Spencer consulted Cooper, the turnkey, who agreed that the leg was not set correctly and sent for the surgeon. Again Robert Higgin turned up, and again he failed to reset the leg. On Monday Baxendale arrived and finally splinted the leg, but when the splints were taken off, the leg was not set properly and the bones overlapped. Spencer again sent for Mr. Howitt, who finally arrived and agreed that the leg had been badly handled, but advised against having it broken again.

Baxendale's testimony amounted to a simple denial. His "senior pupil" Robert had attended to the leg properly, so he had merely continued the treatment. Spencer was very intemperate and subject to gout; the inflammation this disease caused in his leg had interfered with the cure, but his pupil had made no mistakes. Howitt, however, stated uncompromisingly that in his opinion the job had been botched.

Faced with this professional disagreement, the commission retreated precipitately. It simply accepted Baxendale's assertion that the healing of the leg was hampered by gout and intemperance, and dismissed the complaint. The commissioners even failed to examine other possible witnesses on the subject, such as Cooper or Robert Higgin himself. Nor did they call in a third doctor to examine the leg. Although Spencer's charges touched John Higgin's own conduct only marginally, the commission's reluctance to investigate them thoroughly leaves it open to accusations of bias and must stand as its greatest failure.

After considering several minor matters, the commission finally turned to its real raison d'être, Rawlinson's death. It immediately became clear that, as Wardell had charged, the coroner's inquest and the whole manner of dealing with the body after death had been utterly inadequate. The coroner, having been told that Rawlinson committed suicide by strangling himself, had treated the inquest as a mere pro forma proceeding. He did not call in a surgeon to examine the body, nor did he do any more himself than glance at the mark around Rawlinson's neck and the "upper part" of his body. The jury he called consisted of six debtors and six stonemasons working on the Castle. Higgin told the commission that it was customary to choose the jury from people employed on the Castle works, "though I can't say I quite approve of it."[21] The jury was simply left in the room with the body, which was covered by a sheet, and informed that anyone who wished could have it uncovered. Not unnaturally, no one did. For this reason, neither the coroner nor the jury could testify as to whether the body bore marks of ill-treatment. They rapidly came to the conclusion that Rawlinson had committed suicide and disbanded. The coroner did not even keep minutes.

Nevertheless, in the end there was not much doubt about how Rawlinson died. Wardell had suggested that no one ironed as the lunatic had been could have strangled himself, but the commission put a man in the same irons, equipped him with the rough knife found on the body, and found that it was possible for him to cut up his stockings and strangle himself. Wardell's hint that Rawlinson died from the beating he had received and that his suicide was a fabrication seems extremely unlikely, since by all accounts he was in rude health for several days after being beaten. Wardell's suggestion that Rawlinson was not really a lunatic at all was patently absurd; he had been found insane by a jury and his behavior was extremely erratic. Any vestiges of credibility that Wardell retained were destroyed when Hankin stated that Wardell had intended to bribe the two discharged prisoners who had laid out the body, Thomas Lee and Richard Smith, to testify against Higgin. This claim is borne out by the fact that Wardell named Smith to Burdett as a possible witness, although when they were called, both men strongly defended Higgin.

After the hearing had ended, a former turnkey submitted a letter he had received from Wardell. "The commissioners," he wrote, "spoke to me *confidentially*, and I had four interviews. . . . You lived as turnkey some time here; I have *an authority* to offer you a very *considerable sum*, if you will disclose certain communications touching the Crown side, and which will be remitted you at a moment's notice, and an additional assurance of *Government*, indemnifying you from any *inconvenience*. I speak *officially*; and as the sum would be an object to your family, I think it is worthy of your best consideration."[22]

The commission described this letter as "totally destitute of truth," and it must be said that in writing it Wardell convicted himself of dishonesty and of attempting to suborn witnesses.

The only remaining question is how severely Rawlinson was beaten on the evening of May 2. No one denied that he was beaten; some degree of physical force was both inevitable and acceptable in the days before the insane could be controlled by medication. In fact, the beating resulted from Higgin's desire to permit as much freedom as possible to his charges. If, according to the traditional practice with lunatics, Rawlinson had been so heavily ironed as to preclude free movement or had been chained to the wall of his cell, he could not have been so active or posed such a threat to the turnkeys.

This, at least, was the opinion Higgin expressed, in his only real comment on the case. In a letter he wrote to Edward Wilbraham Bootle in July, he said:

I am aware that Lunatics may be kept like wild Beasts chained fast to a Wall, or to the Floor, without the use of a Whip, but with such a filthy mode of Treatment their Health is soon injured. The Turnkey cannot let out a madman with any degree of safety unless he is master of him. Rawlinson had not received the slightest degree of correction during several preceeding months, but he was then in frenzy and striving to conquer the Turnkeys, which for his own comfort could not be allowed. My directions to Birch . . . is never to whip them on the body however unruly. I have now one Lunatic, viz. Richard Coleman, who has been here *10* years, another James Mort 8 years, and another Martha Whewell 8 years. If they had been vigorously treated they would not have been in existence at this moment, especially when we take into Consideration that the place . . . in which they are confined is not calculated for their Health and Comfort, but merely for their safe custody. . . . I am not ashamed to acknowledge to you that I cannot attend to them in a manner consonant with my own feelings, or desire, if I did, more important matters would be neglected and I should be ruined. . . . It would be a great relief to my mind if Government would direct that these unhappy Objects should be removed to St. Luke's, or to one of the Lunatic Asylums at Liverpool, or Manchester, where they could have medical aid.[23]

Until May 2 Rawlinson was not handcuffed and enjoyed considerable freedom of movement. The question is whether the force used to subdue him was excessive. Although the evidence does not offer an unequivocal answer, it favors the turnkeys. The prosecution could not find a single person able to testify to seeing any bruises on the body, while the defense found at least six witnesses ready to swear that they had seen Rawlinson unmarked. No one outside the small circle of Wardell's intimates was willing to suggest that Rawlinson could have been ill treated, and Wardell never formally charged such treatment. It seems likely that if the debtors really believed that Rawlinson had been brutally beaten, a few independent men would have been willing to give evidence.

The commission's report cleared Higgin of all the charges against him, although it did criticize minor aspects of the prison regime. The officers came in for censure for their failure to keep adequate books. The commission approved the justices' conduct of the June hearing as well as their decision to cut off the allowances of the seven witnesses, although it did not approve the decision of the Annual General Session to advertise publicly the names of the recalcitrant debtors. The coroner was criticized for his carelessness. The commission commented on Higgin's "inadvertency" in moving Rawlinson's body but also gave him almost fulsome praise:

He has passed through the trial in a manner which cannot but confirm the good character he had before acquired. . . . Every circumstance which came under our observation has evinced his disposition to administer relief to those who were suffering under the pressure of sickness or extreme indigence, or of that frequent cause of mortification and misery among prisoners of debt, the ill-treatment they receive from those with whom they are forced to live; his readiness to give assistance and advice for the settlement of differences among them; . . . and the correct and proper application of such charities as are distributed under his recommendation. . . . A succession of debtors in the gaol . . . presented themselves with great earnestness to bear their testimony to the humane and generous conduct of their gaoler, whom they represented as the father and the friend of the indigent debtor.[24]

No disciplinary action resulted from the commission's report. Cooper had sued Unthank and Wardell for slander at the September Assizes and won damages, but the hearing was well over before the report appeared. The commission showed some bias in favor of Higgin from the start and tended throughout to judge witnesses on the basis of their "appearance and demeanor," but there seems no reason to dismiss their report as a whitewash. Whatever the rights and wrongs of its findings, however, the report is valuable for its detailed picture of an administrative system in the process of reform. It offers a graphic example of the paradoxical effect of this period of change, which left the gaoler both extraordinarily powerful and extremely vulnerable.

Higgin and his staff were vulnerable for three reasons. First, they lived in an age of great political tension, tension that was reflected in the prison and made it difficult to govern harmoniously. Political disputes were common among debtors; Unthank and Drummond fought over politics while the majority of the pro-Higgin debtors taunted Wardell and his allies with cries of "Burdett's men!" This was the summer of the Luddites; political activists were trickling in to join the criminal prisoners and more were to arrive in the fall. Since Burdett and his allies found it politically advantageous as well as morally desirable to campaign against prison abuses and to air prison scandals, even a conscientious man could find himself caught up in a whirlwind of party enmity.

Second, the gaol staff were vulnerable simply because of overcrowding in the prison. In 1812 the Castle was at bursting point. Among the debtors this crowding caused stress and endless quarreling. It caused disputes about the admission of debtors to rooms on their arrival; the occupants of whatever room the newly incarcerated debtors entered were likely to resent the newcomers for taking up space. Overcrowding made it difficult for inmates to cook their food properly and to eat their meals. It forced them to share beds. The admission of wives and children became a cause for dispute, especially when the wives wished to sleep with their husbands in rooms full of other men.

Higgin tried to avoid the petty disputes and to be impartial in judging the more serious ones, but inevitably some of his decisions displeased one of the parties. Most of the leading anti-Higginites had a particular outstanding grievance: Wardell because Higgin had refused to send for a magistrate to decide his dispute with another debtor, the Mallalieus because of disputes over the admission of debtors to their room, Spencer and Unthank because they had lost their allowances for fighting, William Rideal (another June witness) because he had previously been cut off for writing "spiritedly" about the admission of a debtor to his room, Goulden because he had been cut off for selling ale and had failed to apologize.

Third, the staff were vulnerable because standards of conduct were changing, leaving them without a straightforward code of behavior. They were in the same position as Trollope's Warden of a generation later: accustomed to the old ways, publicly judged by the new, and uncertain themselves of how they should act. Higgin wished to maintain a high standard of personal conduct, yet, with the full approval of the justices, he built a family empire that seemed indefensible to radicals such as Hunt. Cooper returned ostensible bribes but carried on a little "agency" in bread for the debtors. The coroner and the prison officers kept records in a perfunctory manner that suited the magistrates but appalled the commissioners. Higgin found it necessary to assist the debtors with their financial and legal affairs, if only to help them get out and so relieve the congestion, but this role naturally placed him in an equivocal position. Everyone, in dealing with the prisoners, had difficulty in drawing the proper line between informal friendliness and a starchy, impersonal professionalism.

Even more evident than Higgin's vulnerability, however, was his enormous personal and official power. It is important to realize that he did not gain this power by enforcing a reign of terror, but though his methods were relatively gentle, his authority was extensive. Part of this authority certainly resulted from his nepotism. He had relatives both above and below him in the prison. Although his Houseman brothers-in-law took no part in the inquiries into his conduct, the relationship could only have added to the reluctance of their colleagues to pry too closely into Higgin's affairs. Higgin could also claim a rather tenuous relationship with Justice Bradshaw, who gave strong testimony in his defense and took an active role in the administration of the gaol; however insignificant the connection may have seemed to Bradshaw, it offered aggrieved prisoners reasonable grounds for doubting his impartiality. One of the problems, in fact, with appointing "gentleman" gaolers in the provincial towns of this period was that they were almost bound to have such connections with the local gentry.

It was natural that Higgin, a man with a number of sons, living in a country town, would take one as his own assistant and apprentice the others to respectable professional men whom he knew in the course of business. When he sent one son to the school run by the prison chaplain it made little difference, but the results in three other cases were unfortunate. The first was the use of his son as a deputy, a practice so common in this period as to be unremarkable. The second was the apprenticeship of Robert Higgin to the Castle surgeon. This meant that prisoners were treated by the gaoler's son, who was hardly likely to preserve an independent attitude toward possible medical hazards. Nor, if he made a mistake, did prisoners find it easy to appeal. The third was John Higgin's entry into the law and his agreement to act as solicitor for some of the prisoners. John maintained, and provided evidence to prove, that he took on many cases for poor debtors gratis, from charitable motives, and that his relationship with the gaoler only helped the debtors. Even if he never took a fee from a prisoner, however, John's willingness to get prisoners freed on his father's or brother's recommendation can only have increased both their power over their charges and the resentment of the less favored. The distribution of alms can support as real a power as the use of menaces.

Higgin II could control not only his son John's services but also many similar benefits. To some extent the reformers intended to provide gaolers with this power; in their anxiety to encourage the prisoners' reformation they allowed the gaoler to make little discretionary rewards for good behavior. Charitable bequests further enabled the gaoler to reward the well-behaved. Reforming magistrates had tried to make the debtors' allowances another means of controlling behavior, resolving that these should be withdrawn in certain cases, such as drunken or irreligious conduct.

In theory the gaoler himself had no authority to withdraw or grant allowances. The commission report frequently pointed out that three of the petitioners had no quarrel against Higgin, since it was the magistrates, not he, who had withdrawn their allowances. In fact, however, the magistrates could only assess the behavior of prisoners according to the gaoler's information, and ordinarily they accepted his recommendations as a matter of course. Higgin himself, to his credit, distributed charity lavishly, both from the Charity Fund and from his own pocket. When Wardell wrote of the 114 debtors who had signed the petition in Higgin's defense, he added that they all owed the gaoler money! Even Wardell was in his debt. From the testimony of other debtors we know that Higgin often paid the room entrance fees of poor debtors, gave coal to the poorer rooms in winter, and supplied clothing and cots, sometimes from his own house, for the destitute. It is clear that his good will made all the difference to the lives of the poor debtors. Higgin had become the only source of the funds that prisoners had previously collected and administered themselves.

However just was the dismissal of Wardell's charges, there was some truth to his complaint that no one in Lancashire could obtain a fair hearing against Higgin. The commission's report shows that the checks, both traditional and reformist, on the gaoler's conduct were extremely weak. The coroner's duty to hold an inquest on every prisoner who died in the gaol was one such check, but this had clearly become a perfunctory matter and the jury, consisting of debtors and Castle workmen, was not disinterested. It is no wonder that some prisoners, seeing such laxity, became suspicious or apprehensive.

The justices should have offered another check, but their attitude toward Higgin is summed up by the fact that they ascribed their failure to inspect the prison or require written journals to "that perfect confidence which their knowledge of the gaoler and the high character he has acquired during his long course of service had led them to repose in him."[25] In fact, the justices' anxiety to scotch criticism of Higgin led them to publish three separate vindications of his character after the June hearing and to publicize the names of the debtors who had "by Effrontery and Intimidation" interfered with his duty, as well as to suspend their allowances. Although Higgin seems to have deserved their trust, such partisanship, however well intended, was likely, as one of the protesting debtors wrote, to "deter any witness from giving evidence upon any subject that may hereafter be brought forward against the said gaoler, and there can be no safety in a place where such authority is exercised."[26]

Demagogue Radicals and the "Black Catalogue of Traitors": Politics and the Prison, 1812-1832

The commission's exoneration of Higgin and his fellow officers, however welcome to them, did nothing to alleviate the underlying tensions caused by overcrowding and the bitter political rivalries of the Napoleonic period. The population of the Lancashire prisons continued to rise steadily for a generation. The opening of a third house of correction, Kirkdale, near Liverpool, in 1820 offered only a temporary alleviation of the problem. When overcrowding was combined with the public events that took place in Lancashire during this period, the tension in the prison could only increase.*

During Higgin's tenure of office there were four main waves of political agitation in Lancashire, each of which left a flotsam of captives in the local prisons. The first came in the already tense year of 1812, the year of the Luddite disturbances. The spring of that year brought a rash of food riots, arson, and illegal organization. During May and June a special commission in Lancaster tried 58 people, imprisoning 7, transporting 17, and executing 8. In June 38 men were arrested for administering an unlawful oath to Samuel Fleming, a government spy. Their leader was John Knight, a Saddleworth manufacturer, described by John Foster as a "determined Jacobin."† Knight was first imprisoned in 1794 and lived just long enough to become a Chartist in 1838; he was probably the most important of the local radical leaders. To the disgust of the authorities, the "38," ably defended by James Scarlett, John Williams, and Henry (later Lord) Brougham, were acquitted after a ten-week imprisonment.

The next wave came during the unrest of 1817. After the abortive march of the "Blanketeers," 29 men were arrested. Most were hastily released, but 9 were committed for trial, including John Bagguley and Samuel Drummond, reputedly the most violent and hotheaded of the radical leaders.[27] They were held for five months in extreme discomfort because of the severe overcrowding at the Salford New Bailey. One of the justices admitted to the Home Office that since no free beds were avail-

---

*In 1816 Higgin was so concerned about overcrowding that he begged the undersheriff to send a military force to guard the prison, claiming that he was having great difficulty keeping the prisoners under control and was "obliged to go armed into the prison. We are at a loss to know how we are to get over this winter. . . . Should an insurrection take place you must be well aware that our lives and assistants would have little or no chance amongst such a set of desperate fellows" (PRO, HO 6/1, Dec. 12, 1816). I am grateful to Judge Eric Stockdale for sending me this reference.

†John Foster, *Class Struggle and the Industrial Revolution* (London, 1974), p. 139. According to Foster, Knight, born in 1763, was first imprisoned in 1794 for two years. In 1801 he was on the county executive of the United Englishmen. He edited the *Manchester Political Register* in 1816 and the *Manchester Spectator* in 1818; in both cases his work ended in his arrest under the act suspending habeas corpus. In the 1830's he worked for the Trade Union movement, particularly for Doherty's spinners, and in 1831 he became secretary of the Oldham Political Union. Shortly before his death he became the Oldham treasurer for poor relief. For different stages of Knight's career, see also J. L. Hammond and Barbara Hammond, *The Skilled Labourer, 1760-1832* (New York, 1967; orig. ed. 1919); Donald Read, *Peterloo: The "Massacre" and Its Background* (Clifton, N.J., 1973; orig. ed. 1958); and Robert Walmsley, *Peterloo: The Case Reopened* (Manchester, 1969).

able, the prisoners had been put in a storeroom and given fresh straw. Eventually they were released without trial because the justices could not substantiate any of the charges against them.

Parliament, meanwhile, had passed an emergency act suspending the provisions of habeas corpus. The government took advantage of this act to rearrest Bagguley on suspicion of high treason, along with John Knight, Samuel Bamford (another well-known local radical), and fifteen other Lancashire men. In all, 37 men were arrested throughout England. The prisoners were taken to London for a brief hearing and then scattered in prisons all over the country. Their presence often unnerved local officials, who were well aware that any slip would be attended with publicity and who knew that the state prisoners would be disruptive. In Gloucestershire, the Whig justice Sir George Onesiphorus Paul protested the heavy use of certain "model" county prisons for these men, "thereby making the county of that prison a party in the war with printers; in which it has no particular concern."[28] The Tory Higgin was equally disconcerted when he learned that he was again to receive John Bagguley. Although he received exceptionally privileged treatment, Bagguley later tried to arouse a scandal over his imprisonment.

A third group of prisoners came in 1819. A spinners' strike of 1818 led in January to the imprisonment of their leader, John Doherty, in Lancaster Castle, where he immediately began to petition Peel on behalf of the misdemeanants there. In August he was joined by the leaders of the meeting that ended in the Peterloo massacre. They included "Orator" Hunt, the day's speaker, and James Moorhouse, his host; Joseph Johnson, a sponsor of the meeting; John Knight; John Thacker Saxton, a reporter for the radical *Manchester Observer*; Samuel Bamford; Bamford's friend "Dr." Healey, an illiterate apothecary; and three other local radicals. As they arrived at Lancaster, the debtors greeted them with handshakes, "a shout and many good wishes," according to Bamford.*

Hunt and Knight were released on bail the next evening, while John-

---

*Samuel Bamford, *Passages in the Life of a Radical*, ed. W. H. Chaloner, vol. 2 (London, 1967; orig. ed. 1844), p. 3. According to one local historian, the inmates collected stones in one of the gateway turrets as part of an attempt to rescue Hunt, but there is no record of any actual disturbance. Perhaps Hunt's release on bail forestalled the intended riot (William Oliver Roper, "Materials for the History of Lancashire, II" [Chetham Society, 1907], p. 240).

The Peterloo massacre took place when a committee of Lancashire justices, headed by Hulton, ordered first the amateur yeomanry and then the professional hussars to charge a largely peaceful crowd gathered to hear Hunt speak. Eleven people were killed.

son and Moorhouse had obtained release in Manchester, but the other prisoners seem to have remained in the Castle until their trial seven months later. At the trial in York, with Scarlett this time prosecuting, Hunt, Johnson, Knight, Healey, and Bamford were all convicted and sentenced to imprisonment; the other five were acquitted. The convicted prisoners were again scattered among different provincial gaols.

Hunt, however, did not drop from public view. He soon sent a characteristic letter from Ilchester to Johnson, Bamford, and Healey at Lincoln. He was querulous about their luck: "your time will pass pleasantly away, it is a mere nominal imprisonment." He himself, on the other hand, was suffering in the two best rooms in the gaol, having a "very good Bed Room and a very good sitting Room" to himself but a yard only ten paces square. A prisoner was sent in daily to act as his servant but *"mine is literally solitary confinement."*[29]

The government soon had reason to regret sending Hunt to what it believed was a model prison but that he described as "the worst Jail in England." From what he persisted in calling his "dungeon" he sent sharp attacks on the gaol and its "reforming" governor, William Bridle. Eventually, his charges were pressed in Parliament. A royal commission verified many of Hunt's allegations of insanitary conditions, flogging, and torture, much to the embarrassment of the government and the Somerset magistrates. The scandal over the "Ilchester Bastille" probably helped bring about the Prison Act of 1823. At the same time another Peterloo participant, Richard Carlile, sent to Dorchester for publishing the work of Tom Paine, was producing a journal, *The Republican*. His charges that prisoners were frequently flogged in Dorchester provoked an investigation that confirmed his allegations.[30] Although John Knight also stood trial with the Peterloo defendants, he was sentenced to Lancaster with five other men—Nathan Broadhurst, George Dewhurst, John Berry, William Fletcher, and John Adamson—on reduced charges of unlawful assembly, stemming from a different meeting.

The final wave of political imprisonments came in the early 1830's, with the initial defeat of the Reform Bill. In 1830 Hunt, after a disgraceful campaign on both sides, defeated the Whig E. G. Stanley at Preston, then a unique borough with universal male suffrage. Soon afterward, Nathan Broadhurst returned to Lancaster Castle, charged, along with several others, with seditious conspiracy and attendance at an illegal meeting. The men were convicted on reduced charges of unlawful assembly and sentenced to a year in Lancaster. In 1832 John Doherty, now the publisher of a radical newspaper, *The Poor Man's Advocate*, also returned to Lancaster after a local clergyman sued him for libel.[31]

Once inside the walls of Lancaster, each of these four waves of prisoners, which in some cases comprised the same men, succeeded in raising fundamental questions about the way in which the prison was administered and the prisoners treated. Their radical activism, combined with John Higgin's Tory sympathies, aroused a storm of controversy, renewed with each new wave of prisoners, that was to last a generation. In the course of the controversy, two issues became inextricably entwined. The first was the question of whether political prisoners were entitled to special treatment. The second, although raised by the political prisoners, was over what rights, if any, were possessed by all prisoners, and in particular over their right to free communication as a safeguard against abusive treatment.

Until the end of the eighteenth century, the question of how political prisoners were to be treated did not emerge as a major problem, because no rules prescribed special treatment for any prisoners save debtors. Prisoners had certain legally established rights, such as the right not to be tortured, but the conduct of their daily lives was left to their own determination. Many fewer restrictions were placed on ordinary activities such as seeing visitors, corresponding, speaking with other prisoners, working, and idling. Some restrictions were imposed for security reasons, but what privileges there were, such as special rooms, were allocated to those who could pay for them. Prisoners were not distinguished in any but the roughest fashion by the crime they had committed, and the man of means, whatever his crime, could live like a lord.

The Howardian reforms, however, established classes of prisoners based on the seriousness of the crime they had committed. To some extent the different groups were treated differently; some felons, for example, were sentenced to "hard labor," while each class was lodged separately. Many activities that had formerly been permitted to everyone were now either prohibited or allowed only as privileges for certain classes. It was not until all prisoners were classified in this way that the issue of how to class political prisoners could arise. It was standardization that created the demand for differentiation.

The question of whether political prisoners are entitled to special treatment has caused controversy ever since, partly because it is so difficult to determine just who is a political prisoner. Although by this time in England people were rarely imprisoned for their religious beliefs (apart from some prosecutions for blasphemy and a few other miscellaneous cases), there were several sorts of political prisoners.*

The first group consisted of those held by executive fiat. These were political prisoners pure and simple. With habeas corpus suspended, these men were held on a warrant from the home secretary on suspicion alone, without trial. They were not formally charged with any specific illegal acts, nor were they informed of the grounds on which they were held. The only long-staying Lancashire prisoner in this category, during this period, was John Bagguley, the Blanketeer leader arrested in 1817. There can be no question that he received special and highly privileged treatment.

The second group consisted of those who were publicly tried and convicted of specific acts that were widely acknowledged to be political crimes—in general, the nonviolent expression of opinions dangerous or inimical to the state, such as criminal libel against persons in power, sedition, and seditious conspiracy. (High treason might qualify, but traitors were singled out for special execration.) The Peterloo prisoners, who were held on a bewildering collection of charges—which were reduced at intervals until the men were finally convicted of conspiring to hold an unlawful and seditious assembly—were in this category. They experienced varied but on the whole moderately privileged treatment. This group would later include many Chartists.

The third group, then as now, was the one that caused the most difficulty, because it included those who broke ordinary nonpolitical sanctions in pursuit of political ends. These crimes included nearly all violent acts, such as assault and murder, and more importantly, such illegal acts as riot, unlawful assembly, and tumultuous petitioning. There was also a gray area of activities that were more economically than politically motivated, such as attempting to form a trade union, plug pulling, "turning out" factories, arson, or extortion. Depending on the motive of the perpetrator, these might or might not be called political crimes. The man who quarreled with his neighbor and burned his ricks out of malice, or who joined with friends to throw his enemy in a river, might

---

*The last prisoner of conscience I have found in Lancashire was George Connard, an Oldham painter and Owenite who had been arrested for debt. At his insolvency hearing he was remanded to the Castle because he stated that he did not believe in a future state of punishment (PRO, HO 20/8 pt. 2, Joseph Hume to John Russell, Aug. 27, 1839). This claim, according to legal tradition, rendered Connard's sworn statements useless, because they were not made in the fear of God.

be charged with arson, assault, riot, conspiracy, illegal arming, and even unlawful assembly—but he had clearly not committed a "political" crime.

Everyone seems to have agreed that prisoners in the first two groups—state prisoners committed under the Habeas Corpus Suspension Act and prisoners committed for purely political crimes such as sedition—deserved special treatment. The controversy arose over the third, borderline group, to which the vast majority of "political" prisoners belonged. The radicals held stubbornly to the conviction that such prisoners deserved special treatment, but in general, the authorities disagreed. In their eyes the prisoners were being held not for their opinions but for specific illegal acts and ought to be treated in the same way as everyone else convicted for committing the same acts, with whatever motive.

A list printed in the *Parliamentary Papers* in the summer of 1840 of all prisoners being held for offenses such as libel, sedition, and riot makes it clear that by the early Chartist era prison authorities were drawing a firm line between the comparatively few people sentenced for the "political" offense of seditious conspiracy and the much larger number sentenced for the more common crimes of riot, riotous assembly, or riotous assault. The Kirkdale house of correction held nearly eighty prisoners charged with riot, not counting those released either before or just after trial. With two exceptions (one man convicted of an aggravated offense went to Lancaster, another was in poor health), all these prisoners were treated as ordinary misdemeanants, while six of the seven seditious conspiracy prisoners held in Lancaster and Kirkdale received special privileges, being permitted to purchase whatever they wanted. The one remaining Lancaster prisoner and four more at Preston were probably too poor to take advantage of this and engaged in prison work in return for an allowance.[32]

Along with the issue of the status of political activists, the radicals' presence in the gaols aroused a second debate about the rights of all prisoners. The radicals themselves were often ambivalent about the issues raised by prison reform and "model prisons." The only major figure to question imprisonment as such was William Godwin. Carlile's *Republican* argued that prisons were so poorly run that they were not meeting the standards set for them by Parliament and expected by the public. Hunt testified before a select committee on county rates in 1825 that spending on county gaols could and should be cut by more than half, but he expected the savings to come from the elimination of jobbery and corruption in the provision of food and clothing for prisoners, not from the reduction of commitment rates or a complete overhaul of penal policy. Rather than questioning the idea that prisons could reform their inmates through a well-administered regime, the radicals concentrated on arguing that local corruption was preventing such institutions from doing their job properly.[33]

Despite their ambivalence, the radicals' own prison experiences led them to challenge many of the changes in prison life promulgated by the reformers. In particular, they contested the increasing regimentation of prison life, the requirement that all prisoners work, the use of hard labor, and the introduction of separate confinement. "Have not these unhappy wretches been vitiated in youth, and brought up and educated as culprits?" John Doherty asked himself and his readers. "Will hunger enlarge their minds or the tread-mill purify their morals? What pains have been taken to improve these men's minds? What has been done to convince them that their previous pursuits were injurious to society, disgraceful to themselves, and offensive to God?"[34]

Though the Lancashire radicals frequently complained of the conditions of confinement, the center of the debate was the rights of prisoners to communicate freely: to send and receive information without censorship, interference, or oversight by the gaoler and his staff. Without this right, they argued, the petty corruption and misbehavior of local officials could never be brought to light and poor prison conditions would never have a permanent remedy.

It was inevitable that the political prisoners would be the ones to force this issue. They were, almost by definition, disproportionately anxious to communicate with others, while the content of their communications was especially likely to be obnoxious to the authorities and to seem unlawful and dangerous. Finally, because of their abilities and the fact that they had friends in high places, the radicals were better placed than most prisoners to bring their grievances into public view. In the end, though they won a final battle, they lost the war. Yet their conflict reveals some of the underlying divisions, both local and national, of this period and raises important questions about the balance between freedom and security.

The conflict began in 1812, at a time when Lancaster Castle was already experiencing overcrowding and political disputes among the prisoners. John Higgin himself, like most of the justices who had appointed him, was probably a staunch Tory although not an extreme one. The Rawlinson affair in the summer of 1812—when the self-proclaimed "Burdettites" in the gaol obtained support from radicals in Parliament to publicize scandalous allegations about his administration of the prison—can have done nothing to increase his tolerance for either the radicals or Burdett. Meanwhile, throughout the late spring, summer, and fall, Luddites trickled into the prison. Higgin loathed their opinions and made his feelings clear to them. Moreover, he enthusiastically undertook the role of government informer. In the summer of 1812 he passed a number of "communications" from a prisoner named Smith to W. R. Hay, chairman of the Salford Quarter Sessions, a great collector of information who was later to be the chief adviser to the Peterloo committee of justices.[35]

In November Higgin wrote the Home Office directly, saying that he had discovered a "union" among the Luddites that had led him to watch their correspondence closely. He enclosed extracts from their letters that revealed "a Connexion with persons raised above poverty though perhaps not placed in very affluent Circumstances, but possessing fair Education. . . . No doubt remains on my mind that Sir F. Burdett and Major Cartwright were well aware what was going on in the Neighbourhood of Manchester etc. and the various information which my official station has enabled me to connect has impressed on my mind a firm conviction that the late rebellious state of this county and of Yorkshire etc. may chiefly be attributed to the written addresses and inflammatory Harangues of those Persons."[36]

Among the passages Higgin enclosed were several written by John Knight. One of them, to his wife, suggests the way in which Higgin spoke to his charges: "Soon after our arrival here we had the audacity to petition to be indulged with a Newspaper at our own Expence—on which occasion our Governour told us the Bible would suit us better and be more useful to us and with which our Dayroom was furnished."[37] At the time, Knight accepted this rebuff, consoling himself by citing biblical condemnation of the oppression of the poor, but in the future this question of newspaper reading would be a perpetual bone of contention.

It was one of Knight's co-conspirators in 1820, John Adamson, who unintentionally precipitated a major conflict over the issue in Lancaster Castle when he sent an indignant letter to his sister about their trial.

"Look how the Iseralits was oppressed," he wrote, "but nothing to the Oppression of the Presant day—Look at our workhouses Look at our Goals—look at our streets—Rags and wretchedness is the industrious Poor mans Companion—O God when wilt thou hear the Crys of the oppressed. . . . Exodus 2 Ch. 23 to 25 and it came to Pass, In Process of time that the King died and the People sighed by reason of their Bondage."[38]

Despite the evidence that Adamson had been applying himself to the Bible provided for him, Higgin found his letter disturbing enough to take it to the Lonsdale magistrates. The justices, after stating that several such "Letters of seditious, inflammatory and blasphemous tendency" had been written by the prisoners to their friends and then made public, resolved to order the gaoler to prohibit all such correspondence. They also inquired of the Home Office to what extent the magistrates ought to allow letters from political prisoners on misdemeanor charges. Sidmouth's answer apparently favored the magistrates, as Higgin thereafter became even more energetic in censuring and censoring the correspondence of the men whose opinions he detested and whose letters sometimes contained invidious references to himself.[39]

Meanwhile, the radicals began to complain bitterly about their treatment. They objected to being compelled to work on pain of starvation. The Quarter Sessions had authorized the gaoler to punish all felons and misdemeanants before or after trial who refused to work or who worked in a "slovenly or improper manner" by placing them in solitary confinement, withdrawing their allowance of food, or deducting a part of their earnings (although in practice no prisoners were compelled to work before trial). Convicted prisoners who refused to work lost part of their allowances unless they could afford to maintain themselves, in which case the whole allowance was withdrawn.[40] The political prisoners objected to this rule, claiming they had special status. They further complained that Higgin had banned radical newspapers from the gaol.

The man to whom they complained was George Williams, a former soldier and a dedicated radical who had somehow been appointed to the West Derby bench in 1809 and who remained persistently out of tune with his fellow magistrates. The mayor of Liverpool, where Williams three times ran for Parliament with a complete lack of success, described him with disgust as one of those "who are always gratified in having . . . opportunities of making inflammatory speeches to the lower Orders."

He finally entered Parliament in 1832, sitting for three years as the Liberal MP for Ashton under Lyme.*

On June 10, 1820, Williams wrote Higgin that he had received a letter from Nathan Broadhurst complaining that the political misdemeanants were being forced to work and that their newspapers had been confiscated. He claimed that both practices were illegal and added that he was himself sending a newspaper to Broadhurst. Higgin confiscated the paper and cut off the allowances of those prisoners who refused to work, asking his son to write Williams announcing his actions. On June 17 Williams sent an angrier letter to Higgin. Thomas Higgin, he wrote, had pointed out that the stoppage of the newspaper was common in many prisons. Williams, however, would "look to no Precedent or Example, those things complained of are either lawful or unlawful, and right or wrong accordingly—if any Act of Parliament confers a Power on Justices to make Regulations for Prisons, those Regulations I conceive must be in the *spirit of English Law*, or they are not justified in making them, or who knows what solitary Confinement, Fetters or Torture, may not become with some persons, and towards certain offences, wholesome discipline."[41]

Williams was mistaken about what the "spirit of English law" would permit. The censoring of prisoners' mail was an ancient practice. Moreover, the justices of the peace submitted regulations to Assize judges in order to make sure that they were in conformity with the law. Although torture was illegal, both fettering and solitary confinement were accepted, both by law and by precedent, as "wholesome discipline." The "spirit of English law" was not, in fact, heavily weighted in favor of prisoners; once convicted of a crime, inmates, in legal theory, lost most of their rights, while convicted felons lost even their right to life. One can-

*PRO, HO 42/167, John Wright, mayor of Liverpool, to Sidmouth, June 18, 1817. For Williams see William Wardell Bean, *The Parliamentary Representation of the Six Northern Counties of England, 1603-1886* (Hull, 1890). Williams joined the army under Burgoyne at the age of twelve, leaving in 1800 after 25 years of service all over the world. In August 1803 Williams was "drafted" as lieutenant-colonel-commander of the Second Liverpool Volunteers. He was a member of the radical Liverpool Concentric Society. In his 1818 campaign for Parliament he gained only two votes, while the two winners received over fourteen thousand each. He was always active on the bench. A teetotaler, he served on the "Drunken Committee" in Parliament. He was still on the bench in 1848. See Robert Walmsely, *Peterloo: The Case Reopened* (Manchester, 1969); Barbara Wittingham-Jones, "Liverpool's Political Clubs, 1812-1830," *Transactions of the Lancashire and Cheshire Historical Society* 111 (1959): 117-38; Brian Harrison, "Two Roads to Social Reform: Francis Place and the 'Drunken Committee' of 1834," *Historical Journal* 11 (1968): 272-300.

not easily argue that the legal trend in this period was toward increasing prisoners' rights.

Williams was assuming the old radical position that something in the spirit of the constitution protected the subjects' rights against infringement, even when that infringement was permitted by Parliament. It is not clear, however, that prisoners counted as subjects since, like children, madmen, and married women, they suffered special restrictions in their legal rights. In any case, by the time Williams wrote his letter, concern that civil rights be extended to prisoners was being replaced by the desire for more effective prison discipline.

Goaded by Williams's attacks, the justices submitted the case to two northern circuit barristers: Scarlett and Starkie. Both men had helped prosecute Broadhurst and Knight; Scarlett had also led the prosecution against the Peterloo speakers, for which Hunt never forgave him. Scarlett was, however, a liberal who had joined with Henry Brougham and John Williams to defend the Luddites in 1812. He had been a close friend of Romilly's and had supported his campaign to abolish many capital statutes. Many of his associates were prison, as well as law, reformers. He was, therefore, well qualified to judge the magistrates' case. Although Starkie's answers were lost, William Hulton preserved Scarlett's.[42]

The justices had set three questions: could they withdraw food and clothing from convicted persons refusing to work? Could they ban newspapers and political publications from prisons? And, did the gaoler have the power to read prisoners' correspondence? Scarlett's advice was such as might have been expected from a liberal barrister. He agreed that the magistrates had all these powers—although in the case of newspapers his agreement was very grudging. He strongly advised that the justices act with restraint and discretion. Starkie's opinion was apparently more favorable, for Thomas Higgin lost no time in putting it into Williams's hands.

Williams immediately wrote again to Broadhurst, stating that he placed no reliance on the opinions of counsel. Although there was little he could do to alter the situation, he hoped that "the Reformers, who with the Courage of Martyrs, devote themselves to their Country," might someday see how "'Seat Sellers,' and 'Seat Buyers' in adversity, may be trusted in a solitary cell," and how "the black Catalogue of Traitors, under the several Denominations of Spies, Instigators, Blood-money Men, and their Employers, how Murderers who have hitherto eluded Justice—may deport themselves in Solitude and Imprisonment, *begnawn* by their Consciences."[43]

To Williams's dismay, Higgin, availing himself of his newly confirmed powers, promptly impounded this letter. At about the same time, he brought suit against Williams for a libel contained in another letter, no longer extant, to John Doherty. Considering the violence of Williams's language, and particularly the veiled reference to the Peterloo officers in "Murderers who have hitherto eluded Justice," it is no wonder that relations between Williams and his brother justices were somewhat strained.

On August 8 the Annual General Session met in Preston. It provided Higgin with retroactive vindication, ordering him to withhold all newspapers and political publications sent to the Crown side of the gaol. Higgin was also ordered to open and read all letters to or from the Crown prisoners, except for letters between prisoners awaiting trial and their attorneys, and to detain those that seemed improper. The court then heard Williams's letters but deferred consideration of them until he was present. It also ordered that the letters be printed and that copies be sent to Williams and to every other justice in the county. William Hulton seems to have been chiefly responsible for the court's actions. Perhaps he was stung by Williams's contemptuous reference to Peterloo, since Hulton had initiated the attack of the military.

On August 22 the Session again met to consider the issue. Attendance was unusually high—37 justices from all over the county—though the size of the meeting may have been due to the fact that the court was also making appointments for the Kirkdale house of correction; meetings for choosing officers always drew large numbers. Five members of the Peterloo Committee of Nine were present, as well as W. R. Hay, who had advised them. Edward Bootle Wilbraham, a Tory MP and the chief defender of Peterloo in the House of Commons, was also there, but he was a frequent attender and would have come in any case to represent the Kirkdale justices. The court issued and printed a unanimous resolution that Williams's letters to Broadhurst were "peculiarly calculated to destroy all Discipline . . . and are insulting to the Magistrates of the County." Higgin, they said, "exercised a sound and commendable Discretion in withholding" them.[44]

The irrepressible Williams, however, decided to carry the war into a new arena. After an unsuccessful attempt to interest Sidmouth at the Home Office in his case, he brought his son-in-law, W. James, MP for

Liverpool, into the act. In January 1822 James wrote Broadhurst that he believed he, Broadhurst, had been "very harshly and cruelly treated, if I may not say unjustly." He enclosed £5 as a token of his sympathy and wrote a cover letter to Higgin ordering him not to open the letter to Broadhurst since it was a breach of parliamentary privilege to open members' letters.[45] Higgin did open the letter, and James announced a motion in the House of Commons relative to a breach of privilege. The news elicited a small flurry of anxious letters from Lancashire to the Home Office. Among them was a letter from Thomas Higgin pointing out that the rule permitting the opening of letters was in Justice Bayley's own hand and had been drawn up after consultation with the lord chief justice and the lord chief baron. He explained that the rule had been made in the first place in order to have other means of maintaining security than putting the prisoners in irons. Thomas enclosed a letter from his father, who had lost his temper completely:

The practice of inspecting the Letters of persons confined on the criminal side of the Gaol had been uniformly enforced to his knowledge, upwards of forty three years, especially against suspicious persons. . . . No Complaint was ever made to any of the Judges, or Magistrates, before the Demagogue Radicals came here. They have been no little annoyed by the *wholesome restrictions*, because they have not had free scope for their seditious and almost treasonable Expressions used in their Correspondence, even with some Members who, ought to be ashamed of the Encouragement given to desperate Characters, who, under the pretence of Reform seek to Ruin their Country.[46]

James's motion was debated in the House of Commons on February 25. The debate centered on two issues. The first was the magistrates' power to make regulations for prisons. Could they control every aspect of prison life, or only such areas as food and clothing? Did the approval of two Assize judges establish the presumptive legality of the regulations? If the regulations were legal, yet clashed with parliamentary privilege, which ought to prevail? Several members expressed a fear that, in James's words, the House would recognize "two different legislatures; one composed of both Houses of parliament, with the king at their head, and the other composed of judges, magistrates and gaolers."[47]

The second issue was whether Parliament needed to provide prisoners with direct recourse to members. Several speakers brought up the case of Ilchester, expressing a good deal of mistrust about the willingness of justices to deal with prison abuses. They argued that if prisoners had complaints to make, they were entitled to appeal to MPs. If the gaoler could read every letter and if parliamentary privilege could not protect letters to members from censorship, then the gaoler could effectively stifle all public criticism, while the justices could not be trusted to remove the grievance. Brougham spoke in support of James's motion while three Lancashire men—Lord Stanley, Peel, and Samuel Horrocks—spoke against it. When the question was put, it was defeated by a vote of 167 to 60. Although he had raised serious issues, Williams had not succeeded in making Lancaster into a second Ilchester.

Meanwhile, Williams was arrested on the libel charge brought by Higgin. He stood trial at the Lent Assizes on March 23, 1822, and was acquitted.[48] There the matter lay, with the honors roughly divided. The issue, however, and the resentments it had created, did not die. Neither the magistrates nor the radicals forgot the battle. In 1826 the Annual General Session ruled that prisoners might see friends only once in three months. The court also repeated its order that the gaolers prohibit "immoral, seditious, indecent or blasphemous publications," or any others that were "grossly libellous or exciting prisoners to Insubordination or wicked or immoral conduct." It ordered the gaoler to read all letters to and from prisoners, except those of debtors, and to hold back any letter containing improper material. With the chaplain's approval, the gaoler might read the unobjectionable parts of the letter to the prisoner, or explain the objections so that another might be written.

The practice of the prison had withstood every attack. In fact, it had become even more restrictive; henceforth, the gaoler was to bowdlerize mail in accordance with the most fastidious moral code, as well as engage in political censorship. Higgin's successor, for example, confiscated letters from common-law wives. Moreover, similar censorship was being exercised in Lancashire's other prisons, although newspapers soon reappeared. The political attacks of the radicals merely entrenched the prison administrators in a sort of defensive severity that, combined with Victorian censoriousness, resulted in a substantial loss of free speech and expression for the prisoners.

The issue revived in the tense year of 1832, when Nathan Broadhurst, Knight's co-defendant of 1819, returned to the Castle, charged with seditious conspiracy and attendance at an illegal meeting. He had been arrested in London, where he had gone to testify for Henry Hunt, now MP for Preston, in a libel case Hunt had brought against the *Times*. Ten days after the Assizes, on March 27, Hunt presented a petition to Parliament from Broadhurst and three fellow prisoners complaining of their treatment in the Castle. At first they had been given the gaol allowance, but "in consequence of their being unable to do the work assigned to them," they were ordered to find their own food and fuel.[49] Hunt himself complained that Higgin had opened his letters.

As is so often the case in the field of penal policy, the debaters proceeded in complete ignorance of what had been said and done in the past. This time, however, the conflict ended in an indirect victory for the radicals, when a complaint from the debtors paralleled the ones made by the Crown prisoners. On April 4, only a week after the first petition, Hunt presented one from the debtors complaining of Higgin's nonresidence in the Castle. Higgin was, indeed, not living in the Castle and by this time had handed over many of his duties to his son Thomas, although Thomas also had a cotton manufacturing business to oversee. John Higgin had tried but failed to persuade the justices to make Thomas gaoler in his place. He then attempted to bring Thomas in through the back door: John remained the nominal gaoler, but it was Thomas who did much of the work.

However reluctant the justices were to appoint Thomas as gaoler, they winked at the arrangement by which he carried out most of the routine duties at the Castle with his father's advice. When, however, the gaoler's nonresidence was publicly brought to the justices' attention, a committee headed by Edmund Hornby concluded that he ought to live in the Castle. Higgin promised to do so, but while he slept in the Castle, he continued to maintain another house in his son's name. The debtors, led by S. G. Anderton, concluded that they could get no satisfaction from the visiting justices and petitioned Parliament, complaining not only of the nonresidence but also that Thomas had a conflict of interest since his business was a creditor of some of the gaoled debtors. Anderton added that Thomas was embezzling bread shipments and illegally confining complaining debtors in solitary. Commons ordered that the petition be printed, and when the Annual General Session met in September, it agreed that Anderton should send his charges in writing to the visiting justices.[50]

One week later, the *Preston Chronicle* published an open letter from Anderton to John Higgin containing twenty charges. In January Higgin, admitting at least some of the charges by default, resigned. Even the Whiggish *Preston Chronicle* proved sympathetic to him, quoting with approval the comment in the *Lancaster Gazette* that "in no gaol in England has there been better order and regularity observed than this, . . .

owing to the judicious and excellent arrangements of Mr. Higgin and his son."[51] Since John was at this time about 72, he would probably have had to resign soon in any case, although he lived until 1847. He may have resigned simply because he was too old and weary to endure yet another confrontation. A new gaoler, James Hansbrow—like John Higgin a captain in the militia—was soon appointed, apparently without much disagreement.

Although Higgin was forced out of office, it was clear that by mid-century the political prisoners had lost the greater war. By then it had become regular practice to treat political activists charged with such "ordinary" crimes as riot like ordinary prisoners, although prisoners held for sedition still received special treatment. Even they were to some extent hampered by the increasing number of prison regulations. During the controversy, however, the radicals had raised important questions about the lawfulness of prison administration and about the "inalienable" rights of the prisoner that applied to all gaoled criminals.

The parliamentary debates over these issues centered on two questions. First, could prisoners who refused to work be deprived of their food allowances? Second, could the gaoler, with the permission of the magistrates, read and censor correspondence? Neither question applied to political prisoners alone, and ordinarily such problems, though important, would have been normal issues of prison administration to be settled in a routine way. However, because of the extraordinary political bitterness of the period, because those who raised these issues were political prisoners, and because those who supported them in Parliament stood to gain a great deal if the government could be embarrassed over its treatment of prisoners, they became political issues. Time and again they were confused with the question of whether the political prisoners should ever have been arrested at all, or whether, once convicted, they were entitled to special treatment. No one ever forgot that the fall of a Paris prison had symbolized a revolution.

Two of the "ex-cons" in the House, Hunt and Burdett, were especially successful in questioning the treatment of all prisoners, whatever their crimes. These two men had been convicted for political crimes, but once in gaol, they soon became concerned about the whole system of legal coercion and about what they saw as repressive administration. Both men, at various times in the parliamentary debates, drew attention to the unchecked supremacy of the magistrates, claiming that the justices systematically violated fundamental rights of the prisoners under their care. The focus of the debate, therefore, kept shifting between the wisdom of trusting a politically biased magistracy to safeguard the rights of political prisoners and the wisdom of entrusting a socially biased magistracy with prisoners at all.

During this period there were some checks on the conduct of the magistracy. The Assize judges passed on the legality of their regulations for the prisons, a duty that the judges took very seriously, and from time to time they used this power to control general policy. The Home Office, although it snubbed Williams, did exercise a general supervision of the justices' conduct, often demanding reports or explanations about particular charges. Finally, Parliament also debated the justices' conduct and sometimes ordered investigations if it suspected that they were not doing their job.

Moreover, all these issues were debated in the open, in the full glare of intense publicity both in London and in the county. John Higgin, who repeatedly found himself sucked into political controversy, became bitter about the constant inquisitions he endured. A mild, quietly disposed, and sensitive man who disliked quarrels, he spent most of his official life in a storm. That it was often only a tempest in a teacup did nothing to allay his dislike of the men who had conjured it up.

Though the radicals used the openness of the system to stir up controversy, it was that very openness that they were struggling to preserve. Step by step, the prison was withdrawing from the community. Prisoners were more and more isolated not only from each other but from the world outside the walls. Visits were restricted and wives banished. The introduction of prison food and prison dress cut down on contacts with the outside world, as prisoners ceased to barter for supplies and became increasingly identifiable by diet and dress as a race apart. The development of prison labor eliminated commercial contacts.

Partly for their own purposes, the radicals fought to keep the prisons open. They wished prisoners to be free not only to read and write as they pleased but also to complain about their treatment without fear of intimidation. In many other fields the radicals had battled over freedom of speech, of the press, and of petition, so it is not surprising that, when convicted, they carried the battle into the prisons. In the case of prisons, however, the trend was against them and they were repeatedly defeated. Gaolers gained complete control over every point of contact between the inmates and the outside world. This development, in turn, deprived the prisoners of an important protection against mistreatment. "How are we to make our complaint known to the magistrates?" New Bailey prisoners asked John Doherty when he heard that the keeper was cheating them of bread and refusing them writing paper. "Suppose he refuses to inform the magistrates that we want them, what then, will he be punished? . . . How is it to become known?"[52]

In a sense, the radicals were defeated by their own success at agitation. The rules permitting the Lancaster gaoler to superintend correspondence were well established. They might, however, have been relaxed in time if the radicals had not produced papers that simultaneously complained of the restrictions on their speech and criticized the conduct of the magistrates in the most violent terms. The justices, who naturally saw no reason to relax the regulations in order to promote criticism of themselves, dug in their heels and passed increasingly restrictive rules. As a result, censorship in all the prisons increased. Although enforcement varied, the precedent was established. To this day, British prison letters are censored, or their delivery stopped, for the most trivial reasons. Not even petitions to members of Parliament can pass through the prisons unread. Letters to the press, though often smuggled out, are still officially prohibited.

There was another paradoxical reason for the ultimate failure of the radicals. This was their success in using prison affairs as a weapon against the magistracy as an administrative body. The successive investigations into prison management conducted by or for Parliament began to erode public confidence in the county justices, and subsequent events did little to restore it. The radicals were particularly effective in drawing attention to the justices' financial maladministration. Meanwhile, the "philosophic radicals" undermined confidence in the justices' commitment to administrative reform. The combined attack proved devastating and, over the next half-century, the justices lost more and more power to the Home Office. It is questionable whether this process resulted in either more efficiency or more "reform" in the county prisons, although the first step, the appointment of inspectors, was an undeniable improvement. Ultimately, centralization meant a loss of local accountability. The magistrates were guilty of many sins, but at least they often met in public and saw their decisions debated publicly in the local press. Moreover, although they themselves were often remote, they were still less likely than were civil servants in London to be entirely cut off from personal contact with their charges, or from personal experience of the practical problems of running individual prisons.

When Anderton petitioned the visiting justices, he could print his charges in the local press and force Higgin to resign. No such scrutiny could be turned on the secretive Home Office. As the power to make decisions was removed to a central office, local people lost their sense that they had a special interest in local prisons run by a resident gentry. The national newspapers, though continuing to cover issues of prison policy as well as the great scandals, could not pay the sort of constant attention to small administrative problems that the local press provided, while hundreds of local newspapers could not be regularly read and consulted in London, where the decisions were now made.

When people lose the power to discuss and influence decisions made about an institution, they often lose interest in the institution altogether. English prisons are unique in the extent to which administrative decisions are made by the central government. When the prison administrators ceased to be accountable to their own communities, an important check was lost on their activities. Though the prison inspectors continued to issue reports, the reports were probably read less widely. Moreover, through an accident of British law, the central government obtained powers of stifling criticism that the local rulers had never possessed; under the Official Secrets Act it became illegal for civil servants, including the humblest prison guard, to discuss any aspect of their work. As a result, English prisons have never again been as open to scrutiny, or as subject to debate, as they were in the early nineteenth century.

Many prison officials would argue that the restriction of free speech is a good thing; prison staff need some protection against disruption and false or malicious public accusations. Without such protection, able candidates would be deterred from entering the prison service and good officers might be unjustly pilloried by the press.

The experience of the Napoleonic period, however, suggests that a more open policy holds real advantages. The political prisoners of that period were certainly disruptive in the extreme. They did everything in their power to make life difficult in the prisons. They refused to cooperate, sometimes to the extent of staying in bed, slung accusations with great enthusiasm, and frequently used slanderous language to infuriate and provoke. They created constant uproar in the prisons and promoted innumerable inquisitions into the conduct of gaol officers for their own political ends. They also, however, forced debate on issues that desperately needed airing. They questioned the whole basis of authority in the countryside and cast doubt on the justices' competence and fairness. They brought up fundamental questions of penal theory and personal rights; at this time they were almost the only group to question the use of solitary confinement or to maintain that the "spirit of English law" prohibited not merely cruelty but also the infringement of prisoners' rights. They compelled magistrates to account for their actions in Parliament, and in many prisons, such as Coldbath Fields, Ilchester, and Dorchester, they brought about the correction of very serious abuses, such as the use of frequent floggings. Although the cards were stacked in favor of the authorities, the radicals succeeded in discrediting several cruel or incompetent men. Doherty was as good as his word when he promised complaining prisoners in the New Bailey that "the system should at any rate be exposed, if it could not be mitigated."[53] Despite the trouble their relentless criticism caused, the radicals served as badly needed prisoners' advocates behind an iron curtain maintained by increasingly autocratic governors.

CHAPTER 6

Paying for Prisons: County Finance and Administration, 1776-1850

The Rising Rates, 1776-1830

The pace of prison reform depended on the willingness of ratepayers to accept its cost, a factor that could not be taken for granted. One of the great unsolved questions of the history of this period is how the English government, at all levels, managed to raise the revenue to cover rapidly increasing expenditure in a period of generally straitened circumstances. The story of the French fiscal crisis and the role it played in the fall of the ancien régime is well known, but the fact that England faced similar financial problems has not received sufficient attention, although Peter Mathias has found that English taxation was high compared with that of France, and during the Napoleonic wars was three times the French level.[1]

At the same time that Cobbett was writing that "the *cause* of our present miseries . . . is the *enormous amount of the taxes*, which the government compels us to pay for the support of its army, its placemen, its pensioners etc. and for the payment of the interest of its debt," that Orator Hunt was proclaiming that "everything they ate, drank, wore, and even said, [was] taxed," and that Bamford was explaining to the Privy Council that land taxes hurt the poor by raising the price of bread, county rates were also rocketing.[2] This movement was largely concealed behind the growth of the poor rates; under the provisions of the County Rate Consolidation Act of 1739, the churchwardens and overseers of the poor collected the county and poor rates together, handing the county's share to the high constables. In their collections they merely demanded

Fig. 1. Money issued by county rolls, 1787-1815. Source: *PP* 1814-15 X.

the total sum owed, without distinguishing to the taxpayers how much went to the poor and how much to other local expenditure.[3]

Because the poor rates were so large, ratepayers took many years to realize that the county budgets were rising much faster than even the poor rates, although the justices who superintended the spending of the money were well aware of the problem. After 1800 the increase accelerated. By 1825 national concern had led to the formation of a parliamentary Select Committee on the Expenditure of County Rates. The committee found that the rates were rising chiefly because of a combination of increased prosecution rates and new prison building to hold the growing number of convicts. In the counties making returns to the committee, prosecution costs had risen from £3,977 in 1792 to £76,647 in 1823.[4]

TABLE 8

Percentage Cost of Categories of Expenditure, County Only,
Selected Periods, 1744-1850

Object of expenditure	1744-49	1787-88	1800-1801	1810-11	1821	1841-50
L.C. repairs	16%	—	0.2%	2.8%	11.0%	16.3%
L.C. improvements	—	11.7%	16.0	4.6	—	—
L.C. prisoners	10	28.9	11.0	9.2	6.9	—
L.C. salaries (incl. county treas.)	—	5.4	3.8	6.3	5.0	1.8
Taking offenders to gaol	—	6.4	11.2	7.3	10.2	5.5
Vagrants	52	21.1	8.8	6.9	12.3	2.0
Coroners	—	7.0	2.9	3.6	3.3	7.3
Corn inspectors, etc.	—	0.4	1.2	0.4	1.8	3.6
Bridges	4	0.3	4.2	1.5	—	—
Militia, etc.	12	—	—	—	0.8	—
Militia families	—	—	14.4	32.3	—	—
Riots	—	—	—	—	4.8	—
Prosecution of felons	—	13.2	22.3	22.2	38.0	40.2
Lunatics' maintenance	—	—	—	—	1.7	6.3
Crown prisoners in Kirkdale	—	—	—	—	—	6.8
Misc.	6	2.5	3.9	2.5	3.8	10.1
TOTAL	100%	96.9%	99.9%	99.6%	99.6%	99.9%
Total for Lancaster Castle, including salaries	26%	46.0%	31.0%	22.9%	22.9%	18.1%

Because of Lancashire's rapid growth during this period, these developments were even more pronounced there than in England as a whole. The amount collected by county rolls went from about £1,000 a year in the mid-eighteenth century to more than £4,000 by 1787 and £30,000 by 1815 (see Fig. 1). Five years later it had risen to £47,000. Expenditure on the Castle and its prisoners rarely took less than a fifth of the total collected by county rolls; in 1787 repairs, improvements, prisoners, and county salaries (most of which went to the Castle gaoler, chaplain, and surgeon) took nearly half (46 percent) of the total. In only one year of those listed in Table 8 did the combined costs of the Castle and the prosecution of offenders take less than half the total. By 1796, according to the deputy county clerk, about £26,000 had been spent on the Castle construction.[5] A second spurt of building at the gaol between 1814 and

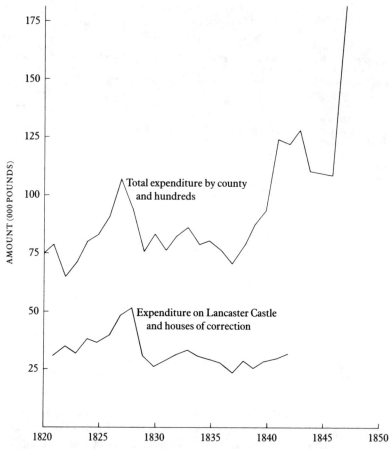

AMOUNT (000 POUNDS)

Total expenditure by county
and hundreds

Expenditure on Lancaster Castle
and houses of correction

Fig. 2. Total county and hundred expenditure compared with expenditure on
Lancaster Castle and the hundred houses of correction, 1820-1847. Sources:
PP 1850 XIII; Robert Hindle, *An Account of the Expenditure of the County Palatine of Lancaster for a Period of 23 Years . . . with Remarks* (London, 1843).

1823 helped account for part, but not all, of the great rise in expenditure
in those years. After that, as new items such as the care of lunatics and
the county constabulary appeared on the budget, the Castle took a
smaller proportion.

   This, however, is only a small part of the story. Because of Lanca-

TABLE 9
Expenditures of County and Hundreds, 1820-1842

Object of expenditure	Percent of total expenditure	Amount (000)
Prisons	38.7%	£763.9
Prosecutions	19.6	387.4
County and private lunatic asylums	11.1	219.4
Bridges	10.2	202.0
Conducting offenders to prison	4.3	85.9
County constabulary	3.5	70.0
Coroners	2.4	47.8
Passing vagrants	2.4	47.7
Law expenses	1.3	24.9
Inspectors of weights and measures	1.0	20.7
Riots	1.0	19.3
Miscellaneous	4.3	84.5
TOTAL	99.8%	£1,973.5

shire's peculiar method of allocating expenditure among the hundreds, many items that were included in the budgets of other counties, such as the houses of correction, were accounted for separately and did not appear in the county budget. By 1820 total county and hundred spending on items usually included in county budgets elsewhere had reached £75,000 a year. It would rise to £180,000 a year in 1847 (see Fig. 2). The county houses of correction and Lancaster Castle combined took between a quarter and a half annually of this larger sum (see Table 9). This sum, in turn, was roughly a quarter of the gross total collected for the poor rates, which had risen from about £80,000 a year in 1785 to a peak of about £560,000 in 1818. After 1818 the amount spent on the poor fell, while total county and hundred expenditure continued to rise.[6] In 1828, a peak year of prison spending, the cost of the Castle and the houses of correction alone amounted to over £50,000, or more than a tenth of the total Poor Law assessment of just under £500,000.

Although the county officers and the justices of the peace must have known what was happening, the county budget was not widely publicized and ratepayers for the most part remained ignorant of this element in their poor rate assessments until a few radical critics, assisted by the *Preston Chronicle*, began to campaign about this issue in the 1830's.

The Incidence of Rates and the Reassessments

By the end of the eighteenth century, the greater responsibility and work entailed by the rapid increase in prosecutions and the expansion of county expenditure were creating serious strains in Lancashire's government. Amateur justices began to find it difficult to cope even with routine business, particularly in those areas where there were few gentlemen qualified to serve and a rapidly rising industrial population. Tradition forbade the appointment to the bench of anyone connected with "trade," and the work was so arduous that the few gentlemen living nearby were reluctant to act.[7]

The turn of the century saw a serious crisis in Lancashire's government. The first casualty of the rise in prosecutions was the Sheriff's Board, which the growing business of the Assizes made impossible. Deprived of a central decision-making body at just the time when their need of it was increasing, and harassed by their growing responsibilities, the justices fell to quarreling among themselves. The overworked magistrates of the southern half of the county, who had always resented having to make the long trip up to Lancaster, demanded an annual meeting in Preston to debate and settle all general county business. The Lonsdale justices, jealous of Lancaster's privileges as the county town, resisted fiercely.[8]

In 1795 the Lancaster justices finally forced the issue by dismissing the county treasurer. After an attempt at reconciliation failed, the three southern benches agreed to bring a bill into Parliament providing for an annual meeting to transact county business at Preston. Despite the efforts of the Lonsdale justices, the bill became law in 1798 as the Lancashire Sessions Act. Thereafter, county business was transacted at Preston by the Annual General Session, attended by all the Lancashire justices who chose to come. A formal meeting in June received reports and accounts; these were then published and a second meeting in September discussed them and made resolutions.[9]

The crisis did not end with the passage of the Sessions Act. The regional divisiveness that had developed during the bitter struggle over its passage made the rural justices especially sensitive to the way county expenditure was rising and to the unequal way the rates were apportioned. In the hard year of 1801, when spending reached a sharp peak, the justices went so far as to prepare a case in support of an act of Parliament to reassess the entire county, but then times improved, spending declined again, and the discontent temporarily subsided.[10]

It is no wonder that ratepayers were dissatisfied with an assessment unchanged for nearly two hundred years; the question is why widespread resistance did not appear earlier. By 1800 the incidence of rates had become extremely capricious; the thinly populated rural areas of the north were paying many times the assessment of the large industrial complexes that had grown up in the south. Several Lancashire parishes had become so small in the intervening years that they regularly paid more to the county rate than they did to support their own poor.[11]

Local observers agreed that the rates fell on the land, although it was the cities that were responsible for many of the problems that created expenditure, particularly a high crime rate. In this period the bench overwhelmingly represented landowning rather than mercantile or professional interests, and the overtaxed, lightly populated rural areas were disproportionately represented since they were more suitable for gentlemen's seats. Although the precise incidence of the rates cannot be determined, it seems that the great expansion of the county rates at the turn of the century and the extensive building programs were supported by the very men whose estates bore a disproportionate part of the costs, paid either from their own pockets or from those of their tenants. Until 1815 the antiquated rating system prevented any attempt to tap the new industrial and commercial wealth springing up around them. It is difficult to understand how the county managed to sustain the increase of services and facilities provided during these years, particularly since the wars, the income tax, and the poor rates were placing taxpayers under considerable strain.[12]

Part of the answer no doubt lies in the fact that landlords also benefited from the Industrial Revolution. Several Lancashire estates developed profitable collieries, while many were able to market their produce to the large new urban markets. The price of corn more or less kept pace with the rises in money wages. It is also true that inflation made the real rises in the rates a good deal smaller than their pound totals. Nevertheless, many Lancashire estates were ill placed to take advantage of such opportunities; in general, Lancashire's farms were small, unproductive, and inefficiently run. As a result, throughout the period, Lancashire became more and more dependent on imported corn. The harvests were extremely poor in 1792 and 1795 and from 1798 to 1800. Because of the

TABLE 10
Percentages Paid by the Hundreds to a County Rate, 1739-1841

		1815		1829		1841	
Hundred	1739, Pct.	Amount (000)	Pct.	Amount (000)	Pct.	Amount (000)	Pct.
Lonsdale	16%	£278.2	9%	£282.4	7%	£302.0	5%
Amonderness	19	258.1	8	295.0	7	364.5	6
Blackburn	18	278.9	9	373.9	9	497.5	8
Leyland	9	171.1	5	172.3	4	199.9	3
Salford	14	918.4	30	1,554.3	37	2,703.3	44
West Derby	24	1,201.4	39	1,536.7	36	2,124.9	34
TOTAL	100%	£3,106.1	100%	£4,214.6	100%	£6,192.1	100%

wet climate and poor soil, oats, never popular with urban workers, were the largest crop. Farm labor was scarce and became scarcer as the war and industrial opportunities pulled men away.[13]

Though it is easy to understand why the rural justices and the ratepayers they represented might have felt aggrieved by the beginning of the nineteenth century, it seems odd that Liverpool—by common consent the most under-rated community in Lancashire—was the place that chose to force the issue. Whatever the reason, in 1807 the borough refused to contribute to the county rate on the grounds that the county assessments were unequal.[14] Prodded into action at last, the county again resolved to bring a bill into Parliament for a new county assessment. It was forestalled, however, by a national act of 1815 establishing a pound rating system.[15] Almost immediately, Lancashire carried out its first general assessment in nearly two hundred years, basing it on receipts and rents from 1812. This assessment greatly increased the contribution of the industrial south. By 1827 Liverpool was protesting that it had been over-rated, and its appeal forced a second valuation in 1829. The further valuations that took place in 1840 and 1852 steadily increased the contribution of Salford and lowered that of the northern hundreds (see Table 10).[16]

The southern manufacturers who were beginning to trickle onto the bench in some numbers by the 1830's, as the exclusionary policy of the government broke down under pressure, never looked favorably on these new rates.[17] Owing to a legislative anomaly, the act establishing the county rate assessment required that valuations be based on the full, or gross, income of the properties concerned, while the assessments for the poor rate were made upon net income, after insurance, repairs, and depreciation. Moreover, assessors rated urban property at 8 percent of its cost and rural property at 3 percent. The fact that the city property owner had to devote a larger proportion of his income to costs was recognized by the poor rate assessors but not by the county rate assessors. To some extent this inequity was counterbalanced by the fact that only real property, not machinery or stock in trade, was assessed, but the mill owners ignored this consideration.[18]

Aside from the irritation it caused year in and year out, the difference in the rating systems had serious repercussions in bad years. The county rate was reassessed only rarely, but the poor rate, being a strictly local tax, was assessed annually. Between new assessments for the county rate the system worked just as it had in the past; that is, every section of the county paid a fixed proportion of the amount to be levied, according to its share at the last general assessment. The rate was actually collected, however, as a percentage of the poor rate and along with it. In bad years, many large enterprises gained reductions in their poor rate assessments, since their net income had fallen. The area as a whole, however, still owed the same amount to the county rate. In years of real hardship, when enterprises gained reductions in their poor rate assessments and many buildings were simply abandoned, the remaining solvent ratepayers had to find not only the money for an increased expenditure on their own poor (because of the hard times) but also to pay an increased percentage toward the county rate. Except in very bad years, however, it is difficult to believe that the urban areas were seriously over-rated; the four northern hundreds contained 26 percent of the population in 1831 and, under the assessment of 1829, paid 27 percent of the rates.[19]

Prices were in general dropping throughout this period. The price for manufactured goods fell especially sharply during the "hungry forties" immediately after the last assessment of 1841, which had been based on 1840 prices. The fact that county spending failed to follow suit was a further irritant to angry ratepayers. After reaching a sharp peak in the 1820's, by the mid-thirties spending had fallen back only to the level of the earlier 1820's, and after 1838 it again began to shoot up. By the early 1830's an organized pressure for fiscal reform had appeared.

The Attack on the Rates

The years after Peterloo saw the development of a sustained radical attack on county government. When the radicals turned to the subject of the rates, they found natural allies among the disgruntled ratepayers of the large industrial conurbations. Although the two groups often failed to agree about purely local issues, it was easy for them to unite in hostility toward an unrepresentative and repressive rural oligarchy that was flinging away hard-earned money on unpopular causes while sheltering behind the bounty of the Corn Laws. Even the radicals accepted the mounting county expenditure on prosecutions as unavoidable, so they concentrated their attack on the less easily defensible expenditure on local prisons and prison salaries. Their leader was George Williams, who took the county to court three times with appeals against the misapplication of the rates. In one case the money had been intended for the erection of army barracks, a particularly obnoxious allocation for the veterans of Peterloo. According to Williams he won at King's Bench each time, but the county refused to reimburse his legal costs, and the expense finally forced him to drop this method of compelling economy.[20]

By this time Williams was convinced that the only way to force the justices to be more responsible financially was to make the position of justice an elected post. He wrote to the Commission for Enquiring into County Rates in 1835 that this "ancient and constitutional right of the people" to elect their justices was now even more necessary, since the revenue had grown in Lancashire from £1,000 in 1770 to nearly £100,000.[21] His campaign in favor of elected justices received support from the radical MP for Middlesex, Joseph Hume, who introduced a bill for the establishment of separate elected boards to administer county expenditure. The bill foundered after several members pointed out that it was virtually impossible to separate the judicial and executive functions of the justices; few Englishmen were prepared to accept an elective judiciary. Lancashire was to take the lead in reviving this issue in the late 1840's.[22]

One of the county's problems was that it had made several long-term commitments—particularly for salaries—at a time when prices had been higher. These salaries, most of which went to prison personnel such as the governor, chaplain, taskmasters, matron, and surgeon at all four institutions, now seemed excessive to the man in the street. Many justices, however, were reluctant to lower the amount paid to people who had served the county well for many years and who had in many cases taken on more obligations to suit their anticipated incomes. Although by the 1830's such salaries represented a relatively small proportion of total expenditure (for example, payments to the Lancaster staff and the county treasurer combined took between 2 percent and 5 percent of the county rolls), the reformers returned again and again to the extravagance of the sums involved.

On this issue the bench was divided, with the most liberal and active justices favoring reduction while the conservatives, such as W. R. Hay and William Hulton, opposed it. In 1829 a committee of five justices, including Thomas D. Hesketh and Thomas Batty Addison, both long-serving chairmen of the Annual General Session, proposed a reduction in most county salaries that would have saved about £1,700 a year, out of a gross county and hundred expenditure of about £76,000 a year. The committee's report was printed, but the Session resolved to debate each salary separately as positions became vacant. For some time it seemed as if the committee's suggestions would be brushed aside; when the chaplaincy of the New Bailey became vacant shortly afterwards, Henry Fielding was appointed at the old salary.[23]

In the spring of 1831, however, the *Preston Chronicle* revived the issue. In March a letter from "Rusticus" appeared, supporting the committee and complaining bitterly about the profligate spending on prison salaries: "I am convinced no satisfactory reason can be adduced, why the salaries of Chaplains of Gaols should have been fixed so high; for most of the men with whom they pass away their time are very ignorant;—their learning, therefore, need not of necessity be *profound*; nor is there any demand for their dress to be very expensive. Why, then, should salaries be allowed which make it very desirable for a clergyman to have the *privilege* of labouring all his life-time within the walls of a prison?"[24] On April 9 Rusticus returned to the attack. He begged the justices to abolish the office of county treasurer entirely and in that way save the £600 a year his salary cost. Even greater savings would come from reducing payment to "the family firm of Messrs, the Gaolers of Lancaster Castle. Who would ever imagine that these persons, good gaolers no doubt, ought to be paid 1300 pounds annually?"[25]

Although most ratepayers probably agreed with Rusticus, Addison and his committee were generally unsuccessful in persuading the justices to reduce salaries when making new appointments. Despite the appearance in 1833 of a book entitled *Remarks on the County Expenditure* by an angry Preston accountant named Robert Hindle, which was warmly praised by George Williams, agitation over the county rates was temporarily subsumed by local debate on the incorporation of Manchester and by more pressing national issues, such as the Reform Bill. Meanwhile,

Parliament took some of the pressure off the justices by following the recommendation of the Commission for Enquiring into County Rates that the national government undertake to pay half the costs of county prosecutions. These costs continued to be listed in the county budgets but were no longer raised on the county rates.[26]

At the end of the 1830's the rates again began to rise, although not nearly as rapidly as total county expenditure, since the national funds took an increasing share of the burden. In 1839 the Annual General Session voted to raise the salary of John Clay, the chaplain at Preston, by £100 to £350, though not without a battle and claims that the vote was miscounted. In the same year, Lancashire decided to establish a police force; this expense was to become a bitterly contested issue until the justices divided the county into several police districts and permitted each to determine the size of its force. In 1840 a third county assessment increased Salford's share by 7 percent.

In 1843 Robert Hindle produced a second book, *An Account of the Expenditure of the County Palatine of Lancaster for a Period of Twenty-three Years . . . with Remarks*. The "remarks" were extremely scathing, while the "account" itself contained many damaging quotations from such authorities as the inspectors of prisons. As a whole, it amounted to a complete indictment of magisterial government. The book received wide publicity and circulation, not least among the justices themselves. Partly because of its influence, they decided in 1844 to establish a permanent finance committee in order to keep a closer watch on expenditure.

Meanwhile, the prison buildings were becoming older and more dilapidated, prison committals were still rising, and penal theory was changing. The combined and strenuous efforts of the prison chaplains and the inspectors finally overcame the determined prevarication of the justices, who agreed to build new ranges of cells at Preston and Kirkdale. In 1846 a committee of magistrates met with Captain William John Williams, the inspector, and Joshua Jebb, the surveyor general, and concluded that further drastic alterations would be necessary, including the conversion of Lancaster Castle into a women's prison. The justices managed to put off further action for several years, partly on the grounds of expense; the ratepayers were already complaining bitterly about the cost of the new wings at Preston and Kirkdale. According to rumor (which in this case was nearly accurate), the justices had spent almost £8,000 on the Kirkdale chapel alone.[27]

The final explosion came in 1847 and 1848, when the county found itself embarked on several building schemes. The rates, which did not even represent the entire cost of the projects concerned, shot up dramatically. From £59,617 in 1845-46 they rose to £95,613 in 1846-47 and £103,739 in 1847-48. Though expenditure for general purposes rose about £10,000 during this interval, most of the increase came from the Preston/Kirkdale building (£12,000 in 1846-47 and £21,000 in 1847-48) and from the two new lunatic asylums necessitated by recent legislation (£31,000 in 1846-47 and £11,600 in 1847-48). In 1847-48 the Poor Law Union of West Derby paid £3,517 for its poor rate and £5,439 for the county rate. The general finance committee reported to the Annual General Session in 1848 that total spending for the past year, including amounts contributed by the national government, had been nearly £180,000.[28]

In January 1849 the guardians of the Poor Law unions, who were responsible for collecting the county money along with the poor rates and who thus bore much of the odium caused by the increases, held an indignation meeting at Newton. They eventually agreed to bring a bill into Parliament establishing a county financial board. Justices would make up one-third of the board, and the other two-thirds would consist of representatives elected by the Poor Law unions.[29] Despite initial enthusiasm, the bill, introduced first by Hume and a second time with changes by Thomas Milner Gibson, failed for several reasons.[30] Many members shared the contempt of the Poor Law guardians that the Rev. J. S. Birley of Bolton expressed before the committee on the bill:

Elected guardians may be respectable men, but many of our boards of guardians are composed of persons who were overseers under the old system of the Poor Law; they are persons of very narrow-minded views; and I know one or two cases in Lancashire where their very rough manner and their proceedings have driven some of the magistrates away from the board; very few of the magistrates . . . do attend the boards of guardians. . . . I am afraid that instead of taking an enlarged view of any matter or question, we should be led away just by the opinion of the hour, and that they would be very often penny wise and pound foolish. My opinion of the judgment exercised by the Poor Law guardians in Lancashire is not very exalted.[31]

By this time also, the Lancashire justices were putting their own house in order. In 1850 they compelled their incompetent treasurer, William Hulton, to resign.[32] Social, economic, and political tensions eased, and interest in the bill dropped. Perhaps the most important influence within Parliament was Sir John Packington's shrewd cross-examination of the witnesses before the committee on the act. Packington succeeded in showing that rates in Lancashire were actually lower than they had been in the 1820's, both on a poundage and a per capita basis. He demonstrated, to the satisfaction of a majority of the committee reporting on the bill, that the justices had had little choice but to authorize the building program that had forced the rates up. Several justices also testified that they had tried but failed to obtain government loans that would have spread the costs more gently over several years. In its report the committee stated that the justices had conducted their financial affairs "with proper attention to economy, with just regard to the public interests, and with all the publicity required by law."[33] It found that discontent arose either from the adoption of police, in which case experience had mitigated complaints, or from the costs of gaols and asylums, in which case the justices had no choice but to approve spending to comply with acts of Parliament. Parliament rejected the bill and, the economy having improved, for the time being the "ratepayers' revolt" was stifled.

There can be no question that the Lancashire justices spent money with a relatively liberal hand. Lancashire's prison staff earned more than any other in England, except for the staffs of York Castle and of London-area prisons such as Newgate and Coldbath Fields.[34] When Higgin was drawing £1,000 a year he was probably the most highly paid gaoler in England, although the gaolers of some of the larger urban prisons, especially in London, may well have earned similar sums in fees. Higgin's huge salary was to some extent an accident of geography: it had been settled in lieu of conveyance fees and other perquisites and, because of Lancashire's position and terrain, conveyance fees had always been extraordinarily large. County chaplains, however, were also very well paid. Though Lancashire's justices avoided the extravagance of the Yorkshire justices, who spent over £100,000 at Wakefield and about £200,000 at York Castle within a short period at the end of the 1840's (enough to buy a separate mansion for each prisoner), they spent more on one complex of buildings at Kirkdale than the Poor Law guardians did for whole workhouses designed for several hundred inmates.[35]

To some, even this expenditure seemed niggardly. John Clay always felt that his salary was inadequate, and he criticized the parsimony that made the magistrates hesitate to build additional separate cells in the early 1850's. The refusal of the justices to make large outlays persistently hindered attempts at wholesale prison reform. Although Frederic Hill objected to the costs of the separate system, the inspectors in general, and the Home Office as well, complained constantly about the dilapidated state into which the local prisons were allowed to fall. Even Hill at one point said that the New Bailey was not fit to hold a single prisoner.[36] Inevitably, the justices were caught between the united force of the chaplains, governors, surgeons, prison inspectors, and the government, on the one hand, and the irate ratepayers, on the other.

In many cases the justices got good value for their money. The Lancaster Castle gaolers, Higgin and Hansbrow, were both outstanding for their humanity. The bench's greatest failings were the uncritical loyalty it displayed toward those it appointed and its leaning toward nepotism. For able and well-connected gaolers this support could be an invaluable source of strength, permitting them to exercise a firm and consistent discipline in an uncertain world, but incompetent or cruel officials were also able to shelter both themselves and their sons beneath this dispensation. A related problem was the lack of adequate provision for superannuated staff, which made the justices reluctant to discharge officers who were too old to fulfill their duties adequately. Although difficulties cropped up at all three houses of correction, serious scandals were rare, in marked contrast to the borough prisons at Liverpool and Manchester. Lancashire also succeeded in finding prison chaplains of exceptional energy and ability, including not only Clay, who achieved a national reputation, but also Fielding at Salford and Appleton and Horner at Kirkdale.

It seems certain that if the guardians and the urban ratepayers had had their way, outlay would have been drastically cut. In the similar Poor Law institutions, almost every item of expenditure was smaller. The cost of the buildings was lower (though this was to some extent due to the greater need for security at the prisons and to the development of cellular confinement), staff salaries were considerably smaller (the highest salary on record for a workhouse master was £150), and expenditure per inmate was less.[37] A letter in the *Liverpool Courier* in 1837 pointed out that the weekly per capita expenditure on food at Kirkdale was 5s. and in the Liverpool workhouse, 2s. ½d.[38] As a result of such economy, the workhouses were largely staffed with incompetent and sometimes cruel men and women, both in Lancashire and throughout the country. As one historian has written recently, "on the whole, . . . the Poor Law service did not attract men and women who were well-qualified, much less dedicated, largely because the rates of pay were from the first ridiculously low."[39]

Where city councils ran the gaols, they often tried to practice a similar frugality. Heather Tomlinson described such a state of affairs in Yorkshire, where a committee appointed by the York city council refused to accept the justices' recommendations on the expenditure for the gaol and "took refuge in instituting cheeseparing and petty measures" such as limiting inmates to bread and gruel for the first fourteen days of confinement. According to Tomlinson, "they did not merely fail in their attempt, but also succeeded in creating greater problems which eventually led to the prison's closure."[40] Lancashire's justices had a good case for their greater liberality.

This story contrasts with the usual model of social reform, employed both by conservative and radical historians, in which a "rising middle class" seizes the initiative from the aristocracy in order to achieve reform. In the traditional version, the middle class is inspired by its increasing self-confidence and the need to overthrow "old corruption" and to reform corrupt institutions. In the radical version, it acts upon its anxiety over the mounting threat of social disorder from the lower classes, and the result is the creation of repressive social institutions. What this model overlooks, however, is the fact that these institutions could not exist at all unless someone paid for them, that control of their finances meant control of the number and quality of the institutions, and that such control remained firmly in the hands of the gentry. Although the gentry was far better able than the urban middle class to insulate itself from the dangers of crime and disorder, it continued, however reluctantly, to create these institutions and to provide them with the level of financial support necessary, although the cost of prison reform aroused protest against the rates and ultimately against the gentry's authority. It was the urban middle class, personified by local accountants, Poor Law guardians, and ratepayers, that bitterly opposed all new prison building or expenditure.

A bench that contained both Hulton and Williams obviously contained a wide spectrum of opinion on the value of social institutions and on the way they should be managed, but the justices were constrained in their activities by the weight of their responsibilities. Whatever individual justices might think, the bench as a whole had to come to some sort of consensus in order to make day-to-day administrative decisions. Fur-

TABLE II

Amount Raised by Rates (County and Hundred),
Five-Year Averages, 1829-1849

Period	Amount
1829/30 to 1833/34	£71,255
1834/35 to 1838/39	58,220
1839/40 to 1843/44	88,977
1844/45 to 1848/49	78,454

thermore, the range of their decisions was circumscribed by the law; when acting as judges they had little choice but to commit certain offenders to prison even if they were apprehensive about the growth of penal institutions. Similarly, they were constrained by Parliament to create asylums, which placed a heavy burden on the rates. Once these institutions had appeared, the justices tried to maintain a certain minimal standard of decency in their administration.

In general, they were successful in controlling expenditure after 1815, and there is no evidence that the rates themselves were unreasonable, nor that they fell most heavily on the middle classes.[41] In Lancashire between 1821 and 1841, the population rose by two-thirds, from a little over one million to 1,667,054. During the period from 1815 to 1841 the total assessed wealth of the county doubled from about three million to about six million pounds.[42] During this period, the county expanded the services it provided, introducing, in particular, the rural police and enormously improved provision for lunatics. Because of greater national government contributions, however, the total actually levied by county and hundred rates did not rise appreciably on average, even including the special rates for the constabulary divisions (see Table 11). Because of the rises in assessed value, the pound rate actually dropped considerably. Even when gross expenditure is used, accepting the complainants' argument that what they received from the nation in one hand they paid back with the other, total expenditure went from an average of £92,926 in the period 1824-28 to £128,472 in 1844-48—an increase of one-third, or less than the increase in either population or assessment.[43] Even allowing for a drop in prices, the burden cannot have become significantly heavier.

If this is the case, then we are left with a paradox. In the first period of building, the 25 years between 1790 and 1815, rates multiplied tenfold.

The payments unquestionably were allocated unequally and did not benefit from industrial growth. The men on whom the rates fell most heavily sat on the bench and approved the increases. Aside from proposing a reassessment in 1801, a proposal that came to nothing, these men made no attempt to alter the situation until the most under-rated community in the county protested. In the second period of building, from about 1821 to 1859, expenditure rose more slowly and its effect was largely dissipated by industrial development and national contributions. At the same time, several other taxes, particularly the poor rate, were falling, thus easing the pressure on taxpayers. Yet throughout this second period there was continuous bitter criticism of the rates.

Part of the explanation for this paradox lies in the fact of representation. Whatever may have been the actual incidence of the rates toward the end of the eighteenth century, the landowners and gentlemen sitting on the bench believed that they themselves were paying the lion's share. This belief helped justify their claim to rule, since it was the payment of taxes that determined the "stake" one had in government. At the beginning of the next century, they successfully redistributed what was becoming an intolerable burden, but only at the cost of undermining their exclusive claim to authority. As the nation moved to broaden the suffrage, the existence of a body of appointed but hereditary rulers in the counties—a "rural House of Lords" without even a balancing House of Commons—became increasingly unacceptable to the urban ratepayers, who were now paying their full share of county costs. The presence on the bench of a handful of the wealthiest and most successful mill owners did little to allay this discontent. Together the radicals and the ratepayers launched an attack against the justices on the points where they seemed most vulnerable: the way they ran their prisons and the way they spent the county rates. Far from increasing the power of the "ruling class," the heavy cost of prison reform and other social institutions proved both politically and socially disruptive. By the end of the nineteenth century the effort of the justices, under pressure from Parliament, to provide new services and new institutions for the inhabitants of their counties would cost them their local power.

CHAPTER 7

The Nineteenth-Century Prisons

Though historians are divided over the effects of the reforms of the late eighteenth century, there is a more general consensus on those of the nineteenth century. Peel's Act of 1823, which abolished all fees, provided for prison instruction and religious services, and established a formal classification system, is usually seen as a step forward. The act sponsored by the Duke of Richmond's committee in 1835, which increased central control over the prisons—providing in particular for appointed prison inspectors—is also seen as beneficial. In general, however, from the introduction of the treadmill in the early 1820's, and especially after the development of the theories of separate and solitary confinement in the mid-1830's, the historians' picture is of an ever-growing repressiveness in which the chief concern of prison officials was to come up with more effective ways to "break the spirit" of their charges.

This interpretation rests on these writers' generally hostile attitude toward Benthamite radicalism, at least as revealed in its prison policies, and on a distaste for middle-class Evangelicalism. To Michel Foucault, "le panoptisme"—the "endless interrogation" made possible by the new form of Benthamite prison—was simply another instrument of social control, like factories, schools, or hospitals, in fact, like all the institutions of the welfare state.[1] To Gertrude Himmelfarb, Bentham's "haunted house" was a vehicle for a fantasy of personal aggrandizement.[2] To Ursula Henriques, the reformative efforts of earnest Evangelicals "might nowadays be called brain-washing." "There was indeed," she writes, "a flavour of self-deception, if not of deliberate hypocrisy, about much of the propaganda for the separate system. . . . For many nineteenth-century reformers religion was an instrument of social discipline, for application to other people, especially the lower orders, not to themselves. . . . Their stock adjectives for inflicted suffering were 'wholesome' and 'salutary' and the stench of unctuous sanctimony still rises from their pages." Even Bentham, she explains, was willing to employ the religious sanction, because "he had been frightened by the French Revolution."[3] This picture has some truth, but it overestimates the extent to which prisons were run by ideas rather than by men and underestimates the problems with which the administrators were grappling. It dismisses the reformers' good intentions as a mere screen for class oppression, while it greatly overestimates their success in attaining their disciplinary goals. In concentrating on the writings of nationally important reformers, it ignores those men, such as the county justices, who were actually implementing and administering the reforms. These men have sometimes been portrayed as mere agents of the parliamentary, inspectional, or bureaucratic will. More often, they are depicted as playing a purely reactionary role. Both these views are misleading. The county bench had a mind of its own. Its members sat in Parliament and enjoyed both power and patronage. Their decisions were as significant and as representative of English intentions as were the writings of the middle-class reformers. The justices were often willing, sometimes even anxious, to implement reform, but under their guidance the counties rarely adopted the radical measures of control suggested by the more zealous national campaigners.

The standard historical view also neglects a second group that had a critical role in the decision to adopt reforms, in the day-to-day administration of the gaols, and in the strictness or kindliness of their regime: the individual prison governors. Finally, it underestimates the success that the prisoners themselves often had in forcing compromises on administrators or in undermining their efforts. The influence of these groups, along with the inevitable compromises imposed by problems of finance, overcrowding, and administration, meant that nineteenth-century prisons were profoundly different not only from their eighteenth-century predecessors but also from the stringent penal fantasies of idealistic reformers.

The Buildings, 1816-1845

During the war years little prison building had gone on, but construction resumed again in 1816. Under the pressure of an increasing number of inmates, Salford more than doubled in size, and Lancaster, which had already constructed a new felons' prison, added an entire women's prison within its walls.[4] Although Preston had been presented in 1816, work did not get under way there until the 1820's. In 1817 the Ormskirk and Wigan Sessions moved to Liverpool, and in 1818 the justices decided to construct an entirely new house of correction at Kirkdale, a nearby suburb. Eventually, South Lancashire received a separate Assize as well.

Although the cells built at the end of the eighteenth century were hailed at the time as a great advance, they had many deficiencies. The new buildings often followed a "contagionist" plan, with small groups of separate cells arranged in squares around a central yard, corridor, or workroom. These were much harder for staff to supervise than either the old-fashioned large wards or the panopticon and radial cell wings of the future. Although the cells were intended to house single prisoners, the pressure of rising numbers filled them with up to five inmates each.

The felons' prison at Lancaster proved especially inconvenient. It consisted of two towers, each containing eight sleeping cells to a floor. The cells were built back to back, four on each side, around a thick masonry core and opened onto a corridor going around the circumference of the tower. Since they were on the inside of the tower, with the corridor between them and the outer wall, they had no windows at all, only a small ventilation hole over the door to the corridor outside. Since the towers consisted of ten very small floors surrounded by extremely thick stone walls, it was difficult to provide moving air, either for ventilation or for heat. It was impossible for a prison officer to see into a cell unless he mounted the stairs and looked through its door; nor, if he was on one floor, could he easily hear anything at all on other floors.[5]

Samuel Bamford, who was imprisoned in Lancaster after Peterloo, graphically described his experience of these cells in his memoirs:

During the day . . . I had imbibed a favourable opinion of this prison. The day-room and yard were clean and airy, and whilst the attendant was sweeping out the cells and making the beds, I had gone in, and found them with their doors all open, lighted with the forenoon sun, and as white and sweet as a constant application of quick lime could make them. . . . At the head of the cell was an iron slab, full of perforations, and resting on the projections from the wall; a sack with straw in, a couple of blankets or so, and a good horse-rug, made up our bed, and the whole being apparently clean, I promised myself a sleep as sound as a king could enjoy. . . . A capital prison thought I. . . . Besides, I had heard that these felon-dungeons were constructed under the direction of the celebrated "humane Howard." . . .

We turned in, and . . . I began to feel as if I were being smothered. My old complaint on the lungs had gone with me to this place. . . . I now began to feel as if I was closed up in a coffin, and not a breath of air above and around me. How dreadful were my sensations! . . . My chest heaved for air . . . and I stood leaning on my bed, pumping and gasping, in the close suffocating den.[6]

Henry Hunt also commented that his cell was "most infamously close" and that "I thought I should have been suffocated for some time after I entered it."[7]

Even in successful designs, eighteenth-century reforms created a number of intractable architectural problems. The open wards of the "unreformed prison" were often close, dark, and difficult of access, but these problems were relatively simple to remedy. It was not too difficult to break through walls to let in light and air. A single officer could take in a room full of twenty or more persons at a glance; locking up, unlocking, and delivering food were all relatively rapid operations. The commitment to nightly cellular confinement complicated these activities, even before there was any interest in the complete separation of prisoners. It was the eighteenth-century development of cellular confinement that provoked a corresponding emphasis on the need for "inspection," since previously this had been a less difficult procedure.

Bentham believed his Panopticon solved this difficulty. Along with the innovative plan itself, Bentham introduced many novelties to make it function properly. For instance, he replaced solid masonry with structural iron and provided duct heating, running water, and water closets in every cell—refinements that are still missing in many English prisons today.[8] In many ways, the Panopticon represented a revolt against what Bentham considered a cruel system, and particularly against the sensual deprivations and discomforts imposed in the reformed prison. He objected to the meagerness of the diet, the dark cold cells with their tiny, high gratings, the monotony and unhealthiness of prison labor, the multiplication of petty rules, the solitude, and the enforcement of unprofitable activities merely to harass the prisoners. A design that made it easier to observe the prisoners, he felt, would enable him to increase their comfort without endangering security.[9]

The more humane elements of Bentham's plan, however, were ignored. No one ever paid much attention to his bitter criticism of such reformed prisons as Wymondham. The two disciplinary elements of his scheme, inspection and industrial labor, were simply added on to the existing reformed prisons. Most of the new building carried out in Lancashire during the early 1820's followed his plan of a circle of cells arranged around a central inspection station. Kirkdale opened with two semicircular wings enclosing airing courts. At Salford the male felons' wards followed a similar plan, as did the treadwheel yards, the male misdemeanants' airing yards, and the female felons' cells.[10] At Lancaster the women's penitentiary and the male felons' dayrooms were built closely around a central station, a plan that won the grudging approval of the Society for the Improvement of Prison Discipline.[11]

In general, however, the SIPD preferred the "new" radial prison plans, where cells were built along long corridors radiating out from the center. Though officers sitting in the center could not see into each room, it was possible to arrange large numbers of cells, along with dayrooms and workrooms, in such a way that they could be easily superintended from the center. Radial plans had been common in hospitals since the Middle Ages, when religious foundations adopted cross-shaped plans to increase the number of patients while still permitting views of the central chapel. With the revival of miasmatism in the early nineteenth century, this layout again became popular, since it promoted ventilation while permitting good supervision and avoided the need for patients and nurses to travel outside in the cold between buildings.[12] Blackburn experimented with this design in his plans for the National Penitentiary in 1782 and for the Liverpool borough prison built between 1795 and 1797, but apparently without much success.[13] By the 1840's, however, it had become the standard prison plan. Lancashire was slow to adopt it, although Preston gradually extended its wings and added new ones to become a radial prison. A radial plan was also chosen for the rebuilding of Kirkdale in the late 1840's.

Though Lancashire adopted the panopticon plan, however, it did not follow Bentham's suggestion that rooms be made large enough to hold several prisoners comfortably. Prisons, like hospitals, had partially retreated from the insistence of the reformers of Howard's generation that inmates be separated completely at night, and Peel's Act merely enjoined classification of prisoners into groups, not cellular separation. In designing prisons, however, reformers were still dominated by the fear of moral if not physical contamination and built single night cells. As a result, the nineteenth-century cells were nearly as uncomfortable as their predecessors. Being designed for only one person, the cells were quite small and were usually built of stone. They were too small to heat individually (until the development of efficient gas fires), and the early Victorians did not have a technology adequate to heat them collectively, particularly when the development of the theory of separate confinement made acoustical isolation desirable; this precluded the introduction of hot air ducts and pipes.[14] Some prisoners complained that their cells were "close," but most complained of the cold. At Salford there was a constant battle between the administration, which was determined to maintain ventilation for health, and the prisoners, who were equally determined to stop uncomfortable drafts by stuffing their unglazed windows with rags. The small, cold, dark, and rather clammy cells can only have exacerbated the symptoms of lung disease, especially tuberculosis, though the partial separation of prisoners may have impeded its spread. On the whole, the provision of an acceptable level of comfort in single cells arranged so that their inmates could not communicate with each other required a level of technology that was not available in the early nineteenth century.

Lancashire's prison capacity frequently lagged behind the population of prisoners; when by necessity the cells were stuffed with extra men they became hot, noisome, cramped, and claustrophobic. In 1813 Higgin wrote that the Castle was holding 325 prisoners and "there is not room for another."[15] The parliamentary return of 1818 showed that the Castle, which by then had an estimated capacity of 390 prisoners, maintained a daily average of 466. The opening of the women's penitentiary with a suggested capacity of 120 prisoners temporarily eased the pressure. In 1823 the Castle reported a capacity of 136 separately housed prisoners, an absolute capacity of 495 with several prisoners to a cell, and a prison population of 286, well within its span. In 1827, however, the population rose to 457. The greatest number at one time in 1826 was 578 and in 1827, 545, well beyond the capacity of the gaol even when several prisoners were crammed into a single cell.[16]

For the next decade, the total population of the Castle remained relatively stable. Except for a drop in 1837, the criminal population rose steadily from the time of Peterloo to the hungry forties, but a slight reduction in the number of debtors helped smooth out the overall change. This was only a limited advantage, because criminals could not be assigned to debtors' rooms. In the depression after 1837, the population again began to rise rapidly; by 1841-42, the *average* population was 515, well above the official capacity, and at one time in 1842 there were 629 prisoners. At some time during every year between 1830 and 1843, Lancaster held 495 prisoners or more.

Though none of the other three county prisons regularly exceeded its official capacity, the number of prisoners rarely dropped below the total number of single cells. For example, Kirkdale had between 334 and 384 single cells seven feet four inches wide at one end, six feet eleven inches at the other end, and six feet nine inches long. On the day that the prisoners were counted for the annual returns to the secretary of state, there were frequently over 600 prisoners and the total once reached 737.[17] Attempts at classification only exacerbated the shortage of space, since fluctuating populations meant that some classes had too many cells while others went short. For example, the 23 vagrant boys at Salford in 1837 must have been reasonably comfortable in 29 double-bedded cells, but what of the 60 female vagrants sharing 10 such cells? Although the massive construction efforts of the postwar years made it just possible for Lancashire's buildings to contain their inmates, their numbers placed an obvious strain on the county's institutions and administrators. Lancashire was not the only county to experience overcrowding: the Duke of Richmond's committee reported in 1835 that of the 136 supposedly reformed prisons covered by the act of 1823, only 36 (possibly only 24) could separate prisoners at night.[18]

Yet though many people went to prison, few stayed for long. The average term of confinement in the 36 largest English county prisons between 1838 and 1842 was 46 days. Salford was slightly below the national average, the other three Lancashire gaols a little above.[19] It was difficult for the staff even to visit the prisoners and learn their names, let alone "reform" or "institutionalize" them. It is no wonder that Salford, once a model for the nation, rapidly became notorious for its discomfort and disorder, or that its beleaguered administration eventually abandoned any pretense of classification (except to separate men from women). A county that had counted its committals by tens in the eighteenth century saw them regularly exceed ten thousand by the 1830's and rise to over forty thousand by 1858, the first year for which complete figures have survived. Under such constant stress, it is no wonder that the prisons and their administrators often failed to justify the reformers' hopes.

Diet

Because prisons were self-contained and because imprisonment was widely thought to pose a special threat of disease, the better-run prisons rigorously enforced such protective measures as washing the floors, liming the walls, fumigating clothes, bathing new arrivals, and separating the sick, long before similar measures appeared in the poorer quarters of the cities that surrounded them. Moreover, prison surgeons tended to rely on relatively simple remedies, particularly food and bed rest; on the whole this treatment probably benefited their patients.

On the other hand, precisely because they were controlled, crowded, and isolated communities, prisons were subject to special hazards. The diet of five hundred prisoners could be suddenly altered, almost at the stroke of a pen. Such control made mistakes disastrous. Prison communities were now large enough to foster epidemics. Gastroenteritis posed a special problem, not only because infected cooks in a central kitchen could spread the disease but also because there was little knowledge of the special hazards involved in the preparation of very large quantities of food. The substitution of cellular confinement for the large wards where prisoners had prepared their own food increased this hazard.

The essential constituents of a healthy diet had not yet been established. Even the connection between diet and scurvy was not universally accepted. In 1822 the committee administering Millbank prison cut the inmates' diet severely, yet the resulting outbreak of scurvy was attributed by many to Millbank's unhealthy location; it took some time for doctors to persuade the committee to introduce oranges, and even then the doctors' opponents were not convinced.[20] Serious scurvy was rare in Lancashire until after the adoption of the government dietary of 1843, which reduced the allowance of potatoes. In 1847-48 the Kirkdale surgeon reported between twenty and thirty cases of scurvy, "a disease we never knew before."[21] Nutritional deficiency also contributed to other diseases, either by lowering resistance or by creating specific symptoms such as cirrhosis of the liver, "debility" or "exhaustion," anemia, and, possibly, "fits." It certainly increased the irritability of the prisoners, though Victorians believed that a "low" diet decreased "animal spirits" and made prisoners more tractable.

Some prisoners were malnourished on arrival. In 1847 Millbank sent nine boys to Preston. Their average age was nearly sixteen, their average height was four feet eight and two-thirds inches, and their average weight was eighty-three and one-half pounds. They gained an average of six and two-thirds pounds each in eight months of imprisonment. The surgeon reported to the prison inspector Frederic Hill that these boys were deficient in energy, rickety, and scrofulous, but all he gained for his effort was a rebuke from the Home Office for failing to enter their condition in his journal and to use the proper channels (the visiting justices) to report their condition.[22] Prisons also held many diseased prostitutes and emaciated alcoholics along with the unsturdy poor.

However inadequate it may have been by modern standards, the prison diet, combined with the medical services available there and the short average term, was good enough to attract many of the poor. This assertion sounds like a piece of Chadwickian propaganda in favor of lesser eligibility, but it is so well documented as to be beyond doubt. There were occasional cases of deliberate entry in the eighteenth century, but these were generally men who had themselves committed for debt to avoid other obligations, such as service in the army. By the 1830's, however, deliberate entry had become very common. Every county prison saw such cases. One woman had been committed to the New Bailey more than two hundred times; she came there "generally to recruit her health."[23]

John Clay, at Preston, attended a dying woman who, "sinking under disease, and recollecting the attention she had received, some years before, in the hospital of the prison, . . . committed a trifling theft in order to obtain admission to it again."[24] Captain Hansbrow recorded many similar cases, such as the woman committed for being drunk and disorderly who, the day before her release, "exclaimed in a passion of tears, 'Oh! Sir, if I only had such food outside as I have here, you would never see me in a prison.'"[25] In 1843 he discharged an epileptic who "wept bitterly *at being put out of gaol*, having no prospect before him but that of the workhouse."[26] In 1847 he reported on Bridget Campbell, who had been sentenced to transportation but remained at Lancaster because she was unfit for removal. "I have more than once asked her if she wished to petition the Magistrates . . . for her liberation; but she answered she was better off where she was."[27]

Vagrants knew perfectly well that many prisons were more comfortable than the workhouse, and in the fall the prisons filled with men who had chosen their offense to provide them with a winter's lodgings. It was also common for young men in the workhouse to break its windows or commit other petty vandalism in order to move to the prison. "One of the most serious and increasing obstacles to good discipline," complained inspector William John Williams in 1837, "is the common practice of tramps and prostitutes, when infected with foul diseases, (not admitted into the public infirmaries), committing some slight offence for the purpose of obtaining medical treatment in prisons. Their committals are generally for one or two months to hard labour, which they seldom or never undergo, oftentimes passing the entire of the term in hospital; and many of the females are scarcely discharged a month, ere they return again for surgical care. Such prisoners are more disorderly in behaviour, more pernicious in example, and more difficult to control, than any other class."[28]

Throughout the period there was a constant seesaw between the desire of the authorities, both central and local, to cut the diet in the interest of making imprisonment less attractive and their need to keep prisoners in good health. In the 1820's the prisoners found a strong ally in John Smith, the Lancaster surgeon. In 1829 he reported to the visiting justices that recent cuts in the diet had more than quadrupled the number of deaths. Between 1822 and 1824, he pointed out, only four inmates had died. At that time the weekly diet for working prisoners had included seven pounds of bread, two and a half pounds of oatmeal, ten pounds of potatoes, four ounces of cheese, four ounces of salt, a half pound of boned beef, one quart of broth, and one quart of stew. Women also received a pint of milk daily. Prisoners could spend part of their earnings on food or receive gifts from friends. The Prison Act of 1823, however, contained a section that the justices interpreted to mean that prisoners should be confined strictly to the prison diet. According to Smith, the ban on gifts and purchases of food had visibly damaged the prisoners' health. Moreover, in 1826 the justices themselves decided to reduce the Lancaster diet in an attempt to make the four county prisons more uniform.

The death rate rose immediately. In 1825 there had been only one death per 123.5 prisoners. In the four and a half years after the reduction, the average was one per 39.75. The surgeon concluded that "insufficiency of food is the principal if not only cause of all the mischief which has ensued."[29] His efforts finally persuaded the justices to improve the dietary. After two successive increases, by 1829 working prisoners received a diet similar to that of 1822, while prisoners who refused to work received seven pounds of bread, two and a half pounds of oatmeal, four and a half ounces of salt, and ten pounds of potatoes per week (see Table 12).[30] For several classes of prisoner this final version was a much more generous diet than the one the government introduced after 1843. This "Graham dietary" divided prisoners into classes according to their length of stay, ranging from one week to four months and over. Since most prisoners stayed for a relatively short term, this system considerably reduced the total provision of food at many institutions.[31]

After the diet was increased in 1828-29, the Castle death rate dropped. From eleven deaths a year in 1829 it fell to eight in 1830 and then to five in 1831. It averaged a little under four and a half per year from 1830 to

TABLE 12
Weekly Dietaries for Lancashire Prisons, 1835

Lancaster	Salford
Convicted male prisoners:	Male prisoners:
7 lbs. bread	8¾ lbs. bread
2½ lbs. oatmeal	31½ oz. dry oatmeal
10 lbs. potatoes	(for 14 qts. cooked)
1½ lbs. beef	5 lbs. potatoes
5 oz. rice	1 lb. beef
1½ gills of peas (3/8 pint)	2 qts. pea soup
4 oz. cheese	3½ oz. salt
2 oz. onions	1 qt. stew
3½ oz. salt	Female prisoners:
Convicted female prisoners:	7 lbs. bread
7 lbs. bread	3½ oz. salt
2½ lbs. oatmeal	7 pts. stew
5 lbs. potatoes	14 qts. gruel
1 lb. beef	
5 oz. rice	*Kirkdale* (for six days)
1½ gills of peas	7 lbs. bread
3½ oz. salt	3 lbs. potatoes
	3 pts. stew with 3 lbs. potatoes,
Preston	meat, salt, and pepper
8¾ lbs. bread	12 pts. gruel
2 lbs. oatmeal	2 qts. broth
5 lbs. potatoes	4 oz. bacon
1 lb. beef	
3 gills of peas	
4 oz. cheese	
4 oz. salt	
¾ lb. stew	

1843.[32] A comparison of the incidence of disease in the two periods before and after 1829 does not, however, suggest that a poor diet played a role in the incidence of any one disease. The late 1820's were bad years at other institutions as well, and it is difficult to relate this fact to any dietary changes. The surgeon of Kirkdale wrote in 1827 that more inmates had died there in the past year than in any other year since the opening. A miasmatist, he explained that this death rate did "not arise from disease generated in the Prison but has been the effect of a particular state of the atmosphere from which cause all the Hospitals and publick institutions for the relief of sick persons have suffered more severely than at any previous period for a number of years."[33] His list of the causes of death does not suggest any single cause: dysentery (two cases), typhus, gradual decay (someone aged 75), exhaustion, diseased knee, smallpox, cancer of the womb, apoplexy, venereal disease, peritoneal inflammation, inflammation of the lungs, and "mortification."

It is not evident in Lancashire, therefore, as it is at Millbank, that a single decision to reduce the diet resulted in an outbreak of disease. Yet though the changes in diet may not have had an obvious effect, it does seem clear that the diet as a whole, both before and after the change, was lacking in variety and balance, and that the increasing strictness with which prisoners were confined to the gaol diet was not to their advantage. Many prisoners stayed in gaol for such short periods that the effect was not serious, but it was still there. It also seems clear in this instance that though increasing central supervision benefited prisoners in marginal institutions, it also harmed many others.

The story of prison diets in the nineteenth century is complex. There is no single trend but a series of backward and forward movements, the product of three interacting and sometimes conflicting trends: the continuation of eighteenth-century policies to equalize the condition of all prisoners by outlawing the purchase of special comforts and by attempting to make different prisons more similar by state regulation; the limitation set by administrative frugality and a need for lesser eligibility; and an increasing scientific understanding of human nutritional needs.

Health

Concern for the health of prisoners had been the chief precipitant of the prison rebuilding undertaken in the Age of Reform. How well did the prisons fulfill the hopes of reformers? It is difficult to extract useful information from the raw data that are available. When the surgeon of Millbank, William Baly, tried to collect data for an article on prison mortality in 1844, he could obtain adequate information (from the *Parliamentary Papers*) for only about five years, between 1838 and 1842.[34] (Captain Hansbrow, however, sent him a complete return of Lancaster deaths, causes of death, and average population for the entire period from 1825 to 1843. Lancaster and Millbank, where Baly himself kept records, were the only two prisons in England with such complete records.) I have been more fortunate than Baly in obtaining average daily populations for all of Lancashire's prisons, which were published in 1843 by Robert Hindle for the period from 1820 to 1842.[35] These averages can be compared with the number of deaths in each prison in each year after 1823, which were published in the schedule B returns in the

TABLE 13
Lancashire Prison Death Rates by Period, 1823-1846
(Avg. death rate per 1,000 prisoners)

Period	Lancaster	Preston	Kirkdale	Salford	Total
1823-42[a]	17.64	7.55	15.73	13.41	13.58
1823-42	17.94	7.67	17.92	14.76	14.57
1823-31	20.30	7.08	15.45	11.96	13.61
1833-42	15.24	7.92	15.99	14.72	13.47
1838-42	14.43	6.22	17.16	17.68	13.87
1838-42[b]	15.94	5.39	16.96	16.86	—
1840-46[c]	8.46	3.10	14.92	10.83	9.33

NOTE: All data are mine except as indicated.
[a]Excludes 1832.   [b]Baly's data.   [c]*Parliamentary Papers.*

Parliamentary Papers.[36] Unfortunately, Hindle's averages run from June to June while the returns were calculated from Michaelmas to Michaelmas, but the yearly fluctuation in population was probably small enough to be insignificant when the results are averaged over several years. For the period between 1840 and 1846, calculations of the death rate appear in the *Parliamentary Papers* for three Lancashire prisons and can be estimated for the fourth (Preston), but these figures are not strictly comparable with those from 1823 to 1842. For the years that Baly also covered, I was able to compare my calculations with his and found that mine were about one death per thousand higher; I am unable to account for the discrepancy. Unless otherwise noted, the rates given in Table 13 are based on my calculations.

Several additional technical problems arise in using these figures. The first is the use of a yearly average of daily populations. In other words, the deaths are compared with total "prisoner-days" divided by 365. This is an appropriate basis, but it is not the only appropriate basis. Another possibility would be a comparison based on total committals. Since the average term served was falling during this period, the number of committals was rising even when the average yearly population stayed more or less steady. The effect of this on death rates is difficult to gauge. This problem of using yearly average populations to calculate institutional death rates aroused heated debates in the nineteenth century, but it probably did not create serious distortions in prison death rates.

The second problem is the question of infants. One prison, Salford, listed infant deaths separately in its returns from 1833 to 1841. The other three did not, and it is impossible to estimate their number. After some hesitation, I have decided to exclude the Salford infant deaths. This may cause Salford's death rate to be artificially low compared with that of other prisons. Many women bore children in prison or brought them in with them, and infant deaths could form a significant fraction of the whole: there were two infant deaths out of a total of eight at Salford in 1836, five out of a total of seventeen in 1840, and three out of a total of fourteen in 1841.

A third problem is the question of whether to separate criminals from debtors. Baly attempted to do this, but the schedule B returns do not list debtors' deaths separately. Since I wished to evaluate the administration of the prison as a whole, the health of the entire population seemed an appropriate base. Criminal death rates were higher in the gaols than in the houses of correction because the gaols contained some convicts sentenced to very long terms.

A fourth problem is the treatment of deaths from cholera. Cholera was a disease whose incidence was more or less out of the control of prison administrators and physicians; its causes were not understood at this time and few treatments were effective. If the cholera deaths of 1832 are included in averages they may skew the final results, making a prison that was ordinarily healthy appear comparatively unhealthy. For example, Kirkdale, which ordinarily had between 7 and 8 deaths a year, had 35 in 1832, raising its overall death rate for the 20 years between 1823 and 1842 by more than two deaths per thousand. Salford also suffered in the epidemic of 1832, but Lancaster and Preston escaped. Following Baly, I have calculated separate death rates for all four prisons both including and excluding the deaths in 1832, a year that also provides a convenient midpoint for comparisons of the two halves of the period.

A fifth problem is the demographic bias of the prison population. With the exception of debtors, prisoners tended to be young men in the healthiest part of their life span. There were, however, some important qualifications to this advantage. First, the prisoners tended to be poor and to come from sections of the cities with relatively high death rates. Second, there was that unknown number of pregnant women and new-born infants, who were at very high risk. Third, certain activities that posed a serious risk to health were also grounds for committal to prison, particularly public drunkenness and prostitution. Finally, there were those few prisoners who deliberately sought committal to take advantage of the prison hospitals. In addressing this problem, Baly decided to compare the incidence of death among prisoners with that of the general adult population (aged 15 to 75), but this was at best an extremely rough comparison.

A final problem is the custom of providing free pardons for prisoners who suffered from a chronic illness and seemed likely to die in prison, a practice that lowered the prison mortality rate. Fortunately, Baly went through the lists of pardons for Millbank and estimated how many of them would have resulted in death before the end of the original sentence: 123 out of 355. Baly then used this ratio to estimate how many of the prisoners pardoned at Wakefield, Liverpool, Preston, Lancaster, Chester, and Derby would also have died. He went through the same process for the thirty-six most important English prisons, except that he also had to extrapolate from the six prisons named above to obtain a probable pardon rate. This procedure produced a rather rough estimate, but one that no modern writer is likely to better. According to Baly's estimate, these pardons would add nearly four deaths per thousand a year to the official mortality rates of the larger provincial prisons. Because terms were much longer at Millbank and the pardon rate consequently higher, there was a difference of nearly thirteen per thousand there.

Baly used these calculations to show that the prisoners in Millbank, with an official death rate of 18.147 per thousand (not counting deaths from cholera) and a corrected death rate of 30.976 per thousand, were considerably less healthy than the adult population of London, with a death rate of 15.391. He also proved that death rates increased very rapidly after the first year or two of imprisonment. When these figures are applied to Lancashire, however, the issue is more difficult to resolve, since the death rate in Lancashire towns was considerably higher than that for either England as a whole or for London, while the death rate in Lancashire prisons was relatively low. For the five years between 1838 and 1842, Baly found an average death rate in 36 British prisons of 19.013. In those five years, however, the rates at all the Lancashire prisons, including the Castle, were lower than the English average. Lancaster's rate was 14.43 (my rate, including debtors; Baly's rate for criminals was 15.94); Salford's, 17.68 (Baly, 16.86); Kirkdale's, 17.16 (Baly, 16.96); and Preston's, 6.22 (Baly, 5.34).

These figures represent the actual prison death rates, which were lower than the annual total mortality rate of Preston (31.08) or Liverpool

(33.88 in 1841) and lower than the annual adult mortality rate of Liverpool (18.19). If to these are added a little less than four deaths per thousand per year, Baly's estimate for pardoned prisoners, then Lancaster, Salford, and Kirkdale all have mortality rates similar to that of Liverpool's adult population, although still well below the total mortality (including children) of Lancashire's industrial areas. In 1851, total Lancashire mortality was 31.25.[37]

Preston's consistently and extraordinarily low death rate presents a special problem. It was independent of changes in staff and discipline, although the relatively greater separation between prisoners no doubt helped. Preston was smaller than the other Lancashire prisons, being only a third the size of Salford. Like the Castle, it largely escaped the cholera of the early 1830's, but in the period studied by Baly, cholera was a relatively minor cause of death. There is no evidence that a high pardon rate was responsible; between 1841 and 1843 Preston had two prisoners pardoned on the grounds of health while Lancaster had eight; nor do sentencing policies and average terms of confinement explain Preston's achievement. John Clay often referred to Preston's remarkable healthiness in his reports. In 1844 Clay and the other authors of the *Report on the Sanitary Condition of Preston* pointed out that the adult death rate in the town was five times that of the prison, suggesting that many lives were lost unnecessarily.*

On the whole, the average person's chances of dying probably increased slightly upon commitment and rose with the length of imprisonment, although this was not true for certain groups of prisoners, particularly those in Preston and those already sick or starving. The average person was less likely to die in a Lancashire prison than in many other, though not all, large county prisons. Baly's calculation of death rates in county gaols varied from a deplorable 45.751 at York Castle to 11.981 at the Gloucester county gaol. His rates for the houses of correction tended to be somewhat lower than those in the county gaols, although the next lowest, Devizes, at 10.989, was double that of Preston. Considering the comparatively large size of Lancashire's institutions and their relatively

---

*Harris Library, Preston, John Clay, *Report on the Sanitary Condition of Preston* (1844). For Clay's views on cholera see *Cholera Morbus: A Sermon Preached on the 21st. Day of March, 1832* (Preston, 1832). March 21 was the day appointed by Parliament for national fasting and prayer to avert the cholera. Clay could not quite bring himself to say that God sent cholera as a retribution for sin, so he suggested it was most frequent among the sinfully dirty.

long term of imprisonment, their record was creditable, particularly given the surrounding population's general state of health.[38]

A comparison of the average death rate of the period between 1823 and 1831 with that of the period between 1833 and 1842 shows an increase in the death rate in the three houses of correction. At Preston and Kirkdale it was less than one death per thousand; at Salford it was nearly three deaths per thousand. At Lancaster, however, the death rate fell by about five deaths per thousand, from 20.30 in 1823-31 to 15.24 in 1833-42. It seems likely that the death rate thereafter fell substantially at all four institutions. At Lancaster between 1843 and 1846, only ten prisoners died and the rate fell to 6.7. At Preston only two prisoners died and the death rate fell to a remarkable 3.2. Because of the great variation in mortality rates from year to year, however, the trend one sees depends heavily on the precise terminal years chosen.

Information on Millbank's morbidity is poor and difficult to evaluate, but Baly did examine the incidence of fatal diseases there. He compared Millbank's diseases with those of London and concluded that though slightly more prisoners died of fever in the prison than in the town, by far the greatest cause of death and the most important cause of the difference between Millbank's and London's death rates was tuberculosis. In the county prisons the pattern was different. Baly constructed a table of actual deaths in prison in sixteen large county prisons, including Lancashire's four. The dates covered varied considerably, ranging from nineteen years for Lancaster to only one year for Exeter and Winchester, but Baly added up the annual average of prisoners for each year in every prison where data were available and used this figure to calculate overall deaths per thousand live prisoners. The variation in the numbers of years covered would have distorted the incidence of disease slightly, since it fluctuated from year to year, but except in the case of cholera this factor probably did not make too much difference to the final result. Because of the state of the records, Lancashire's pattern of morbidity received disproportionate weight.[39]

Tuberculosis remained the greatest killer in the county prisons, although its incidence was much lower than at Millbank and did not account for the discrepancy between prison and external death rates. Consumption, or respiratory tuberculosis, accounted for 102 out of 499 deaths, for a death rate of 3.933 per thousand live prisoners. Other tubercular diseases took a further seven lives. The next most important causes of death were the other respiratory diseases, including asthma, bronchitis, pneumonia, and pleurisy. Together they took 101 lives, for a death rate of 3.895.

Typhus was still a very serious problem, despite the complacency with which Victorians referred to Howard's "fever-ridden gaols." In 1817, for example, Preston suffered an epidemic that killed three prisoners and infected at least seventeen more, forcing the establishment of a "lazaretto" on the other side of town. In 1822 67 Crown prisoners at Lancaster caught typhus in one week.[40] At the time of Baly's compilation, typhus alone took 62 prisoners out of the 499 who died, or 2.391 per thousand. It was inevitable that typhus should appear in the prisons, because it had never been eradicated from the poor and filthy Lancashire slums, but the prison surgeons had grown more skilled in treating it and containing outbreaks.

"Bowel complaints" was the next most important category of disease. This included cholera, dysentery, diarrhea, enteritis, ulceration of the bowel, and intestinal disease. Dysentery and diarrhea together took 38 lives, cholera only 5, and the entire group took 54 lives, or 2.031 per thousand. Prison surgeons were mystified about the causes of these ailments, though for the milder cases opiates offered an effective treatment.

Baly argued that these figures seriously underestimated the incidence of tuberculosis in English prisons, for two reasons. First, since tuberculosis was a slow, chronic disease whose course was easy to predict, patients who were likely to die of it in a relatively short time were more likely to obtain pardons than were prisoners killed by other diseases. Typhus and other fevers killed so quickly that if prisoners died of them at all they would die in gaol. Since there were no adequate statistics for the number of tubercular patients pardoned each year in the county prisons, Baly could not adjust his figures for this factor. Second, because tuberculosis was a slow disease and because the average term of imprisonment in the county prisons was relatively short, persons infected with tuberculosis when in prison would not have time to die of it before their release. The only prisoners dying in gaol of consumption were those who already had the disease upon commitment or those sentenced to very long terms. Baly cited indirect evidence suggesting that tuberculosis was often caught in prison, and argued as well that the known conditions of prison life were likely to encourage the disease's spread. He listed these causes as "1st, deficient ventilation; 2nd, cold; 3rd, want of active bodily exercise, and sedentary occupations; 4th, a listless, if not dejected state of mind; and 5th, poorness of the diet." He also argued that many of these conditions, such as "cold, scanty food and bad air," were not necessary to imprisonment and could be corrected.[41]

Baly's recommendations for remedying the situation reveal the shift that had taken place within English medicine from the contagionism of the late eighteenth century to a more miasmatic stance. Baly says little about the need to separate or quarantine prisoners, to screen and disinfect them on admission, or to prevent the transmission of disease through cleanliness. Instead, he concentrates on the need to choose a healthy situation for new prisons so as to avoid the effects of noxious miasma. His suggestions also reflect, however, the nature of the diseases that preoccupied him, particularly tuberculosis, against which "contagionist" measures could do little. The body has natural defenses against tuberculosis and, as long as it is otherwise healthy, can usually resist or contain it. Conditions that lower resistance, such as a poor diet, depression, or other diseases, can lead to infection or reactivate a previously quiescent case. Moreover, though tuberculosis bacilli are not affected by cold and can live for months, they are readily destroyed by sunlight. The adoption of Baly's recommendations that the prisoners get more food, exercise, air, and heat would have helped to mitigate the disease's effect. The complete isolation of all cases would have helped control its transmission, but tuberculosis was difficult to diagnose in its early stages.

The relentless cleanliness of many mid-Victorian prisons, which some modern writers have found so objectionable, probably helped somewhat to contain the incidence of other diseases, particularly typhus. The prison surgeons were hampered not so much by a lack of will as by ignorance. As Baly himself lamented, speaking of bowel diseases, "in one prison the greater prevalence of the disease in the summer season is ascribed to the use of *old* potatoes; in another, to the use of *new* potatoes. In a third, the gruel is thought to be the *cause*; while in a fourth, a bason [*sic*] of gruel at night is given as a *preventative*."[42] Despite these setbacks, it seems likely that the "reformed" prisons lived up to the purpose that had guided their foundation: to reduce the mortality of prisoners below the level that had prevailed in the late eighteenth century and to bring it close to that prevailing in the outside world, so that a sentence of imprisonment need not be tantamount to a sentence of death by fever. The death rates make it clear that the prisons still had a long way to go before they could be considered healthy places, and the variations in death rates between prisons show that to some extent the death rate could be affected by deliberate policy decisions. Nevertheless, epidemic disease could never be eliminated from the prisons until it was controlled in the population outside.

The Debtors

Debtor self-government at Lancaster Castle persisted into the early nineteenth century largely unchanged. The central association continued to run a mock court, punish offenders, appoint officers, and subscribe to newspapers, but as the century progressed it seems to have gradually lost much of its importance.[43] The central courtroom was lost in 1807 because of overcrowding. Many of the association rules were incorporated into the official rules made for the debtors by the justices, and later by the Home Office, and were thereafter enforced by the gaoler rather than by the debtors themselves. Under the rules of 1841 the governor gained complete control of all charitable contributions and the right to punish debtors for quarreling and disorderliness.[44]

Whatever happened to the central association, the system centering on the different rooms continued to flourish. When new debtors arrived they were shown around the debtors' side of the Castle, known as the "half-crown side." They then chose the room they wished to enter and paid their "room money" to the "room's man." In 1843 the room money varied from 5s. for the Constables, a large room set aside for the poorest debtors, often from the Court of Requests, to 35s. for Number 4 and Number 8, which held only eight prisoners each. There were 32 rooms in all, two being set aside for women. The popularity, cost, and status of a room at any given time depended on its inhabitants and the skill of its room's man.[45]

The room's man filled a role similar to that of the landlady of a boardinghouse. Several made a good profit from their position. One room's man was said to have earned £800 by acting as a moneylender. In the 1860's the Quakers, a large room in the Lungess Tower, became the most popular because its enterprising room's man (who spent 32 years in the Castle) had furnished it in style with "easy chairs, sofas, a piano, and every thing to make the room look comfortable." The rooms' men of the wealthier rooms could count on a good profit from providing full board for their charges, who paid 7s. to 10s. a week for cooked meals and a daily bottle of ale. The wealthier rooms also offered such amenities as books, newspapers, games like dominoes and checkers, and even waiters at meals.[46]

While rooms' men held their posts until released from the Castle, other officers were elected monthly by every room. The Quakers had a chairman, a vice-chairman, a secretary-treasurer, a constable, a postman, and a cock-catcher, whose job was to introduce new members to the room. A popular method of separating incoming debtors from some of their money was to elect them president; a newly elected president was expected to provide dinner beer for three days and a special dinner on Sunday. The more gullible were then accused of misdeeds by the constable, tried, found guilty, and demoted. They were then urged to apply for a fresh trial, vindicated, reinstated, and forced to supply more beer and another Sunday dinner.[47]

Each room had its own rules and regulations, covering such items as cleanliness, clothing, mealtimes, indecent language, quarreling, writing on the walls of the water closet, and damage to communal property. The constable was responsible for keeping a record of all charges made. In the Quakers all accusations were heard at a weekly court, which had the power to punish offenders with fines or by "sending them to Coventry." Members of the room prosecuted the cases; the accused either defended themselves or chose defenders. A mock court also assembled to try the cases of debtors entering at the suit of hostile creditors in order to advise them whether to compound for the debt or go to court. In the Quakers it was an offense to make any complaint to the governor or the turnkeys unless the court had previously heard the case.[48]

Despite the many rules against drunkenness, gambling, profanity, quarreling, and misbehavior, the debtors' side of the prison was always relatively disorderly. Neither the inmates nor the officers objected to a certain rowdy conviviality as long as it was kept within reasonable bounds, but the prison inspectors complained of that atmosphere again and again. "The debtor," William John Williams lamented in 1837, "gradually loses his self-esteem. From want of occupation he descends to the association of those around him, and participates, by degrees, in their low and . . . intemperate enjoyments. He becomes . . . careless in person, dress, language, and habits. . . . Very few, I fear, are discharged, after a long sojourn, without having their sensibility seared, or their principles weakened, by daily contact with misery and vice."[49] Frederic Hill, Williams's successor, expressed a similar disgust: "Instead of being a place of rigid economy and sober reflection, the debtors' side of Lancaster Castle is like a somewhat noisy tavern and tea-garden;

the prisoners idling about, smoking, drinking, talking in a loud voice, and playing at skittles and pitch-farthing."[50]

Though it was almost impossible to control the debtors' consumption of alcohol, the evidence suggests that extreme drunkenness was less common by the 1840's than it had been at the beginning of the century. Hansbrow noted in 1843 that he had locked up a drunken debtor, "a rare occurrence this now-a-days."[51] Few entries in his journal compare with the epic drunken battles to be found in Higgin's. Gambling remained common, and Hansbrow did not make very strenuous exertions to stamp it out, merely confiscating the cards used and on one occasion remonstrating with the players for wasting their time indoors on such a fine day.

Many debtors spent their time in more innocent ways. Music and bowling were popular. A guide of 1843 offers a glimpse of the activities going on in the Constables: "in one of the windows is perched an industrious cobbler, . . . in another an unfortunate tailor. Over a fire of no ordinary dimensions, about half a dozen are leaning; in different parts of the room are groups in earnest conversation; here and there a few lie at full length on their bedsteads; . . . a party in a corner are exceedingly busy at a draught board; and . . . the room is nearly filled with tobacco smoke, emanating from a small knot of furious politicians."[52] One debtor, Edward Slack, occupied himself profitably by drawing the scenes around him and published a book of sketches on his release.

The high point of the debtors' year, although the prison inspectors no doubt disapproved, was a mock election to choose the "representatives of the ancient borough of John of Gaunt." Hustings were erected, deputations waited on potential candidates, election squibs were plastered all over the pump, and hopeful candidates offered bribes and treats on a large scale. The average expense of an election was estimated to be £50. The Conservative candidates invariably won.

On the whole, the condition of debtors changed little in the course of a hundred years. As late as 1835, debtors on the county allowance still received their pound of bread a day and ten pounds of potatoes a week; the only addition had been two pounds of oatmeal a week. They still lived in Norman towers, although a few new rooms and an arcade had been added for their benefit. They could still bring in their own bedding, now subject to inspection for cleanliness, and they still cooked over the open fires in their rooms. They still, if they wished, pursued a multiplicity of trades and shopped for meat, vegetables, and fish at the market held within the Castle. As they were not clothed by the county, many were still to be seen in rags, with "care-worn and haggard visages which express all the horrors of a withering poverty."[53] The gaoler had gained a little more formal control over their behavior, and the institutions of self-government had lost some of their strength, but these developments had not made any major alterations in their daily lives. Prison life had become slightly safer and more peaceful, mirroring changes in the outside world, but on the whole, prison reform had passed the debtors by. As far as they were concerned, the only really significant nineteenth-century reform was the complete abolition of imprisonment for debt in 1869.

The Criminals

To radical historians, the middle of the nineteenth century represents the apotheosis of the strictly regimented prison. Michael Ignatieff gives a vivid account of the solitary life of a Pentonville convict, implicitly comparing it with the freer existence of the eighteenth-century prisoner.[54] "The opening of Pentonville in 1842," he writes, "represents a point of culmination in the tightening up of social controls underway since 1820."[55] The implied comparison is not entirely justified, since Pentonville was a national prison, built to hold men who in the previous century would have been executed or transported. Nevertheless, many elements of the Pentonville regime were also apparent in the county institutions, which by then were holding increasing numbers of felons.

All the Lancashire prisons claimed to follow a daily schedule that was relatively similar to that at Pentonville. At dawn in winter or at a fixed hour in summer, a bell would ring. After ten minutes the cells were unlocked and the prisoners went down to wash. They then worked until breakfast (8:30 at Lancaster). After breakfast they went to chapel for about thirty minutes and then returned to work until lunch (noon at Lancaster). A period of exercise followed lunch, then labor again, then supper. After supper, some prisoners were locked up, some took exercise, and some had a period of relative liberty.[56]

Such a schedule sounds rather forbidding in the official reports, but the entries in the governors' journals and the perpetual complaints of the prison inspectors show that the prisons often failed to live up to their strict routine. On the whole, prisoners probably suffered more from boredom than from overexertion. Lancaster Castle claimed a winter workday of seven hours, but in midwinter it was probably closer to five. Even after Preston converted to the separate system, many convicts there continued to work in large communal shops and suffered similar restrictions on their hours. William John Williams pointedly quoted the comment made by a hatter as he was being discharged from Lancaster: "I must now work a great deal harder than I have been doing here."[57] Any remaining impression of strict discipline is dispelled by such entries as the following in the Lancaster gaoler's journal: "The female crown prisoners reported for having returned their cotton unpicked. I am quite sure this is the result, not only of idleness, but of misapplication of time, for when I yesterday visited the penitentiary, the women were playing at blindman's buff in one shop, while those in the other were dancing."[58]

Lancaster Castle's old buildings, which were generally comfortable if difficult to supervise, and its humane but not strict government made it by far the most popular of Lancashire's prisons among seasoned criminals. Williams persistently demanded that the Castle impose silence, abolish paid convict labor, and institute compulsory instruction to clear itself "from the moral obloquy of being preferred by the criminal population to the other prisons of the county."[59] When Frederic Hill in 1847 asked inmates at random what they thought of the prison, he received answers such as "We are all very comfortable," "We are well attended to," and, at greater length, "My bedding is very clean. It is cleaner and better than I could get outside the prison. . . . If I was to work hard from Monday morning till Saturday night, I could not keep myself and my boy in the same comfort that I am kept in here. . . . The officers are all nice well-behaved men."[60] "The prisoners," Williams complained, "are frequently heard to declare themselves a great deal worse off out of the prison than within."[61]

Though the other three Lancashire prisons were less comfortable, their discipline also left a good deal to be desired. Despite the praises of visitors to Preston it seems evident that by 1820 its keeper had become corrupt and had taken to playing cards with his charges. Later keepers did little to improve matters until the mid-1840's, when Clay finally succeeded in persuading the justices to adopt some of his radical suggestions. In 1839 Williams wrote that he regretted that "some endeavours have not been made to place this prison in a more creditable state of discipline. The defects and improprieties . . . are still unsupplied or unchecked, and are quite independent of the question whether this or that system of discipline should be introduced, being such as ought not, with propriety, to be tolerated under any. If I am not greatly mistaken, there is a disposition to employ physical rather than moral means in the government of this establishment. . . . I am persuaded that, in many instances, imprisonment here is looked upon as the reverse of a punishment."[62] Lancashire, which had been in the forefront of reforming counties in the late eighteenth century, was growing tired, its prisons were growing shabby, and their management had been overwhelmed by the endless tide of bodies.

The discipline at Salford, in Williams's eyes, was vestigial:

From the variety of employments carried on in various parts of the prison, and their want of concentration, it is quite impossible that any effectual supervision can take place. During the day prisoners of both sexes are continually traversing the yards. . . . The matron states—"I have found a great inconvenience in the number of the male prisoners who come to the female side. . . . They bring . . . shoes to bind, wool to pick, cotton to wind, and every morning coals into the cookhouse, where they see the female cooks. . . ." When I was visiting them a male prisoner was engaged in painting the exterior window sashes, women being at work within, without an overlooker. Tobacco in large quantities is thrown over the walls.[63]

The radical publisher John Doherty, briefly imprisoned in Salford in 1832, claimed that he found lice in his bedding. The beef for the prisoners' dinner "stunk most intolerably; so much so, that after . . . smelling several lots, I was obliged to go into the air to prevent me being sick."[64] As late as 1850, Hepworth Dixon was writing that the Salford New Bailey, once a monument to Howard, was "thoroughly *bad.*" Silence was enforced only partially, prisoners were not classified, the labor was unproductive, little instruction was offered, and the discipline was "loose, irregular, and unsatisfactory."[65] The New Bailey was probably the least popular of Lancashire's institutions among the prisoners themselves; the cells were overcrowded, the food was scanty, and the prisoners were especially likely to prey on one another.

In the eyes of the inspector, however, Kirkdale was the worst of all. On early visits, Williams found treadwheel prisoners talking loudly to each other without proper supervision and "in a most filthy state, their legs and feet encrusted with dirt."[66] Tobacco was everywhere. The workrooms were untidy and neglected. A group of prisoners in one of the dayrooms was brewing coffee that had come over the wall. Thefts were frequent; one of the turnkeys admitted that "there is an idea among the prisoners that they can obtain offices . . . such as that of cook, for money."[67] Breaches of discipline were rarely reported to the governor. At least one of the monitors, a prisoner, carried a leather thong for punishing the boys under his charge.

Williams concluded that

> the general discipline, and entire system of management in this prison is . . . most faulty, and calculated rather to encourage crime than repress it. Scarcely any of the penalties awarded by the law are inflicted with due severity. . . . Imprisonment here generally, from the prettiness of the garden, the temporal advantages, and the constant communication which takes place between all classes of prisoners, is little more than nominal. The chaplain . . . states "that a female prisoner . . . appeared greatly distressed at coming in, but . . . seeing the garden her grief vanished, and she exclaimed with astonishment, 'Dear me, what a pretty place!' "[68]

The real problem at Kirkdale was the reluctance of the justices to discharge the governor and matron, who had grown too old and frail to carry out their duties. When Williams returned the following year, no improvements had been made. The many improprieties, he wrote, "plainly manifest either gross neglect of duty in the officers or something worse."[69] Williams, however, had little influence with the justices. It was not until his tenth report, written in 1845, that he finally had the satisfaction of noting that a general improvement had taken place in the management of Kirkdale since the replacement of the gaoler and matron.

It is difficult to escape the conclusion that Lancashire prisoners were seldom strictly regimented during the day. The prison buildings were too old or too poorly designed, the prison staff too small, the justices too anxious to save money by assigning prisoners to maintenance work or to trades they already knew, for the constant vigilance that would have been necessary. Only at Preston, for a brief period, was an order imposed that Hepworth Dixon found "admirable; in fact too admirable," because the prisoners' eyes never wandered from their work.[70]

Though the prison days offered many diversions, the prison nights were often intolerably long. In the winter prisoners might be locked in for as many as seventeen hours at a time. Legislation had prohibited the assignment of only two prisoners to any cell; the cells could hold one prisoner or three or more. When prisoners were alone they suffered intense boredom. When several prisoners shared a cell they were uncomfortable: the cells were too small, they got on each other's nerves, and they were often afraid of one another. Serious assaults were comparatively rare in the prisons, although they did take place occasionally; an insane prisoner at Preston kicked a fifteen-year-old boy to death in 1842.[71] Higgin and his staff had once gone in constant fear of the gangs of desperate convicts who perpetually plotted to overpower their guards and escape. Such attempts had become much less common by Hansbrow's day; aside from occasional episodes of pushing, turnkeys were rarely assaulted, although they were often threatened.

Entries in the gaolers' journals and the occasional comments of prisoners themselves show that the communal life they led was not always idyllic or cooperative. Three Lancashire prisoners testified before the Select Committee on Gaols and Houses of Correction in 1835, when it was considering converting prisons to the silent system.[72] One inmate from Lancaster Castle stated that he shared a yard and dayroom with 20 to 30 others. No officer was present. At night they slept either one or three to a cell and there was

noise and singing for Two or Three Hours. . . . Some of all Sorts were there; much Talk about Crime; much swearing and indecent Talk; some had been in Prison before, some had been transported before, and some who seemed to take a Delight in telling what they had done. . . . A wretched bad Place altogether, . . . worse before Trial than after Trial . . . for Contamination; nothing to do, and always contriving Mischief. . . . Had rather be in a Place by himself, or in total Silence, than be amongst such a rough Set; it is the biggest Punishment to be amongst such; always quarrelling and fighting, and no Peace.

An eighteen-year-old thief who had spent ten weeks at Kirkdale before his trial and twenty weeks after said he "spent the day in Idleness. . . . There was very bad Talk; the longer a Man stops in such a Place the worse he is." The third witness stated that at Preston no officer was present in the ward to keep order and to protect prisoners from their companions.

Even for prisoners who were cynical to begin with, or who had become "hardened" by frequent internments, there were many sources of fear and tension. Even after the establishment of county lunatic asylums, prisoners who were insane or "half-crazed" posed a constant hazard to their companions and presented a persistent conundrum to their harassed gaolers. Lunatics remained common in the houses of correction, which continued to serve as convenient dumping grounds for problem cases. Seven of the thirteen visits to Kirkdale made by the visiting justices in 1844-45 were to see insane prisoners.[73]

Lancaster Castle was by this time supposed to be free of lunatics, but they frequently appeared nevertheless. Juries were often reluctant to acquit even distinctly eccentric offenders on the grounds of insanity. Official ineptitude accounted for the presence of others, much to Hansbrow's annoyance. In 1846 he wrote that he had received a "perfectly insane" convict from Preston. "I am at a loss," he added, "to understand why . . . the Preston authorities have not effected his removal to an Asylum . . . and . . . avoided the painful exposure of an unfortunate and irascible being in a Court of Justice."[74]

Once insane prisoners had been sent to gaol, they were unlikely to be removed. Even when the gaoler was convinced that a prisoner was genuinely mad, the transfer process was slow and unreliable. In July 1845 Hansbrow wrote that a female felon had had another access of insanity and had been placed in the hospital with some difficulty. When he visited her he found her "quite frantic—screaming, dancing etc." He noted that he intended to take steps to remove her to the asylum, but she was still in the Castle on October 9.[75] Because malingerers hoping to avoid the full penalties of the law often chose to simulate insanity, prison administrators, unable to distinguish the false from the true, preferred to err on the side of skepticism. In 1843 a Lancaster felon named Ann Ray, whose behavior had already been bad, assaulted one of her companions, beating her severely about the head and trying to kill her. Ray was brought before a visiting justice and "behaved most violently" when he sentenced her to 25 days' solitary confinement. A few days later Hansbrow wrote that she had refused to eat for three or four days and that "whenever I have visited her . . . I have found her singing wildly, and in other respects acting like a maniac." The justices and two doctors came to see her but decided that she was only simulating insanity. "If so," said Hansbrow, unconvinced, "she is acting her part very skilfully."[76] Within four days, Ray was in the hospital, where she and a companion were so violent that the matron was forced to put them in straitjackets. Even then, she managed to break four panes of glass.

Insane prisoners posed the most dramatic threat to the tranquillity of the prison and to the safety of their fellow prisoners, but they were not the only discordant element in prison life. Less visible but more pervasive were the effects of the inmate subculture. This was organized around the bartering or purloining of food and the exchange of contraband such as tobacco, writing paper, extra clothing, and, occasionally, opium. The extent of such trading depended on the conditions in the prison and the vigilance of the staff, but it was present everywhere. At

Lancaster the chief sources of trouble among the criminals were the boys, who traded their bread to some of the older men in exchange for protection from the other prisoners. The head turnkey told Williams in 1843 that "the boys give their food to some of the men, and those men side with them. No man dare complain of the boys, for he is sure to be beaten or annoyed." Two of the monitors confirmed this, and a prisoner asked to be put into solitary because: "I am ruptured, and the boys are always jeering me about it." Another prisoner said, "I have no fault to find with the officers. . . . If the boys were quite away from us there would be no reports. The men induce the boys to commit faults; there would be no more complaints than from the other wards if the boys were away from us."[77] That summer the boys were more fully segregated in a silent shop of their own, which alleviated this source of irritation.

This problem with boys and their older "protectors" may suggest homosexuality. Patricia O'Brien has found considerable evidence of sexual and sentimental attachments among French prisoners in the nineteenth century.[78] Evidence of such activity in Lancashire prisons is very scarce, however, both in the inspectors' reports and in the gaolers' journals, which might be expected to be more frank. The biggest sexual problem was keeping the women separate from both the male prisoners and the male prison staff. The county was very slow to hire female matrons and turnkeys for the women's side of the prison, and a female convict in Lancaster created a scandal in 1820 when she accused a turnkey of making improper advances to her.[79] I have found only one unambiguous reference to homosexual advances. William John Williams included in his 1839 report on Kirkdale an extract from the chaplain's journal about "an abominable crime committed by two young men." Four days later the boys were brought before a magistrate and charged with robbing younger boys of their provisions and beating and kicking them. Further charges stated that they were guilty of a "crime formerly capital" and that one of them had made an attempt on another boy who had reported it to a turnkey and refused to share the same cell any longer. These charges, however, were dismissed because they rested solely on the testimony of "criminals." Shortly thereafter, all prisoners were placed in separate night cells.

Clay's biography contains a more ambiguous reference to "vile practices and disgusting profligacy, to which the turnkeys were suspiciously blind."[80] Although the chaplains were far less tolerant of sexual activity than was the secular administration, sexual advances were a potentially serious source of discord and violence among the prisoners and probably encouraged increased segregation. Certainly, the complaints about the "corrupting influence of prison" and the demands for ever more complete separation carry an undertone of sexual anxiety. It is difficult to see how infractions could be prevented, with a staff distinguished by its absence and a magistracy reluctant to accept the unsubstantiated complaints of "criminals." Nevertheless, it seems likely that there were comparatively few cases of brutal aggression in sexual affairs, as in other aspects of prison life, and that the absence of reported instances of homosexual rape bears some relation to reality. In this, as in other aspects of prison discipline, a comparatively low level of violence was due more to the habitual behavior of the prisoners than to any efforts by the staff.

A significant prop of the prison subculture was the sale of food, which supported the underground economy and provided a frequent occasion for violence. Hansbrow vigorously attacked the practice by having suspected sellers take their meals at a special "traffickers mess," which was closely superintended by a turnkey. All uneaten food was returned to the kitchens. The governor believed that in making these assignments he was protecting prisoners from their own folly or from the intimidation of others, but often the prisoners themselves felt they were being singled out for punishment. Food continued to be bartered sporadically at Lancaster, but neither there nor at Preston, where the supply was relatively generous, did the problem attain the proportions it did at Salford, where the diet was poor and the large size of the prison population completely precluded superintendence by the inadequate staff. Doherty contrasted the "thin, tasteless and almost black" gruel, sour black bread, and stinking meat of the New Bailey with Lancaster's "thick and palatable" gruel, "sweet and wholesome" meat, and bread "of the very best quality."[81] Hansbrow wrote that he had disciplined a man for having 2s. 6d. in cash that he had smuggled in from the New Bailey "under the impression that the diet of this Gaol would be as meagre as that of Salford, and that *here*, as he tells me the prisoners did *there, he might purchase his* comrades' food; but that he found *he had no use for his money*."[82]

Quarrels over food, barter, and loans were a frequent source of tension between prisoners, who often felt they had received the short end of the bargain but did not dare to complain. Another source of tension was the hostility that the prisoners showed as a group to those who did not fit in because they were too religious, feeble-minded, or deformed, or because they came from the countryside or another country. In 1844 a felon approached Hansbrow "under apparently very excited feelings" to complain that the schoolmaster "was in the habit of referring to his being an Irishman, which brought down upon him the ridicule of his comrades."[83] Two years later the gaoler wrote that a Jew named Philip Lipman claimed that the persecution of other prisoners had forced him to quit school. He added, "I fear there is too much truth in his complaints—because he is a foreigner."[84]

The communal feeling that sometimes led prisoners to turn on the misfits in their midst also enabled them to act together to protect their interests. Like the workers in the mills outside the walls, the prisoners cooperated to restrict the amount of work exacted of them. Hansbrow wrote in 1845 that a felon complained that potatoes were thrown at him and that he had been threatened because " 'he does *too much* work!' as a Weaver! I really am at a loss to understand the meaning of this."[85] Four months later a felon refused to continue power-loom weaving because his companions threatened him for working too hard. The army-trained governor was incredulous when he heard such tales, but any factory master could have enlightened him.

The prisoners also banded together to air grievances. The most common cause of complaint, even at Lancaster, was the food. In 1843, for example, the Castle prisoners refused to work because they felt they had been given bad potatoes. A visiting justice promised them he would try to obtain a better supply and the prisoners then returned to work. They were reproved but not punished. The most serious incident of this sort recorded in Hansbrow's diaries came in 1848, when a prisoner was taken sick in the night and died two hours later in the infirmary. The next morning the convicted felons refused to work until they saw the governor, the surgeon, and a magistrate. They complained that the turnkey on duty the night before had been slow to answer their call for help. The turnkey denied the charge and Hansbrow reminded the prisoners that officers on night duty were constantly disturbed by false alarms and that he himself had warned them of the danger of "crying wolf." He promised that any prisoner who had something to say would be allowed to testify at the inquest, and they all returned to work. The next day the prisoners on three wards, led by a man named Buck, complained that the potatoes were bad. Although prisoners were always reprimanded for such concerted protests, there seems to have been a tacit understanding that they would not be punished as long as they behaved peaceably and returned to work once they had made their point.[86]

Prisoners were punished, however, for a wide range of other offenses. Evidence about the frequency of such punishments can be obtained from the schedule B returns in the *Parliamentary Papers*, although the accuracy of this source is open to some question. Nevertheless, when the records of the four county prisons are viewed together, some facts seem evident. One is the relative infrequency with which any prison resorted to the harsh corporal penalties of whipping or ironing. Irons were nearly always reserved for men who attempted escape; their use is probably a better indicator of the security a prison maintained than of the severity of its discipline. Whippings, however, are another story. They were reserved for prisoners who had committed serious offenses and remained unmoved by other penalties. The average number of whippings at the New Bailey, which had been 1.4 per year from 1823 to 1837, suddenly rose between 1838 and 1845 to 14, suggesting that the governor was anxious to reimpose discipline on an essentially disorderly institution. The prison had failed, but the staff was not yet ready to admit defeat. By contrast, both Lancaster and Preston consistently imposed minor punishments with few whippings (about one per year at Lancaster and two every three years at Preston), suggesting the relatively gentle maintenance of order. Kirkdale, after seventeen whippings in 1825, imposed few punishments at all until 1841, suggesting that the staff had simply given up altogether.[87]

Few convicts ever experienced a whipping. Except at the New Bailey, there were rarely as many as six in one prison in a year. The milder punishments, however, were much more common. Governors had the right to sentence offenders on their own authority to up to three days' confinement on bread and water in a dark cell. They also administered a number of other minor penalties, of which the most important was the stoppage of some or all of a prisoner's food. Early reformers, such as Bayley, had encouraged the use of dietary sanctions, but in the early 1850's, as a result of several well-publicized scandals, including one at Manchester borough gaol in 1851, dietary penalties were banned.[88]

At Lancaster Castle, the incidence of most punishments remained relatively stable between 1823 and 1847, despite a change of gaolers in 1832. In each of the houses of correction, however, there was a year in which the number of minor punishments suddenly increased to a much higher level, remaining high or even increasing thereafter. At Salford, the total number of punishments went from 373 in 1835 to 2,369 in 1836 and to 4,181 in 1837. At Preston the total rose from 458 in 1842 to 3,089 in 1843, and at Kirkdale it rose from 521 in 1843 to 2,910 in 1844. This increase seems to have been due as much to accident and new staff as to the consistent application of a new policy. The rise at Preston coincides with the period of Clay's ascendancy and, in particular, with the completion of a wing of separate cells and the enforcement of the silent system in 1843. Preston also had a new governor that year. Similarly, an increase of penalties at Kirkdale in 1844-45 corresponds with the appointment of a new governor there who was attempting to correct the very lax administration of his predecessor. At both of these institutions, the adoption of the silent system brought an immediate increase in the number of penalties, since speaking became a punishable offense. It was this irritating proliferation of minor punishments for natural infractions that was the chief complaint of the silent system's critics.

The New Bailey had four different governors in the 1840's, but the significance of any changes in the number of punishments there is obscured by the returns' patent unreliability in recording minor penalties before 1834. The returns for the 1840's, however, show a relatively high incidence of minor penalties in an institution that was making only a lackluster attempt to enforce silence: prisoners were told not to speak on the treadwheel but were not supervised by an officer, while prisoners in the wool-picking rooms were allowed to speak in low tones. Hepworth Dixon, who visited the New Bailey in the late 1840's (probably in 1848), commented on the large number of punishments there, which had reached 8,407 a year by the date of his visit. He blamed this "monstrously high" figure on the poor design and bad discipline of the gaol.[89]

The general level of punishment was quite low at all three houses of correction until the early 1840's. This fact suggests that the prison staff were not making any effort to "reform" the prisons in the direction of a more stringent discipline until the Pentonville period. The reasons for the rapid escalation thereafter are diverse, but even a relatively large number of punishments was compatible with a very old-fashioned regime. Even if they had wished to, the New Bailey staff could hardly have enforced discipline on a Pentonville scale; in 1843 the total staff numbered 27, including professional men like the surgeon and chaplain, administrators like the governor and steward, industrial staff like the miller and the taskmaster, and gatekeepers and watchmen. There were only ten full-time turnkeys trying to maintain order among about 700 inmates, and not all these men were on duty all the time.[90] By the time of Hepworth Dixon's visit the number of staff members had risen, but only to 42.

The other county prisons were similarly shorthanded. In 1843 Lancaster Castle had a total staff of 28 men and women, including 14 "monitors" and "monitoresses" and only 5 turnkeys.[91] Kirkdale in 1836 had a staff of 23, including 10 turnkeys, and Preston in the same year managed on a staff of only 16, including 5 turnkeys.[92] Even Manchester's eventual complement of 42 seems ridiculously small by modern standards. It is obvious that nineteenth-century turnkeys could hope to keep order only with the cooperation of a large proportion of the prison community.

This impression of comparatively mild discipline and the relative infrequency of life-threatening offenses is confirmed by the surviving volumes of the Lancashire gaolers' journals. Most violence occurred in the course of fights between two or three men, and the most dangerous weapons used were the heavy wooden clogs the men wore at work. Most of the offenders who were reported to the governor received a penalty, but most penalties were small: an hour or a few hours in the lockup, rarely more than a day. In one case, Higgin went so far as to forgive a man who had threatened to kill him with a piece of iron. Frederic Hill commented that though Hansbrow's journal contained "scenes of gross misconduct on the part of some of the prisoners, implying a very imperfect state of discipline, several entries in the journal show a habit of patient investigation by the governor, an anxious desire on his part to avoid inflicting unmerited punishment, and a general willingness to render friendly services to the prisoners."[93]

If prison life in nineteenth-century Lancashire was far from being a communal Eden, it was equally far from serving as the highly regimented "machine for grinding men good" evoked by the radical critics of reform. The main problems were the traditional ones: corruption, peculation, overcrowding, dirt, lax discipline, and violence or intimidation directed against some prisoners by others. Increased discipline, and particularly increased cellular confinement, reduced the contact between prisoners and increased their physical security as it reduced their freedom to do and say what they pleased, but with the partial exception of Preston that discipline never came close to altering, manipulating, or controlling prisoners' minds as the reformers had hoped and as the critics have charged.

CHAPTER 8

Toward the Future: John Clay and the Separate System

Prison Labor and William Liddell

However lax Lancashire's other prisons had become, Preston symbolized for the whole nation the fluctuating currents of reform, from "Benthamite" labor regimes to "Evangelical" isolation. The Rev. John Clay, Preston's chaplain, was the chief local proponent of the separate system, and his writings made him a figure of national importance. His effort to introduce the silent and separate systems constituted a sustained attack on the prison community and on the way early Victorian prisons were run. For historians, Clay's explicit social theory and apparent success in implementing it make his work central to the case for a "social control" model in the Pentonville period. An examination of the way in which prison reform was adopted in Preston, however, reveals that even there it was limited in scope and never fully implemented. Even at Preston, reform was bedeviled by the problems of unintended consequences and limited resources. Nonetheless, the dilemmas raised by Clay's approach to crime are still with us today.

Preston began to have a prominent role in national penal policies even before Clay arrived, when it undertook its first great experiment: the enforcement of a comprehensive labor system. Eighteenth-century reformers had been unanimous in calling for the more thorough imposition of labor in the prisons. They frequently referred to the success of the Dutch *rasphouses* in setting their inmates to work and lamented the relative idleness of the English prisoner even in the bridewells established to teach habits of industry. Howard cited with approval the Dutch maxim "Make them diligent and they will be honest." Bayley quoted it to his colleagues.[1]

Lancashire was relatively successful in finding work for its inmates, because the growing textile industry provided steady employment at least until the hungry forties. On his visits to the north, James Neild commented very favorably on the profitable labor of its prisons. Nevertheless, even in Lancashire there was never a time when profitable labor was successfully imposed in all four prisons at once. At Preston, however, it served as the cornerstone of prison life for some years. Its eventual failure is a story of clashing ideologies and conflicting personalities.

Preston's industrial policy was introduced by its keeper, William Liddell, shortly after his appointment in 1817. He later commented that "my reason for setting them to work was this, when the men have been tried, and the jury have found them guilty, the magistrates would ask them what they had to say for themselves; they would say, 'I could not help it, I was a sailor and could not get a ship; or I could get nothing to do, and I went to the parish officers and they gave me a shilling and turned me away:' and I then determined I would give them a trade."[2]

Three Preston textile firms employed the Preston inmates to weave cotton and cambric. They were encouraged by an allowance of one-fourth the gross value of their work and by the occasional offer of an extra noggin of gruel. Only those with terms of six months or more, or with previous training, became weavers; the others were employed in batting and picking cotton or other simple tasks. The looms of Preston soon became a national symbol of industrious imprisonment. In 1819 Liddell testified before the Select Committee on Gaols as an expert witness. Elizabeth Fry and Joseph Gurney, who visited Preston at about the same date, praised his efforts. "The Governor," Gurney wrote, "has met with great success in two respects. He has, by his kindness, gained the hearts of his prisoners . . . and he has contrived to provide them all with full employment. The consequence is, that he governs with comfort to them, and facility to himself. . . . One thing seems wanting; —namely, more religious care and instruction."[3]

Liddell agreed with Gurney; he acknowledged to the committee that the chaplain came only to hold the Sunday service and that the prisoners received no instruction. Asked whether his system had any effect on their moral character, he replied, "I think a little more religious instruction would be better for them." This suggestion was soon carried out;

under the provisions of Peel's Act, the justices appointed schoolmasters to instruct the illiterate boys. More important, in 1821 they had replaced the aged and ineffective chaplain with a zealous and energetic young man: John Clay. It was this appointment that brought about Liddell's downfall.

By the early 1820's, many Englishmen were beginning to have second thoughts about the desirability of industrial prisons.[4] The Benthamites, who had little faith in spiritual regeneration, stuck firmly to the value of productive labor, on the grounds that it was the most profitable way of keeping prisoners occupied, that it could do no harm, and that it might lead prisoners to develop good habits. The true Benthamites in prison administration continued to emphasize the advantages of productive labor throughout the first half of the century; among them were William John Williams and the Hill brothers.[5] This policy, however, was under attack from two sides. On the one hand, the "Evangelicals" maintained that labor regimes were hardening prisoners and failing to bring about that creative anguish that alone could transform the spirit and reform the mind. On the other hand, the "common-sense school" regarded with dismay the many improvements in the physical comfort of prisoners that the reforms had created. Prisoners, they pointed out, now had better food, clothing, shelter, and medical attention than did many free laborers. They worked shorter hours, and weaving was not an arduous trade. Imprisonment was actually becoming attractive to the poor.[6]

Though useless hard labor schemes were popular with certain segments of the population, however, the loss of income that they entailed was not. Lancashire magistrates, sensitive to increases in the rates and surrounded by manufacturers anxious to find more labor, were never enthusiastic about demands that they convert profitable prison manufactories into places of worthless and unpleasant activity merely to make prisoners more uncomfortable. Indeed, despite objections from all sides, they did their best to extract useful labor from their recalcitrant subjects and even paid them when necessary to encourage effort. After a certain amount of campaigning by zealous reformers, led by Clay, they did introduce treadwheels into all four county prisons in the 1820's, but the power the wheels provided was applied to practical objects, and their use often depended on the power requirements of the prison rather than on the number of inmates deserving hardship. For example, the Kirkdale wheel ground grain into flour. The Lancaster wheel ran the power looms, a system used nowhere else in England. When crank labor was introduced into Kirkdale's separate cells in 1851, it pumped water for the prison.

To the disgust of William John Williams, Lancashire prisons not only continued to employ prisoners as needed in miscellaneous tasks around the buildings and grounds but also paid them a little extra for such work. At Preston, for example, on August 15, 1836, 21 felons and 35 misdemeanants, out of a total population of 161, were grinding flour on the treadwheel. Forty-three prisoners were weaving, winding, or picking cotton, three were cooking, one was acting as a personal servant to the matron, and twelve were serving as "constables." A joiner, a painter, a barber, a flour carrier, a miller's assistant, two whitewashers, and six laborers were pursuing their trades. Four chapel singers and four gardeners received an extra allowance of food. Williams complained that paying the prisoners was bad enough, but giving them extra food when the diet was ample "appears quite preposterous and likely to encourage the very opposite to habits of frugality."[7] He objected even more strongly to the use of prisoners to maintain the large and beautiful ornamental garden just inside the gate. His successor, Frederic Hill, however, a strong proponent of industrial labor, cooperated closely with the justices to introduce a variety of trades.

Prison officials had initially greeted the treadmills with enthusiasm. Convicts, it was said, loathed them and were staying away from prison in droves. John Clay reported that news of the hated machines was being spread through the poorer classes by means of broadside ballads. The authorities' enthusiasm quickly waned, however. Humanitarians began to rally against the common-sense school, claiming that treadmills were cruel and harmful to health. They stunted growth, overheated the body, caused hernias, and brought on miscarriages. In the meantime, ironically, prison officers discovered that treadmills, when used moderately, were not all that unpopular among their charges. While a fat man might endure agonies climbing the "endless staircase," old lags soon mastered the art of sliding their feet from one rung to the next with a minimum of effort and used the opportunity to converse with their friends. As late as 1850, Hepworth Dixon wrote that "a strong proof of the want of more and harder work in the castle [Lancaster] is—that prisoners *desire* to go on the wheel: they say they are starved in the winter months, and want heavier labour to keep them warm!"[8] His comments were confirmed by bemused justices and gaolers all over England. Humanitarians never believed these reports and succeeded in prohibiting treadwheel labor for certain groups, particularly women and boys, but it continued in use in a desultory way, especially in those prisons where the power it provided was useful.

At Preston, John Clay quickly became disillusioned about the deterrent effect of treadmill labor. He began to seek other solutions to the problem of crime and soon began to oppose Preston's emphasis on profitable labor and its disregard of the sinfulness and spiritual needs of its inmates. His son's description conveys Clay's jaundiced view of Liddell: "a rough and ready bully, with a flavour of good nature, and wit enough to manage the prison cheaply. . . . He had been successively sergeant in the army, butler to a county magnate, and a publican. His military experience, his old master's influence, and (it was said) the excellence of his tap, procured him the post. . . . Economically he worked the prison with success, and being a kind-hearted man, though coarse and violent-tempered, he neither practiced nor permitted cruelty."[9]

Liddell's failure to discipline his staff had become evident shortly before Clay's appointment, in the same year Gurney's journal was published. The Preston Michaelmas Quarter Sessions of 1820 dismissed two turnkeys for misconduct. Disgruntled, these men in turn preferred charges against the gaoler, surgeon, and chaplain, claiming that the bodies of prisoners dying in confinement had secretly been given to Lancaster surgeons to dissect. Two justices found that this had indeed happened, although they cleared the surgeon and other officers of participation or knowledge. They also found that "some irregularities have certainly existed . . . from the want of rules and regulations, of which there does not appear ever to have been any at all sufficient for the . . . conduct of the officers."[10] After this wholesale rejection of the work of the late-eighteenth-century reformers, however, the justices blamed the two discharged turnkeys for most of the "irregularities."

Clay cooperated with Liddell for some time, but it became increasingly clear that the two men's ideas about the governance of the prison were incompatible. Clay's son credited Clay with the appointment of a schoolmaster and a matron, although the fact that both were required by the act of 1823 may have been a more important factor. The matron, however, was a friend of his and he supported her against the governor. Walter Lowe Clay wrote that her appointment "considerably embarrassed" Liddell's "household arrangements" and that Clay's reforms "began to trench on his own privileges." For his part, Clay was disgusted by the "open riot and blasphemy" in the yards—where prisoners stole, gambled, boxed, and smoked with impunity—and even more distressed by the "vile practices" that were ignored by the turnkeys.[11]

About five years after his appointment, Clay wrote to the justices, charging Liddell with misconduct. At first they rejected his charges and publicly censured him for making them. The matter rested there for some time, until newspapers published a story that Liddell had "tortured" an inmate by putting her in a scold's bridle. The fact that this action alone was considered scandalous and newsworthy is a sign of the quiet change that had been taking place in public sentiment during the Age of Reform, despite the superficial complaints about "coddling criminals"; at the end of the eighteenth century scold's bridles had been used without arousing any comment.[12] The Home Office inquired into the matter and an embarrassed justice, Thomas Hesketh, wrote that the bridle had been in Preston for many years but that the justices "were not aware that it had been used in modern Times" until they had investigated.[13]

Once again, the justices initiated an inquiry into Liddell's conduct, urged on by the newspapers and, according to Walter Lowe Clay, by a "fatal suspicion that he was too lenient to poachers."[14] On March 28, 1827, they resolved that Liddell's "general habits . . . were those of intoxication."[15] After three days of hearings, they dismissed him for intoxication, neglect of duty, neglect of classification and cleanliness, gambling, improper delegation of authority, failing to discipline staff, peculation, and improper and unkind behavior to the matron. Oddly enough, Walter Lowe Clay found Liddell's dismissal rather harsh because, he said, no better conduct was expected of the gaolers of the time. Perhaps Liddell seemed better in retrospect, for Clay and the new governor, Capt. Anthony, were almost immediately at odds over Anthony's opposition to the "introduction of educational and religious influences," and his imposition of "Quarterdeck discipline, rough, capricious and tyrannical."[16]

This recurrent conflict at Preston can be seen in several perspectives. In one way it was purely a battle for power between the governor, who officially ran the prison, and the chaplain, who thought he knew how it should be run. On another level, the conflict can be seen as a confrontation between reformers and the unreformed prison. Many people were not as convinced as Clay was that swearing and smoking should be stamped out at any cost, including the prohibition of any speech or communication between the prisoners. The Preston justices had never been great reformers; they had trailed the field in the late eighteenth century and had been prepared to overlook many admitted "irregularities" in 1821. Clay complained, with some justification, that Preston was so comfortable that it was attracting prisoners; the resistance of the justices to his costly suggestions for making prison less pleasant was not necessarily a sign of inhumanity. Walter Lowe Clay himself conceded that Liddell was not a cruel man. Like most reformers, Clay was campaigning on two fronts: to increase physical comfort while simultaneously introducing psychological discomfort to maintain lesser eligibility.

On a third level, the conflict was between two competing systems of reform rather than between reform and tradition. Liddell, after all, was considered a reformer by his contemporaries, although apparently the passage of years had relaxed his energy and honesty. He had undoubtedly succeeded in making his charges industrious, but the "Evangelicals" were no longer prepared to agree that that was sufficient to render them honest.

However one looks at the conflict, three things are clear. The first is the importance of an uncensored press in prison affairs. Liddell had already triumphed in two investigations and the justices had actually censured those who had dared to bring charges against him, when newspapers forced a third investigation. By publishing the testimony the local papers made it very difficult for the justices to retain Liddell, whatever their wishes. The press was an unreliable check, ignoring ordinary, everyday peculation and pouncing eagerly on sensational allegations, but nevertheless, it played an important role in prison life.

The second conclusion is that many of the eighteenth-century reforms had been relatively ineffective. There can be no question that the prisons of the 1830's were very different from their predecessors. In the 1770's Preston had contained a huddle of about a dozen prisoners who lived without water and slept in "eleven Closets." By 1830 it was a large and organized institution that provided food, clothing, baths, employment, medical services, education, and religious training to about 200 prisoners living in 138 sleeping cells and working in a large complex of buildings containing workrooms, common rooms, kitchens, a chapel, a reception wing, a boiler house, bathhouses, a treadwheel shed, a governor's house, sickrooms, and separated airing yards. Yet in many ways the prisons had changed little. The most common complaint made by the prison inspectors was that prison discipline was too lax. For one reason or another it had been easier to improve the physical plant in which prisoners lived than to subject them to a more rigorous discipline. The new buildings had become as dirty and crowded as the old ones had been; the carefully written rules were dismissed by the justices as "not at all sufficient" and were in any case largely ignored.

Measures to prevent bribery and peculation were almost totally ineffective. In fact, the opportunities for such activities had increased; once the state undertook to provide for the needs of prisoners, in place of the earlier direct trading for commodities between individual prisoners and suppliers, the prison staff were in the position of middlemen who could alter the quality of the goods provided to almost any extent. It was difficult to compare what the contractor provided with what the prisoner received. Such peculation was also common among the few prisoners in the privileged positions of cook, clothing supplier, warehouseman, or laborer; indeed, the offense was so common that the offenders were rarely punished severely when caught.

The final conclusion is that the prison staff were gaining in importance. Liddell's story is another example of the fact that the eighteenth-century reforms had increased the power of the governor without increasing the justices' control over prison affairs. Of equal significance in this case was the growing importance of the other professional members of the prison staff: the surgeon who stopped the punishment of the bridled woman, the chaplain who brought charges against the governor, and the matron who testified against him. Though historians have paid a great deal of attention to the national inspectorate's place in the growth of reform movements, they have neglected the development of a professional and experienced group of administrators within the local institutions themselves. Of these, the gaoler or warden wielded by far the most power, but other professional staff members were often more vocal. The comparatively high wages paid to prison staff meant that those posts were far more likely to attract able and ambitious men and women than were such institutions as the workhouses. These staff members were, in turn, more likely to gain a hearing for their demands for further reform. Chaplains and surgeons were particularly well placed to collect the evidence to back up their demands. It was Clay's assiduity in collecting such evidence and in publishing his recommendations that was to make him an effective campaigner for the separate system, both in Lancashire and in England as a whole.

John Clay and the Separate System

Clay arrived at Preston with the very traditional view that the role of prisons was to deter criminals. If anything, his early reports reveal a rather retrograde attitude. While Bentham deplored the use of hard labor, Clay helped introduce the treadmill and praised it highly in his second report in 1825. In the same report, he commended the effects that a sound whipping had on juvenile criminals. Even more extraordinary, at a time when prison administrators were trying to abolish "kangaroo courts" among prisoners, was his complacent remark that the convicted felons' ward had established a set of rules against swearing and irreligious conduct. They enforced these rules by mock trials, punishing those found guilty by whipping them with a leather strap or knotted cord. Further experience and the failure of the treadmill forced Clay to reconsider his theories and to try to discover the causes of crime in the hope of developing more effective remedies.

Almost as soon as he arrived at Preston, Clay had begun to interview convicts on their admission and to collect statistics about them. His first report to the visiting justices, in 1824, included a table of commitments and recommitments and the comment that he hoped crime had not increased with the increase in population of the surrounding area. By 1827 he had carried out a more subtle investigation into the relationship between industrial development and crime, using his carefully compiled statistics.

Lancashire had a long tradition of interest in statistics and their application to social policy, dating back to the work of Percival and his associates a half century earlier. Percival's son-in-law, Benjamin Heywood, and a circle of his friends and relatives would found England's first statistical society in Manchester in 1833. Like them, Clay took a fundamentally optimistic view of Lancashire's industrial society. While modern historians have emphasized the hardship, strain, and class bitterness caused by the Industrial Revolution, these men, most of whom had at least an indirect interest in economic development, saw it as a source of social strength.

To Clay, regular employment was a stabilizing force. He believed that factories were so effective in disciplining their workers that they reduced the need for other institutions of control or authority. The problem came not from factories but from those places where the factory discipline did not reach, especially from the large numbers of men attracted to urban areas by casual employment. These men were particularly likely to have bad habits and to drink whenever they had the opportunity. Since they could afford to drink more when times were good and they had more money, they contributed to a rise in the crime rate in good times. Since many crimes were committed on impulse, by persons who were not well able to weigh the consequences of their actions, deterrent policies were not likely to succeed.[17]

Despite his initial difficulties with the Preston bench, Clay soon managed to convert its chairman, Thomas Batty Addison, recorder of Preston and chairman of the Annual General Session, to his views. In 1827 Addison summarized Clay's ideas in his own general report on the Preston house of correction. Because factory labor provided its own discipline, he wrote, few factory workers committed crimes. It was piece-workers, "who are under no restraint as to the Regularity of their Employment; or the Hours of their Labour," who filled the prisons. Industrialization itself would reduce the need for other institutions of control.[18]

Clay discovered that about three-fifths of the prisoners in Preston had been fully employed at the time they had committed their crimes. He drew a sharp line between "hardened" professional criminals, who supported themselves by regular and systematic thefts and accounted for a great deal of loss but were skilled at avoiding capture, and casual criminals, those who supported themselves by honest labor but committed crimes on impulse. Only a few were driven to crime by need or hunger. Neither factories in themselves nor the periodic industrial depressions that caused severe suffering among Preston's working classes were sufficient to explain changes in the crime rate. Factory hands themselves usually constituted less than one-fifth of all employed prisoners, a proportion that dropped to 14 percent in 1851.[19]

One piece of evidence supporting this view was the explanation that prisoners themselves usually gave for their crime. A relatively large number attributed their offense to drunkenness, while few pleaded need as an excuse. For example, in four months of 1836, 88 out of a total of 198 prisoners—by far the largest segment—attributed their crime to drink, and only 11 to need. In the whole year, among felons alone, 77 out of a total of 187 alleged "drunkenness" and only 12 "want" as the cause of their offense.[20]

Later in his life, as national crime statistics became more available, Clay tried to show that industrial regions were not more criminal on a per capita basis than agrarian ones. He argued that the effects of urbanization should be separated from those of industrialization. He analyzed per capita committal rates for the counties and regions of England, as well as within Lancashire itself, and pointed out that Liverpool, a non-industrial port, was responsible for far more crime per capita than the industrial centers farther north. The four manufacturing towns—Manchester, Salford, Bolton, and Preston—combined had a population one-fifth larger than Liverpool's, but Liverpool's summary convictions for robbery were seventeen times larger than those of the other four towns. Moreover, such agricultural counties as Rutland and Hereford had higher crime rates than north Lancashire.[21]

Clay's most important contention was that there was a direct correlation between the crime rate and the business cycle. When times improved, the crime rate rose—because, according to Clay, a large proportion of crime was caused not by fundamental dishonesty but by drink. When times got hard, fewer working men could afford alcohol and the resulting drop in drink-related offenses (particularly assault) more than compensated for the slight rise in need-related crimes (particularly larceny). V. A. C. Gatrell and T. B. Hadden's recent study of the differential correlations between property and physical crimes and the business cycle in nineteenth-century Lancashire has confirmed Clay's basic analysis of these trends.[22]

Clay was not merely an apologist for industrialization, nor was he a simple-minded moralist. If the immediate cause of crime was human failing, that failing was brought about by the deprivations of poverty. While he found that most criminals were working when arrested, he also found that the average wage was very low. He was an active campaigner for improved public health measures and better housing for the poor; as a member of the commission established by the mayor in 1842 he wrote the *Report on the Sanitary Condition of Preston* used by Chadwick. His tables demonstrated the abysmal ignorance of convicts: for example, only about half of all prisoners could name the months of the year, and about 40 percent did not know who the sovereign was.[23]

In fact, Clay was probably led by his own experience to overstress the environmental causes of crime; though he denied that the poor were necessarily criminal, he assumed that nearly all criminals were poor. He did not adequately consider the possibility that poor offenders were disproportionately likely to be arrested and gaoled. He saw the poor as criminal and the rich as immoral for demanding "indiscriminate vengeance on all sorts and conditions of criminals, as if the comfort and ease of the vocal, self-asserting respectability . . . was altogether to outweigh the rights, temporal and eternal, of the helpless inarticulate mass . . . below."[24] This nascent environmentalism, buttressed by a statistical method that assumed that aggregations of behavior had meaning, led Clay to espouse an uneasy and often shifting compromise between attributing crime to individual moral failure and blaming it on the larger failures of society. It was this compromise that underlay his penal policy.

Clay rapidly abandoned his original belief in deterrence as the primary goal of imprisonment. He argued that deterrence offended against natural justice on two grounds. First, it was unjust to punish convicts merely in order to terrify someone else, because the convicts then suffered not for their own criminal acts but for the propensities of others whom they could not control. Second, criminals were not wholly responsible for the weakened morals that led to their crime. Deterrence was not only unjust but also ineffective, since criminals never expected to be caught, while those who actually were caught were merely hardened by brutal punishment. At the same time, however, Clay complained that under Liddell, Preston had become so nondeterring that the poor committed crimes in order to be gaoled.

By 1827 Clay had begun to campaign for the "American system," a compromise between the silent system of Albany and the separate system of Philadelphia. Though he could not claim to have developed these systems, he was quick to seize on their possibilities. *Encellulement* offered the hope of ending the corruption of prisoners, which had made the prisons less a remedy for than a cause of crime. At the very least, cellular confinement would not make prisoners worse. More than that, it might even encourage reform. Clay did not, like some of his more enthusiastic contemporaries, believe that solitary confinement and private meditation alone would reform criminals. His experience, however, showed that it "softened" the inmates' minds and made them more receptive to the active program of religious teaching and education he wanted to establish. Since prisoners were weak almost by definition, once separated from their bad companions they could be influenced to do good rather than ill.*

Clay seems to have adopted the American system out of despair. As he campaigned for it, however, he found that it had positive aspects. Imprisonment could now be justified as a means of reforming rather than of deterring or punishing criminals. Clay began to refer to the "self-adjusting" nature of the system; since it punished criminals only by leaving them alone with their conscience, the minute the prisoners reformed and their conscience ceased to bother them, they were no longer undergoing punishment. Until that time, however, no punishment could be more severe than the self-reproaches of a guilty person with few distractions and no hope for a better future. Moreover, however terrible their crime or however pure their innocence, the criminals had a right to be protected from contact with other offenders. Finally, although mild enough to be used even for untried prisoners, the system was yet sufficiently severe to deter offenders. Such arguments reveal Clay's own ambivalence; since he could not really determine who was responsible for crime, he was compelled to argue for a system that provided at one and the same time for punishment and for nonpunitive "treatment."

Like many prison chaplains, Clay preferred the separate to the silent system. The latter, he felt, did not produce "that deep and earnest self-examination which is the necessary prelude to self conviction and conversion."[25] After Rev. William Crawford visited the American prisons in 1833, Clay began an intense and prolonged effort to persuade the Preston justices to adopt the separate system, or else the silent system as second best. In 1834 he persuaded the bench to agree to the adoption of a modified American system, but the agreement was not implemented. In subsequent reports he continued to harp on the subject. By 1840 he could report some progress. A number of solitary cells had been made, though they were only certified for one month's confinement, and the

*For the early history of separation see Robin Evans, "A Rational Plan for Softening the Mind: Prison Design, 1750-1842" (Ph.D. dissertation, University of Essex, 1975). See also Philip Collins, *Dickens and Crime* (London, 1965), chap. 5, "The Separate System"; and David J. Rothman, *The Discovery of the Asylum* (Boston, 1971), chap. 4, "The Invention of the Penitentiary." The silent system permitted prisoners to work in groups by day but forbade any communication between them. It was often enforced by prisoners acting as monitors. The separate system, or "Philadelphia system," kept prisoners entirely apart in single cells but, unlike solitary confinement, allowed them books, light, work, a full diet, and frequent visits from prison staff. "Encellulement," the term used by W. L. Clay, is a better description of the Preston system than is "separation."

silent system was in use in much of the rest of the prison. In 1841 he noted that after another year's trial, the system seemed to be working. In 1843, a year after Pentonville opened, a corridor of separate cells appeared at Preston. In his report for that year Clay commented that the discipline of Preston had improved continuously in the years since 1828 (the year of Liddell's departure) and dramatically over the past eighteen months (following Anthony's departure). The silent system was now fully enforced. In 1845 the treadwheel was removed and, for the first time, all prisoners were separated before as well as after trial. By 1848 Clay proudly pointed out that committals and crime had decreased more in north Lancashire than in any other county over the past five years. He attributed the trend to the introduction of the new system at Preston.

Although Clay referred to the discipline he introduced as the "separate system" and argued vigorously for its advantages over the silent system, in fact the separation was so modified that it is difficult to assign it to either category. His son used the word "encellulement." Clay was appalled by the high suicide rate at Pentonville, although Crawford was prepared to write off a few extra deaths as the cost of more effective reformation. Accordingly, Clay altered the system to permit a good deal of silent contact between prisoners. They exercised together, took their lessons together, gathered together in an open chapel, and often worked together in large shops.

Clay had originally opposed the imposition of prison labor on prisoners sentenced to short terms and was later to argue against Maconochie's mark system (differing for once from Matthew Davenport Hill, the recorder of Birmingham) on the grounds that it aimed solely at making men industrious. Preston's convicts were already industrious. By 1851, however, when half the entering prisoners had been unemployed outside, he changed his mind and argued that industrial occupation was essential to preserve mental health and prevent depression.*

*The mark system, or social system, developed by Alexander Maconochie required prisoners to earn their discharge from prison by performing a certain amount of hard labor. Each unit of labor earned them so many marks toward the total set for their release. After a period of separation, prisoners worked in groups of six to eight and marks were awarded to the group as a whole. Matthew Davenport Hill was responsible for introducing the system to Birmingham, but it was discredited in 1853 after a scandal following the suicide of a boy assigned to a defective crank. See Sidney Webb and Beatrice Webb, *English Local Government*, vol. 6: *English Prisons Under Local Government* (London, 1963; orig. ed. 1922), pp. 164-70; and Philip Collins, *Dickens and Crime* (London, 1965), chap. 7.

Like M. D. Hill, Clay began to think of prisons as moral hospitals where prisoners would come to be cured of the moral aberrations engendered by a lack of religious training and education. If prisons were reformative rather than punitive, and if crimes were symptoms of a diseased state, then, clearly, the answer was to send more people to prison earlier in order to nip the evil in the bud and to protect the convalescents while there from further contamination. Clay originally expressed doubt about the value of incarcerating offenders, juveniles in particular, because it just made them worse. As Preston more and more nearly approached his ideal, however, he felt able to recommend incarceration as a universal panacea.

Since imprisonment was no longer imposed as a sort of social vengeance, the idea of simple justice, of fitting the punishment to the crime, became less relevant. Clay believed that only a long spell of reformative imprisonment could truly break criminals of their bad habits, so he advocated ever longer sentences. He was perfectly willing to countenance sentences that, had they been imposed merely for punishment, would have seemed grossly disproportionate to the original offense. The culprits would remain until they had undergone a complete cure. It is possible, though it cannot be proved, that Clay's success in convincing the justices that imprisonment was beneficial increased their readiness to sentence offenders to gaol for such petty offenses as public drunkenness—especially since the number of drunken offenders already in gaol proved the seriousness of the problem. (Lancashire had the highest commitment rate for drunkenness in the country; it accounted for approximately half of all county committals.) This was the danger from reform that Sir George Paul had feared in the previous century.

It was probably owing to Clay's growing influence that the separate system was also partially introduced into Kirkdale and Salford. William John Williams strongly supported the silent system, which had the additional recommendation of cheapness. Frederic Hill, an adamant opponent of silence, also disliked the complete imposition of separation. Several local leaders believed, in the words of the chaplain of Kirkdale, that prison reform was pointless "as long as the state of society remains what it is outside."[26] Nevertheless, old cells were altered and new ones built in order to make at least partial separation possible.

At Lancaster, where architectural barriers made large-scale adoption of the separate system impracticable, Hansbrow was converted by his experiments with his more difficult charges. He began "putting apart" those who broke prison rules on full diet in their cells as a way of evading the regulation that restricted gaolers' punishments to three days of solitary. (Hansbrow frequently found the justices' decisions frustrating; on one occasion a prisoner repeatedly and brutally kicked another, splitting his lip and knocking out a tooth, but the justices refused to punish him on the grounds that he had committed only a single offense, while their jurisdiction was limited to *repeated* infractions of the rules.) Several of these isolated offenders came to thank him for the period of reflection. By 1849 he was noting in his journal that Crown prisoners improved "rapidly and perceptibly" in health and appearance when put apart. He attributed the change to the absence of irritation from other prisoners and to the sequestered prisoners' inability to part with their food.[27] In 1850 he wrote with regret that a felon newly released from solitary had begged to be put apart but that he had no space to do so.

The Home Office was putting more pressure on the local prisons to tighten their discipline and introduce separation. The prison inspectors for the Home District had long since agreed that the separate system should be enforced throughout England, but it is difficult to know what effect they had in Lancashire since they and the surveyor general, Joshua Jebb, were on very bad terms with Williams.[28] Nevertheless, it seems likely that Clay's work was the decisive element in persuading the committee of justices appointed in 1846 to adopt the separate system completely in Kirkdale and Preston and to convert Lancaster into a women's and debtors' prison. (No immediate plans could be made for Salford because the borough of Manchester and the hundred had not yet come to an agreement about city prisoners.) It was the committee's work that inspired the county to embark on the building program that soon aroused loud protests from the ratepayers. By 1851 the county was firmly committed to a policy of separation.[29]

The official adoption of separation by the government, the acquiescence of the magistrates, and the triumph of the reformers should not obscure the limited way in which the separate system was actually implemented. The controversy over the idea has concealed its tenuous existence in fact. The adoption of separation was bedeviled by all the problems that had impeded prison reform since the eighteenth century. The expense of total conversion and the ratepayers' revolt acted as important brakes on its introduction, as did the delay common to all governments and especially to those dependent on unenthusiastic committees of amateurs. By the time Lancashire was actually prepared for conversion, the separate system was again falling out of fashion, in favor of the mark system.

Another difficulty was the unpredictability of prison populations: in 1851 Preston contained 168 cells certified for separation, as well as 108 cells that could not be used for separation and 34 cells too dilapidated for use. Since Preston's average population in that year was 367, it is difficult to see how more than two-thirds, at most, could have been separated even at night. Only 168 prisoners could have been separated by day as well. While the municipalities of Manchester and Liverpool were able to introduce separation (and crank labor) into their newly completed prisons in the 1850's, matters changed little in the county prisons.[30] In 1863 Preston still had only 168 separate cells; Kirkdale, despite much building, had only 162; and Salford, with a population of nearly 500, had 101. The new inspector, Herbert P. Voules, who was now responsible for half of England, supported separation only at night; by day he encouraged industrial labor and open schooling. Lancashire prisoners spent up to five hours a day in associated schooling even when they were nominally separated.[31]

Lancashire was not atypical in this lackluster approach to prison reform. Only one prison in all of Wales had any separate cells at all. The Select Committee on Prison Discipline complained in 1863 that "there are so many interruptions to the regularity of prison discipline, instruction is given at such various times, and the communications which pass between prisoners and other persons are so frequent, that separation, though it exists nominally in many, is really to be found in few gaols."[32]

Nevertheless, the middle of the nineteenth century represents the culmination of a period of continuous change that began in the late 1780's. Several writers have implicitly or explicitly attempted to separate the "good" reforms of the 1780's, which were aimed at improving prison conditions and protecting prisoners, from the more equivocal reforms of the early nineteenth century. There is little justification for this approach. Many nineteenth-century reforms grew out of concerns that the eighteenth-century reformers had expressed as well: a rising crime rate, an apparently disorderly and mobile populace, alcoholism, lack of secular and religious instruction, and a poor environment. Bayley and Clay, though very different in background, religion, and political sympathies, nevertheless worked for many of the same causes: Sunday schools, other education for the poor, prison reform, curbs on drinking, and public health measures. Clay had begun at Preston by campaigning for typical eighteenth-century measures: the abolition of bribery and peculation, the banning of blasphemy and gambling, greater order and discipline, and greater cleanliness. Ever since the introduction of cellular prisons in the late eighteenth century, a trend toward the separation of prisoners had been growing; the separate and silent systems were merely its logical conclusion.

The separate system rested firmly on the "liberal" assumption that prisons should be reformative rather than punitive, and its result was longer sentences. Though Lancashire prison terms remained relatively short, many juveniles were sent to "reformatories" for long periods of time. The probation system was also a direct product of the assumption that the punishment should fit the moral state of the criminal as much as the original crime. Whatever its advantages, the overall effect of probation as it operated in England was to undermine the convict's right to judicial due process, since his sentence was determined not by a judge after trial by jury but by a board of appointed officials whose decision was made in secret and could not be appealed. When this effect was combined with the restrictions on the prisoner's liberty while in prison entailed by *encellulement*, the net effect of this "liberal" theory was increased restriction.

Yet we should not condemn the silent and separate systems and the reforms they brought with them too quickly. There is evidence that some convicts were grateful for changes that not only saved them from being "corrupted" but also protected the weaker prisoners from abuse. It became more difficult for felons to whip each other with knotted cords, or to tease the weak-minded in the hope of provoking an amusing display of fury, or to steal each other's food. Improved prison discipline was protective as well as restrictive.

The adoption of a reform-oriented view of imprisonment also promised an end to the escalation of the harshness that deterrence involved as each new penalty failed and was replaced with something more arresting. If reformation implied the lengthening of sentences, deterrence implied the imposition of unpleasantness, such as the treadmill and crank, merely to "torment" convicts. As fears that prisoners would spread epidemics waned, belief in deterrence also led to a lack of public interest in reducing overcrowding and in maintaining decent prison conditions. This public apathy, which was the prevalent attitude throughout the nineteenth century, also resulted in some cruelty.

Whatever its advantages, however, this "liberal" view of imprisonment as a means of rehabilitation instead of deterrence or vengeance resulted in an advocacy of substantially longer and less certain forms of imprisonment, much greater restrictions on the prisoners' liberty and freedom of speech, the attempted destruction of the last remnants of a prison community, the further isolation of prisoners from the outside world, and an increasing resort to incarceration to solve social problems.

Conclusion

Though prisoners often did suffer in the "reformed" prisons, they suffered from corruption and peculation, bad food, filth, cold, uncomfortable cells, and intimidation by other prisoners. These were old and unsolved problems, not new instruments of manipulation. Lancashire was both the industrial and the ideological heart of the new order, yet with the single exception of Preston for a brief period, Lancashire's prisons bore no more resemblance to the highly regimented model of Pentonville than Lancashire's Poor Law did to the rigorous visions of the New Poor Law commissioners.

As with the New Poor Law, Lancashire's foot-dragging suggests that the theory that links the development of industrialization with the rise of repressive institutions is in need of some qualification. Lancashire—the home of Preston's Gradgrinds and of Manchester's economists, the industrial center of the nation—was, after all, also a center of resistance to Chadwick's principles. As with the New Poor Law, there are several reasons for the fact that Lancashire, after an initial burst of reform, began to lag.

First, Lancashire's county government was still in the hands of an old aristocracy rather than a new bourgeoisie. The county's great wealth, which benefited the gentry as well as the middle class, probably actually helped delay the movement of "traders" onto the bench. Successful merchants finally achieved admission to the bench by the middle of the century, but the old rulers, through a mixture of compromise and hard work, still retained much of their influence. In any case, since the newcomers had specifically challenged the extravagance of the old guard, it was difficult for them to propose any broad new programs involving considerable expense. They were more interested in reducing chaplains to curates' pay than in hiring the most able and zealous young reformers. Gentlemen like Hesketh, or established professionals like Thomas Batty Addison, were prepared to support a good measure of reform but not a complete revolution in prison management. That had been possible only at the end of the eighteenth century, when an absolute crisis, combined with fear, had been exploited by Bayley—who, as a Nonconformist, a Whig, and a Mancunian, was a Lancashire anomaly.

Second, as with the New Poor Law, Lancashire had begun to reform relatively early. In the late eighteenth century, both the gaoler and the justices seem to have been eager to reform the Castle and were in some cases waiting for legislation that would make it possible. The county was quickly prepared to engage in massive and innovative rebuilding at the gaol and the houses of correction. It thus experienced the fate common to many innovators; early experiments were soon overtaken by versions refined by experience, while the experimenters were left with outdated goods that were too new and expensive to replace. Lancaster Castle's architectural intractability saved it from extreme innovations (though the felons' towers were a costly mistake), but Salford exemplified these problems. Built in the first flush of enthusiasm for a plan that rapidly became outmoded, Salford was too inflexible to adapt to the changes in penal theory and prison population. Once considered one of England's most "humane" prisons, it soon became known as one of the worst. Lancashire's heavy early investment in reform made it much more difficult for the county to begin anew.

Third, Lancashire was simply overwhelmed by the extent of the problems caused by industrialization. It resisted the New Poor Law at least in part because no institution was adequate to contain the multitudes displaced by cyclical employment. Urbanization had grown beyond the power of any institution of social control to contain it. Justices and governors were fully occupied just trying to house, clothe, feed, and clean up after the constantly increasing number of prison inmates. They built their new cells on a new plan, but they could not afford to destroy the old ones. Even the new cells soon became so crowded as to preclude separation; in the old cells separation would have been both cruel and illegal. Nor were there ever enough prison officers to enforce an effective discipline. A shortage of staff often forced prison administrators to leave prisoners to their own devices. It was not until the crime rate at last began to ebb, at midcentury, that the justices were able to win enough distance and flexibility to consider major policy changes on a countywide basis. This is not to suggest that reform did not take place. It did. The prisons of 1845 were very different places from their predecessors of three or six decades before. They were larger, more highly and formally organized, and more firmly controlled by a professional staff headed by a more powerful governor. These efforts had improved the prisoners' comfort, security, protection from others, and, probably, health. The traditional historians were correct in recounting these improvements, although they failed to weigh the full costs.

This study suggests that the radical historians have seriously oversimplified their case. In particular, they have failed both to delineate the different groups interested in reform and to appreciate the complexities of their interaction. They have assumed that a united elite was acting with a clearly defined motive, the maintenance of domination, and have failed to appreciate both the multiplicity of intentions and the fact that many actual changes had not been intended at all. The cast of actors with a say in the administration of Lancashire prisons included: a Parliament that on occasion heeded Henry Hunt and Francis Burdett as well as Whigs and Tories; a county bench that contained radicals such as George Williams, reformers such as Thomas Butterworth Bayley, professional clergymen and lawyers such as W. R. Hay and Thomas Batty Addison, conservative country gentlemen such as William Hulton, and reluctant reformers such as Thomas Hesketh; prison inspectors who disagreed violently with each other; the Home Office; Assize judges; gaolers; professional staff members; journalists and their readers; ratepayers; and, finally, prisoners themselves.

If the radical version oversimplifies both the groups involved and their motives, however, it correctly reveals the darker side of prison reform. The radical case may assume an overly conspiratorial elite, but the traditional account is naive in assuming a universal benevolence. For many actors in this story, self-interest and altruism were inextricably mixed. The gaoler sought both greater autonomy for himself and better discipline. The professional staff sought both personal advancement through the composition of impressive reports and better conditions for prisoners. The journalist sought both the correction of scandals and new readers, the politician both reform and adulation, the justice both greater personal security from disease and crime and the better protection of those under his charge, and the prisoner both personal revenge for sometimes imagined slights and greater justice.

The radicals have also performed a service by renewing interest in the painful balance between freedom and security. The Age of Reform may have brought prisoners greater protection from disease, hunger, and violence, but they paid heavily in loss of freedom and community life. The choice between freedom and security is not a simple one, since for many, security is a form of freedom. Hunger and fear impose their own restraints on behavior. Any society that does not to some extent restrain its citizens leaves them free to prey on each other, and such a state of affairs may also severely restrict the choices people can make about their own destinies. Nevertheless, there comes a point at which restraints imposed in the name of security smother other needs and values.

Finally, the radicals were correct in claiming that prison reform succeeded in convincing a large segment of the public that prisons ought to be reformative while utterly failing to fulfill that goal. An unjustified faith in reformation may in turn have led judges to sentence to institutions many who should not have gone to them. Whether this means that we should eliminate penal institutions entirely, or merely that we should recognize that they serve other ends, must be a subject of further debate.

Reference Matter

Notes

Information on the major manuscript collections and parliamentary papers consulted by the author, together with the abbreviations used in citing documents, can be found in Document Sources, pp. 255-59. In citations of LCRO sessional records, "Lanc." refers to Lancaster, "Manc." to Manchester, "E" to Easter, "T" to Trinity (or Visitation or Summer), "M" to Michaelmas, "Ep." to Epiphany, and "AGS" to Annual General Sessions. To avoid confusing the reader wishing to pursue references, all dates given are as found in the documents. That is, all dates are Old Style until 1752, and the Epiphany Sessions meets *after* the Michaelmas Sessions of the same year. This follows the arrangement of the Order Books, which are in volumes covering one year each.

Introduction

1. Erving Goffman, "On the Characteristics of Total Institutions," in D. R. Cressy, ed., *The Prison: Studies in Institutional Organization and Change* (New York, 1961).

2. E.g., David Roberts, *The Victorian Origins of the British Welfare State* (New Haven, 1960); O. MacDonagh, "The Nineteenth-Century Revolution in Government: A Reappraisal," *Historical Journal* 1 (1958): 52-67; Henry Parris, "The Nineteenth-Century Revolution in Government: A Reappraisal Reappraised," *Historical Journal* 3 (1960): 17-37; Jennifer Hart, "Nineteenth-Century Social Reform: A Tory Interpretation of History," *Past and Present* 31 (1965): 39-61.

3. Sidney Webb and Beatrice Webb, *English Prisons Under Local Government* (London, 1963; orig. ed. 1922), p. 247. This superb study is volume 6 of *English Local Government*.

For other studies of local prisons or county prison systems see: James Horsfall Turner, *The Annals of Wakefield House of Correction* (Bingley, 1904); K. Tweedale Meaby, *Nottinghamshire: Extracts from the County Records of the Eighteenth Cen-*

tury (Nottingham, n.d.); P. Styles, "The Development of County Administration in the Late XVIII and Early XIX Centuries, Illustrated by the Records of the Warwickshire Court of Quarter Sessions, 1777-1837," Dugdale Society Occasional Papers 4 (Oxford, 1934); Albert John Rhodes, *Dartmoor Prison* (London, 1933); J. Stevens Cox, *Ilchester Gaol and House of Correction*, Ilchester Historical Monographs 4 (Ilchester, 1949); I. Wyatt and J. W. Wyatt, "Prisoners in the County Gaol, 1789-1814," *Gloucestershire Historical Studies* 2 (1968); M. B. Weinstock, "Dorchester Model Prison, 1791-1816," *Proceedings of the Dorset Natural History and Archeological Society* 78 (1958): 94-109; W. Payne, *Stafford Gaol and Its Associations with a Record of County Crime and Criminals* (Stafford, 1887); Esther Moir, *Local Government in Gloucestershire, 1775-1800*, Bristol and Gloucestershire Archeological Society, Records Section 8 (1969) and Moir, "Local Government in Gloucestershire, 1775-1800" (Ph.D. dissertation, Cambridge University, 1955); Elizabeth Melling, ed., *Kentish Sources*, vol. 6: *Crime and Punishment* (Maidstone, 1969); R. K. Howes, "The Reform of Gloucester Prison," *Gloucestershire Historical Studies* 5 (1972); Royal Commission on Historical Monuments, *York Castle, an Illustrated History* (London, 1973).

See also four recent long studies: Wayne Joseph Sheehan, "The London Prison System, 1666-1795" (Ph.D. dissertation, University of Maryland, 1975); Eric Stockdale, *A Study of Bedford Prison, 1660-1877* (London, 1977); Peter Southerton, *The Story of a Prison* (Reading, 1975); and J. R. S. Whiting, *Prison Reform in Gloucestershire, 1776-1820* (London, 1975).

4. For examples, see Gordon Hawkins, *The Prison, Policy and Practice* (Chicago, 1976), chap. 1, "The Prison and Its Critics," pp. 1-29.

5. Gertrude Himmelfarb, "The Haunted House of Jeremy Bentham," reprinted in *Victorian Minds* (New York, 1968), pp. 32-81.

6. *Ibid.*, p. 77.

7. See L. J. Hume, "Jeremy Bentham and the Nineteenth-Century Revolution in Government," *Historical Journal* 10 (1967): 361-74, and Hume, "Bentham's Panopticon, an Administrative History," part 1, *Historical Studies* 15 (1973): 703-21, and part 2, *Historical Studies* 16 (1974): 36-54; Barbee-Sue Rodman, "Bentham and the Paradox of Penal Reform," *Journal of the History of Ideas* 29 (1968): 197-210; Robin Evans, "Bentham's Panopticon: An Incident in the Social History of Architecture," *Architectural Association Quarterly* 3 (1971): 21-37, and Evans, "Panopticon," *Contraspasio* 10 (1970): 4-18; William C. Bader, "Jeremy Bentham: Businessman or 'Philanthropist'?," *Albion* 7 (1975): 245-54; and Rod Morgan, "Divine Philanthropy: John Howard Reconsidered," *History* 62 (1977): 388-410. Himmelfarb herself explicitly criticized this view during the 1980 meeting of the American Historical Association, at the session on "Social Reform and Social Control in Britain in the Era of the Industrial Revolution."

8. David J. Rothman, *The Discovery of the Asylum* (Boston, 1971), pp. 294-95.

9. Michel Foucault, *Madness and Civilization*, trans. Richard Howard (London, 1967), and *Discipline and Punish*, trans. Alan Sheridan (London, 1977).

10. Foucault, *Discipline and Punish*, p. 268.

11. *Ibid.*, pp. 227-28.

12. Michael Ignatieff, *A Just Measure of Pain* (New York, 1978), pp. 214-15. This book is a revised version of a Ph.D. thesis submitted to Harvard University in 1976. I would like to thank Dr. Ignatieff for permitting me to see early manuscript versions of this thesis.

13. *Ibid.*, p. 209.

14. *Ibid.*, p. 211. For other "radical" accounts, see Morgan, Hume, and Bader. See also Robin Evans, "A Rational Plan for Softening the Mind: Prison Design, 1750-1842" (Ph.D. dissertation, University of Essex, 1975). I would like to thank Dr. Evans for providing me with a copy of this work. For the use of Ignatieff's conclusions by penologists, see Michael Sherman and Gordon Hawkins, *Imprisonment in America: Choosing the Future* (Chicago, 1981).

15. Michael Ignatieff, "State, Civil Society, and Total Institutions: A Critique of Recent Social Histories of Punishment," in Michael Tonry and Norval Morris, eds., *Crime and Justice: An Annual Review of Research*, vol. 3 (Chicago, 1981), pp. 153-92. I am very grateful to Dr. Ignatieff for providing me with an early draft of this article.

16. Peter Linebaugh, "The Tyburn Riot Against the Surgeons," in Douglas Hay et al., eds., *Albion's Fatal Tree* (London, 1975), pp. 65-117: "To the surgeons, their spokesmen, and the lords and squires sitting in Parliament, not only was humiliation at the death of one of the 'Scum of the People' a passing matter, but such further 'Marks of Infamy' as public dissection became a part of the policy of class discipline" (p. 117). Linebaugh offers no evidence in support of this contention, nor does he specify whether "scum" referred to convicted felons or to the poor generally. He also does not explain who was feeling humiliated or why.

17. David Philips, *Crime and Authority in Victorian England* (London, 1977). I would like to thank Mr. Richard Trainor of Glasgow University for bringing this work to my attention. See also John Langbein, "Albion's Fatal Flaws," *Past and Present* 98 (1983): 96-120. For a recent analysis of English legal process in an earlier period that also emphasizes the importance of participation by victims and juries, see Cynthia Brilliant Herrup, "Courts, Crimes and Criminals: Legal Structure and Substance in East Sussex 1594-1640" (Ph.D. dissertation, Northwestern University, 1982). I would like to thank Dr. Herrup for permitting me to see this work.

18. See below, pp. 138-39.

19. Eric Midwinter, *Social Administration in Lancashire, 1830-1860: Poor Laws, Public Health and Police* (Manchester, 1969), p. 61. For classic descriptions of the effects of communal inmate resistance on the implementation of of-

ficial rules, see Erving Goffman, *Asylums* (Garden City, 1961), and Gresham Sykes, *The Society of Captives: A Study of a Maximum Security Prison* (Princeton, 1958). For Lancashire examples, see chap. 7.

Chapter One

1. Sidney Webb and Beatrice Webb, *English Local Government*, vol. 6: *English Prisons Under Local Government* (London, 1963; orig. ed. 1922), p. 31.

2. W. L. Burn, *The Age of Equipoise* (New York, 1965), pp. 176-77.

3. Ursula Henriques, *Before the Welfare State* (London, 1979), p. 157.

4. Bryan Keith-Lucas, *The Unreformed Local Government System* (London, 1980), p. 57.

5. Robin Evans, "A Rational Plan for Softening the Mind: Prison Design, 1750-1842" (Ph.D. dissertation, University of Essex, 1975); Michael Ignatieff, *A Just Measure of Pain* (New York, 1978), pp. 44-79.

6. Rod Morgan, "Divine Philanthropy: John Howard Reconsidered," *History* 62 (1977): 388-410.

7. See, e.g., Douglas Hay et al., eds., *Albion's Fatal Tree* (London, 1975).

8. Jennifer Hart, "Nineteenth-Century Social Reform: A Tory Interpretation of History," *Past and Present* 31 (1965): 39-61.

9. Henriques, p. 261.

10. *Ibid.*, pp. 265-66. Henriques does, however, emphasize the continuing power of the justices.

11. See my Ph.D. dissertation, "County Prison Administration in Lancashire, 1690-1850" (Princeton University, 1980), p. 134, and Webb and Webb, p. 5. Pugh, however, shows that many gaolers were paid to undertake the position (Ralph B. Pugh, *Imprisonment in Medieval England* [Cambridge, Eng., 1968], pp. 165-66). Bribery of sheriffs was prohibited by 12 Rich. II, c. 2; 4 Hen. IV, c. 5; and 5 and 6 Ed. VI, c. 16. An act of 1718 (4 Geo. I, c. 15) explicitly outlawed the sale of gaolerships.

12. R. Sharpe France, "The Lancashire Sessions Act, 1798," *Transactions of the Lancashire and Cheshire Historical Society* (hereafter *LCHS*) 96 (1944): 1-35, is the chief source on the Sheriff's Board and its replacement. The proceedings of the board from 1661 to 1694 are in LCRO, QSV/11.

13. For more about the role of the Assize judges in county administration, see Pugh, pp. 342-43; J. S. Cockburn, *A History of English Assizes, 1558-1714* (Cambridge, 1972); and Esther Moir, "Local Government in Gloucestershire, 1775-1800," Bristol and Gloucestershire Archeological Society, Records Section 8 (1969). For examples of judicial intervention, see Bryan Keith-Lucas, pp. 58-59, and PRO, HO 42/132, Judge J. Bayley to the Home Office.

14. Pugh, p. 191, and Clifford Dobb, "Life and Conditions in London's Prisons," in A. Nicoll, ed., *Shakespeare in His Own Age* (Cambridge, 1965), p. 98.

15. 23 Hen. VIII, c. 2 (1532), and 14 Eliz., c. 5 (1572). On the houses of

correction see W. E. Passey, "Houses of Correction in England and Wales" (M.A. thesis, University of Liverpool, 1936).

16. Walter Joseph King, "The Prosecution of Illegal Behavior in Seventeenth-Century England" (Ph.D. dissertation, University of Michigan, 1977-78), and John Bellamy, *Crime and Public Order in England in the Later Middle Ages* (London, 1973).

17. 22 and 23 Charles II, c. 20.

18. William Oliver Roper, "Materials for the History of Lancashire, II" (Chetham Society, 1907), pp. 227-29. See also DeLacy, p. 53.

19. See William Farrer and J. Brownbill, eds., *The Victoria History of the County of Lancashire*, vol. 8 (London, 1966), p. 6. A drawing of Lancaster Castle in the PRO (MR 15) is attributed to the Elizabethan period. Speed's map of Lancaster also contains a plan of the Castle. A comparison of these images with eighteenth-century drawings reveals no significant change, suggesting that most of the Castle survived Parliament's attempts at demolition. For descriptions of the Castle, see Roper, p. 247; "A Perambulation of Lancaster Castle" (Lancaster, 1973); Edward Higgin, "Memoranda Relating to Lancaster Castle . . . ," *LCHS* 1 (1948-49): 95-102; LCL, plan of Lancaster Castle prior to 1778; LCL, scrapbook 5; City of London Record Office, "Report from the Committee of Aldermen Appointed to Visit Several Gaols in England" (1815-16); and *Parliamentary Papers* (hereafter *PP*) 1812-13 V, Report of the Commissioners on the State of Lancaster Prison, and the Treatment of Prisoners Therein. I would like to thank Mr. K. J. Neale and Mr. Maurice Butters of the Home Office and the Governor, Assistant Governor, and staff of both HM Prison, Preston, and HM Prison, Lancaster, who made it possible for me to visit these institutions and took the time to answer numerous questions.

20. William Harrison, "The Old House of Correction at Hunt's Bank, Manchester," *Transactions of the Lancashire and Cheshire Antiquarian Society* (hereafter *LCAS*) 3 (1885): 89-110; LCRO, QSO, Manc. M 1700; QSO, Manc. Ep. 1720; QSO, Manc. Ep. 1746; QSP, Manc. Ep. 1757; QSO, Manc. E 1773.

21. John Howard, *The State of the Prisons in England and Wales* (Abingdon, 1977; orig. ed. 1777), pp. 439-40.

22. Sylvia Tollit, "The First House of Correction for the County of Lancaster," *LCHS* 105 (1953): 69-90.

23. Howard, p. 439.

24. See DeLacy, pp. 58-59, for a list of larger repairs.

25. T. C. Porteous, "Roger Haydock of Coppull: A Brief Biography and Ten Original Letters," *LCAS* 52 (1937): 4.

26. Historical Manuscripts Commission, Kenyon MSS., no. 527, pp. 159-60.

27. Tollit, p. 77.

28. LCRO, QSP, Manc. T 1703, no. 46.

29. PRO, PL 27/2/2.

30. PRO, PL 27/2, pt. 2; PRO, PL 26/27; LCRO, QSP, Lanc. Ep. 1695. While chained, Arrowsmith was allowed 10*d*. a week, an increase of 2*d*. over his previous allowance.

31. PRO, PL 290, PL 26/45; LCRO, QSP, Lanc. E 1756; LCRO, QSO, Preston E 1756; LCL MS. 3204; PRO, T 90/149 (Sheriff's Cravings) year ending Michaelmas 1755. I would like to thank Miss Joanna Innes of Oxford for referring me to the Sheriff's Cravings, a useful source.

32. PRO, PCOM 2/442: Journal, Feb. 1, 1816.

33. LCRO, QSP, Wigan Ep. 1699, no. 9.

34. LCRO, QSO, Lanc. Ep. 1775.

35. For further discussion see DeLacy, pp. 104-11. I would like to thank the parish of St. Mary's, Lancaster, for permitting me to consult this register in the church. See also the Parish Register Society, *The Registers of the Parish Church of Lancaster*, vols. 2 (Cambridge, 1920) and 3 (Cambridge, 1948).

36. Higgin, pp. 101-2.

37. LCRO, QSP, Lanc. M 1693, no. 20.

38. LCRO, QSP, Lanc. T 1703, no. 9. The gaoler in 1703 was the charitable Henry Bracken.

39. LCL, MS. 6615.

40. LCRO, QSP, Lanc. Ep. 1704, no. 27.

41. LCRO, QSO, Lanc. Ep. 1737, no. 4.

42. LCRO, QSO, Lanc. T 1719, and E 1720; QJB/9.

43. LCRO, Ormskirk E 1715, no. 22: "An Account of the Prisoners that hath the Libtie to worke or Begge in the Towne and what weekly Allowance they have paid them." The eighteen prisoners listed took in a total per week of 16*s*. See also Howard, p. 438.

44. LCRO, QSP, Lanc. E 1711, no. 2; Lanc. M 1748, no. 3.

45. Webb and Webb, p. 18.

46. Wayne Joseph Sheehan, "The London Prison System, 1666-1795" (Ph.D. dissertation, University of Maryland, 1975), p. 239.

47. LCRO, QSP, Manc. T 1703, no. 46.

48. LCRO, QSO, Manc. T 1720; Tollit, p. 76; LCL, MS. 7321 (folder on J. S. Harrison). This figure probably does not include Higgin's earnings from conveyance fees.

49. Tollit, p. 182.

50. Cf. Eric Stockdale, "John Howard and Bedford Gaol," in John C. Freeman, ed., *Prisons Past and Future* (papers given at the Howard Bicentenary Conference; London, 1978), p. 321; LCL, scrapbook no. 2, f. 1; W. L. Clay, *The Prison Chaplain* (Montclair, 1969), p. 113. Though distinguished, Bracken was also quarrelsome. Two disputes involving his household appear in PRO, PL 27/2/2, and a third is discussed by E. Bosdin Leech, "Fovet Medicinam Concordia," *Manchester University Medical School Gazette* 17 (June 1938): 111-14. I do

not know whether this gaoler was related to the Henry Bracken who served from 1699 to 1707.

51. See DeLacy, p. 156, n. 20; LCL, scrapbook no. 2, f. 1; LCL, *Waddington's Guide to Lancaster*, pp. 30-31; Roper; LCL, MS. 7321; LCL, "Biographies."

52. LCL, MS. 7321.

53. See DeLacy, pp. 131-34. Fell tried to have Ellitson indicted at the Assizes.

54. LCRO, QSP, Lanc. M 1695, no. 7; QSP, Wigan E 1699, no. 9; QSP, Lanc. E 1699, nos. 20, 3, 17; QSP, Lanc. E 1703, no. 6; QSP, Lanc. M 1700, no. 13. Similar comments about kind gaolers can be found in other counties, such as Oxfordshire and Bedfordshire.

55. LCRO, QSP, Lanc. T 1730, no. 3; QSO, Lanc. T 1730; QSP, Lanc. M 1748, no. 3.

56. Tollit, pp. 81-84; LCRO, QSP, Wigan M 1689, no. 24; Manc. E 1690, no. 11; Lanc. M 1690, no. 1; Lanc. E 1691, nos. 10, 14. On the Tomlinson affair, see also the *Calendar of State Papers, Domestic*, June 12, 1690.

57. LCRO, QSP, Manc. T 1703, no. 46; Preston M 1703, no. 81.

58. *The Poor Man's Advocate*, July 14 and July 21, 1832.

59. This description of Lancashire rates is based on the following in the LCRO. Rate books: CAV 3 (1793); DDRo (1665); DDX 123/42 (1718); CPV 3 (ca. 1750); DDP (rate book of John Wilcock, 1767); DDX 951/7. Other rate books consulted include: DDF 5 (1645); DDX 603/1 (1752); DDTa 215 (17ᶜ); DDKe 2/17/9 (17ᶜ); DDPt (1622); DDX 114/1 (1675-78); DDT, 2d batch; ZBR 2/2A (n.d., ca. 1640). Many of these books are almost identical, but some have useful prefaces.

Also used were DDGR 0/1, "Case for a New County Rate" (1801), and Robert Hindle, *An Account of the Expenditure of the County Palatine of Lancaster for a Period of Twenty-Three Years . . . with Remarks* (London, 1843). See also G. W. Oxley, "The Administration of the Old Poor Law in the West Derby Hundred of Lancashire, 1601-1837" (Ph.D. dissertation, University of Liverpool, 1966), and Oxley, *Poor Relief in England and Wales* (London, 1974), as well as A. F. Davie, "The Government of Lancashire, 1798-1838" (M.A. thesis, University of Manchester, 1966). See also James Tait, ed., *Taxation in Salford Hundred, 1524-1802*, Chetham Society n.s. 83 (1924), and Edwin Cannan, *The History of Local Rates in England* (London, 1896).

60. 43 Eliz., c. 2, 3. The ox ley is Lancashire's equivalent of the purveyance tax, or "purvey," that formed the basis of Cumberland's rating system. See J. V. Beckett, "Local Custom and the 'New Taxation' in the Seventeenth and Eighteenth Centuries: The Example of Cumberland," *Journal of Northern History* 12 (1976): 105-26.

61. LCRO, DDRo.

62. LCRO, DDGr 0/1.

63. Webb and Webb, p. 9, n. 1.

64. LCRO, QSO, Lanc. M 1695; QSP, Lanc. T 1696; and, e.g., QSO Lanc. E 1699.

65. Keith-Lucas, p. 55; my calculations from his table. Since other counties may have had peculiarities of accounting similar to Lancashire's, this table should be used with caution.

66. For the restraint this placed on prosecution, see King.

67. This paragraph follows David Philips, *Crime and Authority in Victorian England* (London, 1977), pp. 112-13.

68. LCRO, QSP, Lanc. E 1699, no. 23.

69. LCRO, QSP, Lanc. E 1707, no. 13.

70. LCRO, QSP, Lanc. E 1722; Lanc. Ep. 1767.

71. LCRO, QSP, Lanc. E 1711, no. 1.

72. PRO, T 90/159.

73. LCRO, QSP, Lanc. E 1695.

74. LCRO, QSO, Lanc. M 1695.

75. LCRO, QSP, Lanc. Ep. 1699, no. 17.

76. LCRO, QSP, Lanc. Ep. 1721, no. 2; Lanc. E 1722; QSO, Manc. M 1724; Lanc. T 1725.

77. LCRO, QSO, Lanc. M 1737; QSP, Lanc. Ep. 1737, no. 4; QSO, Lanc. Ep. 1737; AGS, 1822.

78. LCRO, QSO, Lanc. E 1742; Manc. E 1748; Lanc. T 1748.

79. LCRO, QSP, Lanc. E 1695; Lanc. M 1683, no. 6; Wigan Ep. 1699, no. 9.

80. Howard, p. 12.

81. Jeremy Bentham, *Panopticon; or, the Inspection-House, with Two Postscripts* (London, 1791), pp. 149-50.

Chapter Two

1. See also Wayne Joseph Sheehan, "The London Prison System, 1666-1795" (Ph.D. dissertation, University of Maryland, 1975), p. 132; and Michael Ignatieff, *A Just Measure of Pain* (New York, 1978), pp. 11-15. Ignatieff sees four early periods of reform: the Elizabethan period, the 1690's, the 1720's, and the 1780's. He bases his conclusion on his national data. My work in Lancashire, carried out before his book appeared, confirms his. On the fluctuations of the "crime rate" see J. M. Beattie, "The Pattern of Crime in England, 1660-1800," *Past and Present* 62 (Feb. 1974).

2. John Howard, *The State of the Prisons in England and Wales* (Abingdon, 1977; orig. ed. 1777), p. 437.

3. Ignatieff, p. 82.

4. Sir Leon Radzinowicz, *A History of English Criminal Law*, vol. 1 (London, 1948), pp. 138-64.

5. PRO, HO 42/4 and HO 42/8. See also Ignatieff, pp. 82 and 85-87.

6. LCRO, QJC. For further discussion see Margaret DeLacy, "County Prison Administration in Lancashire, 1690-1850" (Ph.D. dissertation, Princeton University, 1980), pp. 218-25.

7. For a table of the numbers of debtors filing insolvency papers, see De-Lacy, p. 79, which is a count of debtors calendared in LCRO, QJB. Joanna Innes has informed me that she has compared these numbers with the numbers of debtors listed in the London *Gazette* as filing for insolvency in Lancaster and has found that the numbers seem to bear no relationship to each other. I know of no explanation for this puzzling discrepancy.

8. Numbers for committals of debtors are compiled from the following sources: *PP* 1819 XVII; PRO, PCOM 2/442 (Thomas Houseman Higgin); *PP*, Annual returns of prisons under 4 Geo. IV, c. 64, schedule B. These numbers do not always coincide.

9. Manchester Central Library, Henry Fielding, "Tables Showing the Total Number of Prisoners Committed to the New Bailey, Salford, under the Several Charges Specified . . ." (paper read to the Manchester Statistical Society, 1834-35). I am grateful to the City of Manchester, Cultural Services, Archives Department, for providing me with a copy of this paper.

10. Total committals, Michaelmas to Michaelmas, are in the schedule B returns.

11. The best source for daily average populations is Robert Hindle, *An Account of the Expenditure of the Country Palatine of Lancaster for a Period of Twenty-Three Years . . . with Remarks* (London, 1843). S. Peter Bell calculated his own daily averages in his M.Sc. thesis, "A Social History of Salford New Bayley Prison, 1823-1865" (University of Salford, 1972). Another set of figures is available from the reports in the Annual General Session (LCRO, QSG and QSZ), and miscellaneous figures are available in other LCRO documents (e.g., QAV/3). Unfortunately, due to different calendar years and other variables, there is some discrepancy between the sets of figures. Since Hindle provides the only consistent long series for all four prisons, it has been used whenever possible. See DeLacy, pp. 485-88, for further discussion. Daily average populations are difficult to obtain for most English prisons, and because sentence length varied, total committals are only a rough guide to population levels.

12. I am grateful to Mr. Malcolm Ramsey for enabling me to see a draft of his paper on Paul, read at the 1977 Howard Society Conference in honor of the bicentenary of the publication of *State of the Prisons*. See also Ignatieff, pp. 108-9.

13. Andrew Tennant Scull, *Museums of Madness: The Social Organization of Insanity in Nineteenth Century England* (New York, 1979), pp. 34-36.

14. David Philips, *Crime and Authority in Victorian England* (London, 1977), pp. 112-13.

Chapter Three

1. The chief sources on Bayley are [Thomas Percival], *Biographical Memoirs of the Late Thomas Butterworth Bayley, Esq.* . . . (Manchester, 1802), and Sir Thomas Baker, *Memorials of a Dissenting Chapel* (Manchester, 1884). See also Valentine Arthur Charles Gatrell, "The Commercial Middle Class in Manchester from c. 1820 to 1857" (Ph.D. dissertation, Cambridge University, 1971); Michael Ignatieff, *A Just Measure of Pain* (New York, 1978), pp. 62-64; Sidney Webb and Beatrice Webb, *English Local Government*, vol. 1: *The Parish and the County* (London, 1963; orig. ed. 1906); William Wardell Bean, *The Parliamentary Representation of the Six Northern Counties of England, 1603-1886* (Hull, 1890). Letters from Bayley can be found in the Liverpool papers at the British Library, the Public Record Office Home Office letters, the Wilkes papers, and the Dundas papers in the Scottish Record Office.

2. I would like to thank Joanna Innes for informing me of Bayley's proposal to Miss Wilkes.

3. John Brewer, "The Wilkites and the Law, 1763-74," in John Brewer and John Styles, eds., *An Ungovernable People: The English and Their Law in the Seventeenth and Eighteenth Centuries* (London, 1980), pp. 128-71.

4. *Ibid.*, pp. 166 and 170.

5. BL, add. MSS. 38225, f. 114.

6. BL, add. MSS. 38450.

7. J. L. Hammond and Barbara Hammond, *The Skilled Labourer, 1760-1832* (New York, 1967; orig. ed. 1919), p. 62.

8. Percival, *Biographical Memoirs*.

9. BL, add. MSS. 38447, f. 144.

10. Percival, *Biographical Memoirs*, p. 6.

11. *Ibid.*

12. LCRO, QSO, all sess. T 1781, and Manc. T 1787.

13. LCRO, QSO, Lanc. M 1770; Lanc. Ep. 1772; and Lanc. T 1774.

14. 32 Geo. II, c. 28; 13 Geo. III, c. 58; and 14 Geo. III, c. 20, 59.

15. 16 Geo. III, c. 43, and 19 Geo. III, c. 74. Bayley to Lord Sydney, Jan. 26, 1785, PRO, HO 42/6.

16. 22 Geo. III, c. 64.

17. 24 Geo. III, c. 54, 55.

18. LCRO, QSO, Manc. T 1777.

19. Manchester Central Library, 365 C20; *The Report of Samuel Clowes the Younger, and Thomas Butterworth Bayley, Esquires, of the State of the House of Correction at Manchester* (Manchester, 1783).

20. LCRO, QSB/1.

21. *Ibid.*, deposition of Edward Cowburne.

22. LCRO, QSO, Lanc. Ep. 1784. Manc. Ep. 1784; E 1784 adjourned to

Preston, May 13; Lanc. M 1784; Ep. Manc., adj. to Preston, 1785; and all sess. M 1786. On Harrison see J. Mordaunt Crook, "A Reluctant Goth: The Architecture of Thomas Harrison," *Country Life* 149 (1971): 876-79, 944-47, 1088-91, 1539.

On typhus in Lancashire see [?A. Meiklejohn], "The Putrid Fever at Robert Peel's Radcliffe Mill," *Notes and Queries* 203 (1958): 26-35. Typhus was present in Lancaster town from 1782 to 1784, in Preston from 1781 to 1783, at the Radcliffe Mills from Nov. 1782 to 1784, and at Carlisle in 1781. See also John Heysham, *An Account of the Gaol Fever or Typhus Carcerum* (London, 1782), and D. Campbell, *Observations on the Typhus* (Lancaster, 1785). Campbell was a superintendent of the Lancaster Dispensary. Percival was one of the doctors who were called in to control the Radcliffe epidemic.

On public health in the north, see B. Keith-Lucas, "Some Influences Affecting the Development of Sanitary Legislation in England," *Economic History Review* 2d ser. 6 (1953-54): 290-96, and E. P. Hennock, "Urban Sanitary Reform a Generation Before Chadwick," *Economic History Review* 2d ser. 10 (1957): 113-20.

For further citations see John Pickstone, ed., "Health, Disease and Medicine in Lancashire, 1750-1950, Four Papers on Sources, Problems and Methods" (University of Manchester Institute of Science and Technology, Department of History of Science and Technology), and Pickstone, "Ferriar's Fever and Kay's Cholera: Disease and Social Structure in Cottonopolis," paper read to the Society for the Social History of Medicine (Liverpool, July 1980). I would like to thank Dr. Pickstone for sending me copies of these and other papers and for additional assistance. See also my paper, "Social Medicine and Social Institutions in Eighteenth Century Lancashire" (Social Science History Association, Bloomington, 1982).

23. PRO, HO 42/6, Jan. 1, 1785.

24. [?Harriet Martineau], "Convict Systems in England and Ireland," *Edinburgh Review* 117 (1863): 241-68. I am grateful to Mr. Simon Stevenson of Oxford for this reference.

25. On the Life Table see John M. Eyler, *Victorian Social Medicine: The Ideas and Methods of William Farr* (Baltimore, 1979), pp. 73-74. John Heygarth, *A Letter to Dr. Percival on the Prevention of Infectious Fever* (Bath, 1801), and "Observations on the Population and Diseases of Chester in the Year 1774," *Philosophical Transactions* 68, pt. 1 (1778): 131-54. Heygarth, who was physician to the Chester Infirmary between 1767 and 1798, introduced fever wards to the infirmary in 1783, following the typhus epidemic of 1782. On the Aikins see John Fulton, "The Warrington Academy (1757-1786) and Its Influence upon Medicine and Science," *Bulletin of the History of Medicine* 1 (1933): 50-80. On Currie, see William Wallace Currie, ed., *Memoir of the Life, Writings and Correspondence of James Currie, M.D., F.R.S. of Liverpool* (London, 1831), and Rob-

ert Donald Thornton, *James Currie the Entire Stranger and Robert Burns* (Edinburgh and London, 1963).

26. On this group, see DeLacy, "Social Medicine"; notes 3, 9, and 10 contain further citations.

27. The classic source on contagionism and the logic that led medical theorists to modify or reject it is Charles-Edward Amory Winslow, *The Conquest of Epidemic Disease: A Chapter in the History of Ideas* (Madison, 1980; orig. ed. 1943), esp. chaps. 10 and 11. See also Erwin H. Ackerknecht, "Anticontagionism Between 1821 and 1867," *Bulletin of the History of Medicine* 22 (1948): 562-93; Eyler; and Margaret Pelling, *Cholera, Fever and English Medicine, 1825-1865* (Oxford, 1978).

28. Ackerknecht, "Anticontagionism."

29. Peter H. Niebyl, "The English Bloodletting Revolution, or Modern Medicine Before 1850," *Bulletin of the History of Medicine* 51 (1977): 464-83.

30. Richard Mead, *A Short Discourse Concerning Pestilential Contagion and the Methods to Be Used to Prevent It* (London, 1720), pp. 47-48.

31. *Ibid.*, p. 42.

32. *Ibid.*, quoted in Winslow, p. 187.

33. Sir John Pringle, *Observations on the Diseases of the Army*, 5th ed. (London, 1765).

34. Sir John Pringle, *Observations on the Nature and Cure of Hospital and Jayl-Fevers* (London, 1750); and Stephen Hales, *A Description of Ventilation* (London, 1743), and *A Treatise on Ventilation, Part Second* (London, 1758). On the Newgate incident see Ignatieff, pp. 44-45; Wayne Joseph Sheehan, "The London Prison System, 1666-1795" (Ph.D. dissertation, University of Maryland, 1975); Robin Evans, "A Rational Plan for Softening the Mind: Prison Design, 1750-1842" (Ph.D. dissertation, University of Essex, 1975).

35. John Howard, *The State of the Prisons in England and Wales* (Abingdon, 1977; orig. ed. 1777), p. 243.

36. Erwin Ackerknecht, *Medicine at the Paris Hospital, 1794-1848* (Baltimore, 1967), chap. 1, esp. pp. 4-5. See also Richard Harrison Shryock, "The Medical Reputation of Benjamin Rush: Contrasts over Two Centuries," *Bulletin of the History of Medicine* 45 (1971): 507-53; and Niebyl.

37. Ackerknecht, *Paris Hospital*, p. 5.

38. Ignatieff, p. 60.

39. *Ibid.*, p. 61.

40. John Ferriar, "Some Remarks on Dr. Tattersall's 'Brief View of the Anatomical Arguments for the Doctrine of Materialism,'" in *Medical Histories and Reflections* (Warrington, 1792); Thomas Percival, *Essays, Medical and Experimental* (London, 1770). I would like to thank Mrs. Hanks of the National Library of Medicine for providing me with copies of these works.

41. John E. Ransom, "John Howard on Communicable Diseases," *Bulletin of the History of Medicine* 5 (1937): 131-47; and see Niebyl.

42. Percival, who was a close friend of Priestley and corresponded regularly with Benjamin Franklin and the French *philosophes*, was especially suspect.

43. Thomas Percival, *Medical Ethics*, ed. Chauncey Leake (Baltimore, 1957), pp. 77-78.

44. *Ibid.*

45. John Thompson and Grace Goldin, *The Hospital: A Social and Architectural History* (New Haven, 1975). See also Anthony King, "Hospital Planning: Revised Thoughts on the Origins of the Pavilion Principle in England," *Medical History* (1966): 360-73.

46. *Proceedings of the Board of Health in Manchester* (London, [1805]). I would like to thank Miss Margaret De Motte of the Manchester Central Library, City of Manchester Cultural Services, for providing me with a copy of this work.

47. Percival, *Medical Ethics*, p. 173.

48. On the history of typhus see Charles Creighton, *A History of Epidemics in Great Britain* (2d ed. Totowa, N.J., 1965; orig. ed. 1894); Major Greenwood, *Epidemics and Crowd Diseases* (London, 1935); Ronald Hare, *Pomp and Pestilence: Infectious Disease, Its Origins and Conquest* (London, 1954); and Hans Zinsser, *Rats, Lice and History* (London, 1935).

49. E.g., Gloucester, Worcester, Maidstone (PRO, HO 42/4). Fear of fever is mentioned in petitions from Reading, Portsmouth, Stafford, and Dorset. See also Webb and Webb, *English Local Government*, vol. 6: *English Prisons Under Local Government*, p. 57. William Augustus Guy wrote that Howard saw gaol fever in six prisons and heard of it in twenty-one, "so . . . fever haunted at least one-fourth of our prisons" ("John Howard as Statist," *Journal of the [London] Statistical Society* 36 [1873]: 1-18, p. 3). Some of these episodes, however, were well in the past.

50. Heysham, *Account*, and Heygarth, "Observations." See also M. W. Flinn, "Introduction" in Edwin Chadwick, *Report on the Sanitary Condition of the Labouring Population, 1842* (Edinburgh, 1965), p. 9.

51. Friedrich Engels, *The Condition of the Working Class in England*, trans. W. O. Henderson and W. H. Chaloner (Stanford, 1970), p. 113; and Winslow, p. 359.

52. PRO, HO 42/3 and 42/4. See also HO 42/8 (from Kent) and 42/6, Higgin to T. Stanley, MP.

Chapter Four

1. Copies of the rules for Lancaster, Preston, and Salford can be found in Margaret DeLacy, "County Prison Administration in Lancashire, 1690-1850" (Ph.D. dissertation, Princeton University, 1980), pp. 311-27.

2. See Michael Ignatieff, *A Just Measure of Pain* (New York, 1978), p. 77. I am grateful to Dr. Ignatieff for providing me with a copy of a paper read at the December 1976 meeting of the American Historical Association that also discusses these points.

3. 2 Geo. II, c. 22, and 55 Geo. III, c. 48.

4. *PP* 1812-13 V, Report of the Commissioners on the State of Lancaster Prison, and the Treatment of Prisoners Therein (hereafter "1812 Comm."), p. 34.

5. *Ibid.*, pp. 11, 85.   6. *Ibid.*, pp. 27-28, 34.

7. LCRO, QSO, Lanc. T 1777.   8. LCRO, QSO, Preston T 1785.

9. LCRO, QSO, Manc. T 1786.

10. PRO, PCOM 2/442, April 18, 1817, entry in handwriting of John Higgin.

11. 1812 Comm., p. 68.

12. *Ibid.*, p. 23.

13. PRO, PCOM 2/442, Oct. 22, entry in handwriting of Thomas Houseman Higgin; Joseph John Gurney, *Notes on a Visit Made to Some of the Prisons in Scotland and the North of England in Company with Elizabeth Fry*, 2d ed. (London, 1820), p. 418; LCRO, Testimony of William Liddell Before the Select Committee on Gaols (extract from the *Parliamentary Papers*).

14. LCL, folder on J. S. Harrison.

15. John Howard, *The State of the Prisons in England and Wales* (Abingdon, 1977; orig. ed. 1777), p. 51.

16. LCRO, QSO, Manc. July 1786; Preston M (2d sess.) 1792. See also 1812 Comm.

17. LCRO, QSO, Manc. T 1777.

18. These diets are taken from the rules. See above, notes 1 and 16.

19. J. C. Drummond and Anne Wilbraham, *The Englishman's Food: Five Centuries of English Diet* (London, 1958), pp. 206-8.

20. 1812 Comm., p. 40.

21. PRO, PCOM 2/442, entry in handwriting of Thomas Houseman Higgin.

Chapter Five

1. James Neild, *State of the Prisons in England, Scotland and Wales* (London, 1812), p. 326.

2. *Ibid.*

3. PRO, HO 42/125.

4. The following narrative of the events leading up to Rawlinson's suicide and the commission's investigation closely follows the commission's report.

5. *PP* 1812-13 V, Report of the Commissioners on the State of Lancaster Prison, and the Treatment of Prisoners Therein (hereafter "1812 Comm."), p. 51.

6. *Ibid.*, p. 49.

7. *Ibid.*, p. 65.

8. *Ibid.*, p. 62.

9. *Ibid.*

10. *Ibid.* p. 94.

11. PRO, HO 42/125.

12. *Ibid.*

13. John Howard, *The State of the Prisons in England and Wales* (Abingdon, 1977; orig. ed. 1777), p. 438.

14. *Hansard*, 24: 895-904.

15. PRO, HO 42/125.

16. 1812 Comm., pp. 14-15.

17. *Ibid.*, pp. 15-16, 88.

18. *Ibid.*, p. 17.

19. *Ibid.*, pp. 43-44.

20. *Ibid.*, pp. 64-65.

21. *Ibid.*, p. 69.

22. *Ibid.*, p. 97.

23. PRO, HO 42/126, July 18, 1812.

24. 1812 Comm., p. 21.

25. *Ibid.*, pp. 27-28.

26. *Ibid.*, petition of John Hankin, p. 97.

27. PRO, HO 42/165.

28. J. R. S. Whiting, *Prison Reform in Gloucestershire, 1776-1820* (London, 1975), p. 67.

29. Samuel Bamford, *Passages in the Life of a Radical*, ed. W. H. Chaloner, vol. 2 (London, 1967; orig. ed. 1844), pp. 181-82. See also Henry Hunt, *Memoirs*, vols. 2-5 (n.p., n.d.); Hunt, *Investigation at Ilchester Gaol . . .* (London, 1821); Hunt, *Peep into a Prison or Inside of Ilchester Bastille* (London, 1821); William Bridle, *A Narrative of the . . . Improvements Effected in . . . Ilchester . . .* (Bath, 1822); J. Stevens Cox, *Ilchester Gaol and House of Correction* (Ilchester Historical Monographs no. 4; Ilchester, 1949); and *PP* 1822 IV, Report of the Commission on Ilchester. I would like to thank Miss Joanna Innes for referring me to the Cox pamphlet.

30. On Carlile see Edward Royle, *Radical Politics, 1790-1900: Religion and Unbelief* (New York, 1971).

31. Winifred Proctor, "Orator Hunt, M.P. for Preston, 1830-32," *Transactions of the Lancashire and Cheshire Historical Society* 114 (1963): 129-54. For Doherty see R. G. Kirby and A. E. Musson, *The Voice of the People: John Doherty 1798-1854, Trade Unionist, Radical and Factory Reformer* (Manchester, 1975).

32. *PP* 1840 XXXVIII.

33. *PP* 1825 VI.

34. *Poor Man's Advocate*, July 14, 1832.

35. PRO, HO 42/125, Hay to HO, Manchester, July 26, 1812.

36. PRO, HO 42/129, Higgin to John Beckett (undersecretary of state), Nov. 12, 1812.

37. *Ibid.*

38. PRO, HO 20/1.

39. *Ibid.*

40. LCRO, DDHu 53/59.

41. *Ibid.*

42. *Ibid.* See also Sir Leon Radzinowicz, *A History of English Criminal Law*, vol. 1 (London, 1948), pp. 314 n. 72, 498.

43. LCRO, DDHu 53/59.   44. *Ibid.*

45. PRO, HO 20/1 fol. 124a.   46. *Ibid.*, fol. 102b.

47. These accounts are taken from *Hansard* for the dates mentioned in the text. In many cases they were also recorded in the local press.

48. PRO, PL 28/16; LCL, cause list no. 2, Lanc. Lent Assizes, March 23, 1822 (notes by T. B. Addison).

49. *Preston Chronicle*, March 31, 1832; and *Hansard*.

50. *Preston Chronicle*, Sept. 8, 1832.

51. *Ibid.*

52. *Poor Man's Advocate*, July 21, 1832.

53. *Ibid.*

Chapter Six

1. Peter Mathias, *The Transformation of England* (London, 1979), p. 122.

2. E. P. Thompson, *The Making of the English Working Class* (New York, 1963), pp. 600, 603-4; Samuel Bamford, *Passages in the Life of a Radical*, ed. W. H. Chaloner, vol. 1 (London, 1967; orig. ed. 1844), p. 125.

3. S. E. Finer, *The Life and Times of Sir Edwin Chadwick* (London, 1952), p. 42. *PP* 1836 XXVII (County Rates Committee). The Rate Consolidation Act was 12 Geo. II, c. 29. See also A. F. Davie, "The Government of Lancashire 1798-1838" (M.A. thesis, University of Manchester, 1966), p. 72. I am grateful to Michael Collinge of the Institute for Historical Research for pointing out to me that joint collections probably camouflaged the rises in the county rate.

4. *PP* 1825 VI.

5. R. Sharpe France, "The Lancashire Sessions Act, 1798," *Transactions of the Lancashire and Cheshire Historical Society* (hereafter *LCHS*) 90 (1944): 33.

6. See Margaret DeLacy, "County Prison Administration in Lancashire, 1690-1850" (Ph.D. dissertation, Princeton University, 1980), p. 436.

7. BL add. MSS. 38447, f. 3 (Liverpool Papers), Bayley to Liverpool, March 4, 1790.

8. Sharpe France. This is the main source for the events leading up to the act and I have followed it closely. It is also discussed in Sidney Webb and Beatrice Webb, *English Local Government*, vol. 1: *The Parish and the County* (London, 1963; orig. ed. 1906).

9. Sharpe France, pp. 10-34. LCRO, QSO, Preston T 1794.

10. LCRO, DDGr Box 0/1 (Case for a New County Rate). See also Davie, "Lancashire 1798-1838," p. 54.

11. LCRO, DDGr Box 0/1, and *Fourth Annual Report of the Poor Law Commissioners for England and Wales*, appendix D: Poor Rate Returns, 1838 (London, 1839). According to these returns, 9 of the 22 parishes in West Derby

Union and 5 of the 20 parishes in Prescot Union paid more to the county than to the poor rate. There were only 9 other such parishes in the whole county, however. In 1804 money spent on "Church rate, County rate, highways militia etc" had exceeded total poor-law expenditures for paupers both in and out of poorhouses (not including law expenses) in 12 parishes in Lonsdale, 11 in Amonderness, 12 in Blackburn, 19 in Leyland, 19 in Salford, and 42 in West Derby (LCRO, poor rate abstract, 1804).

12. David Foster, "Class and County Government in Early Nineteenth-Century Lancashire," *Northern History* 9 (1974): 48-61. See also Foster's Ph.D. thesis, "The Changing Social and Political Composition of the Lancashire County Magistracy, 1821-51" (University of Lancaster, 1971).

13. E. W. Gilboy, "The Cost of Living and Real Wages in Eighteenth-Century England," in A. J. Taylor, ed., *The Standard of Living in Britain in the Industrial Revolution* (London, 1975), pp. 1-20. Lancashire's agricultural problems are analyzed in J. Phillip Dodd, "South Lancashire in Transition: A Study of the Crop Returns for 1795-1801," *LCHS* 117 (1966): 89-107.

14. Davie, "Lancashire 1798-1838," p. 54, and see LCRO, QSG (1809).

15. 55 Geo. III, c. 51. See also *PP* 1836 XXVII, and Davie, "Lancashire 1798-1838," p. 54.

16. *The Preston Pilot*, Sept. 15, 1827; A. F. Davie, "The Administration of Lancashire, 1838-1888" (Ph.D. dissertation, University of Manchester, 1968), p. 4; Foster, "Lancashire County Magistracy," pp. 4-5; Robert Hindle, *An Account of the Expenditure of the County Palatine of Lancaster for a Period of Twenty-Three Years . . . with Remarks* (London, 1843), p. 15. This is the source for Table 10. LCRO, AGS, Sept. 1840.

17. Foster, "Lancashire County Magistracy," pp. 4-5, and "Class and County Government." Hindle, pp. 37-45.

18. Hindle, pp. 37-45.

19. *Ibid.*; AGS, June 1842.

20. *PP* 1836 XXVII; Hindle, pp. 222-23.

21. *PP* 1836 XXVII.

22. D. Gregory, "Rates and Representation: Lancashire County in the Nineteenth Century," *Northern History* 12 (1976): 158-71.

23. *Preston Chronicle*, Sept. 10, 1831. LCRO, AGS, Report of the Committee to Examine Expenditure, Dec. 1849, pp. 16-17.

24. *Preston Chronicle*, March 20, 1831.

25. *Ibid.*, April 9, 1831.

26. Hindle, p. 171.

27. *PP* 1850 XIII, Evidence of Edward Gorst and William Roberts.

28. *Ibid.*, appendix. This includes county, hundred, and constabulary rates. For West Derby, see the evidence of John Livesay. LCRO, AGS, 1848.

29. Gregory, pp. 161-62; *PP* 1850 XIII, Evidence of William Roberts.

30. Gregory, pp. 164-71. I agree with both Gregory's analysis of this attempt and his explanation of its failure; the account below follows his.

31. *PP* 1850 XIII.

32. For Hulton's failings, see Davie, "Lancashire 1838-1888," pp. 70 and 281-82.

33. *PP* 1850 XIII, Report of the Committee.

34. Hindle, pp. 302-3.

35. M. Heather Tomlinson, "Victorian Prisons: Administration and Architecture, 1835-77," vol. 2 (Ph.D. dissertation, University of London, 1975), appendix D. I would like to thank Dr. Tomlinson for permission to consult this work and for other assistance. Richard Wildman, "Workhouse Architecture," in Norman Longmate, *The Workhouse* (London, 1974), appendix. The average cost of a new workhouse was about £5,000.

36. *PP* 1850 XIII, Evidence of J. S. Birley.

37. Longmate, pp. 105-6.

38. Eric Midwinter, *Social Administration in Lancashire, 1830-1860: Poor Laws, Public Health and Police* (Manchester, 1969), p. 62.

39. Longmate, p. 105.

40. Tomlinson, 1: 174-75.

41. E. P. Hennock, "Finance and Politics in Urban Local Government in England, 1835-1900," *Historical Journal* 6 (1963): 212-26.

42. *PP* 1850 XIII, appendix B.

43. *PP* 1850 XIII.

Chapter Seven

1. Michel Foucault, *Discipline and Punish*, trans. Alan Sheridan (London, 1977), p. 228.

2. Gertrude Himmelfarb, "The Haunted House of Jeremy Bentham," *Victorian Minds* (New York, 1968).

3. Ursula Henriques, "The Rise and Decline of the Separate System of Prison Discipline," *Past and Present* 54 (Feb. 1972): 61-93, quote from p. 90.

4. See M. Heather Tomlinson, "Victorian Prisons: Administration and Architecture, 1835-77" (Ph.D. dissertation, University of London, 1975); Robin Evans, "A Rational Plan for Softening the Mind: Prison Design, 1750-1842" (Ph.D. dissertation, University of Essex, 1975); and J. Mordaunt Crook, "A Reluctant Goth: The Architecture of Thomas Harrison," *Country Life* 149 (1971): 876-79, 944-47, 1088-91, 1539, for more information on building at these prisons. I am grateful to Dr. Tomlinson for referring me to the Crook article.

5. This tower still stands, although it is no longer used for prisoners' cells. I am grateful to the Home Office, the Governor and Assistant Governor of Lancaster Castle, and the prison staff for enabling me to view these cells.

6. Samuel Bamford, *Passages in the Life of a Radical*, ed. W. H. Chaloner, vol. 2 (London, 1967; orig. ed. 1844), p. 7.

7. Henry Hunt, *Memoirs* (n.p., n.d. but ca. 1820), 3: 628-29.

8. Robin Evans discusses these innovations in "Bentham's Panopticon: An Incident in the Social History of Architecture," *Architectural Association Quarterly* 3 (1971): 21-37.

9. See, e.g., Jeremy Bentham, *Panopticon; or, the Inspection-House, with Two Postscripts* (London, 1791), pp. 148-50: postscript I, pp. 132-33, postscript II, pp. 104-5.

10. Tony Frankland, ed., *Salford's Prison* (Salford, 1978); Society for the Improvement of Prison Discipline, *Fourth Report* (1822), pp. 31-33, and *Fifth Report* (1823). Tomlinson, vol. 2, appendix D, p. 519. I would like to thank the Salford Central Library, Peel Park, for sending me the plans for Salford.

11. Society for the Improvement of Prison Discipline, *Remarks on the Form and Construction of Prisons* (London, 1826), p. 27.

12. John Thompson and Grace Goldin, *The Hospital: A Social and Architectural History* (New Haven, 1975).

13. Evans, "A Rational Plan," pp. 164-66.

14. Tomlinson discusses these problems at length; I am merely summarizing her conclusions. See her "Victorian Prisons," vol. 1, pp. 110-17.

15. LCRO, QJB 58/5.

16. *PP*, Returns under 4 Geo. IV, schedule B.

17. *PP* 1837 XXXII, Second Report of the Inspectors of Prisons for the Northern and Eastern District.

18. *PP* 1837-38 XXXI, Third Report of the Inspectors of Prisons for the Northern and Eastern District. See also Sidney Webb and Beatrice Webb, *English Local Government*, vol. 6: *English Prisons Under Local Government* (London, 1963; orig. ed. 1922), p. 106.

19. Thomas Rogers Forbes, "The Crowner's Quest," *Transactions of the American Philosophical Society* 68 (1978): 33. See also William Baly, "On the Mortality in Prisons and the Diseases Most Frequently Fatal to Prisoners," *Medico-Chirurgical Transactions* (Royal Medical and Chirurgical Society of London), 2d ser. 10 (1845): 113-272, esp. 250.

20. George Holford, *A Short Vindication of the General Penitentiary of Milbank*, 2d ed.; *A Second Vindication . . .* and *Third Vindication . . .* (London, 1825). See also J. C. Drummond and Anne Wilbraham, *The Englishman's Food: Five Centuries of English Diet* (London, 1958), pp. 436-37.

21. *PP* 1847-48 XXXVI, Thirteenth Report of the Inspectors for the Northern and Eastern District.

22. LCRO, QGR 2/41 (chaplain's report, 1847), and QGV 2/8.

23. Second Report. See also S. Peter Bell, "A Social History of Salford New Bayley Prison, 1823-1865" (M.Sc. thesis, University of Salford, 1972).

24. Chaplain's report for 1844.

25. PRO, PCOM 2/445, Aug. 13, 1849.

26. PRO, PCOM 2/443, July 13, 1843.

27. PRO, PCOM 2/445, Sept. 7, 1849.

28. Second Report.

29. LCRO, QGR 1/25.

30. LCRO, QSZ: AGS 1826, 1828.

31. Webb and Webb, p. 135; Drummond and Wilbraham, pp. 437-39. The dietaries printed in Table 12 are taken from the schedule B returns in *PP* 1835 XLIV. These dietaries vary considerably from those reported in the "Digest of Returns" in the "Second Report of the Inspectors," *PP* 1837 XXXII.

32. Returns under 4 Geo. IV, c. 64, schedule B, and *PP* 1843 XXV and XXVI, Eighth Report of the Inspectors for the Northern and Eastern District.

33. LCRO, QGR 3/22.

34. Baly, pp. 113-272. I am most grateful to Miss Valerie Johnston of Oxford for this reference. I would also like to thank Dr. Margaret Pelling of the Wellcome Unit for the History of Medicine at Oxford for her advice on this section.

35. Robert Hindle, *An Account of the Expenditure of the County Palatine of Lancaster for a Period of Twenty-Three Years . . . with Remarks* (London, 1843).

36. Returns under 4 Geo. IV, c. 64. See Document Sources for a list of these returns for this period.

37. Eric Midwinter, *Social Administration in Lancashire, 1830-1860: Poor Laws, Public Health and Police* (Manchester, 1969), p. 74.

38. Baly, appendix.

39. *Ibid.*, Table XX.

40. *Preston Chronicle*, July 10, 1817. PRO, HO 20/1, no. 53, Joseph Baxendale to HO, Jan. 30, 1822. Typhus killed another prison officer at Kirkdale in 1835 (LCRO, QGR 3/38, surgeon's report).

41. Baly, pp. 234-35.

42. *Ibid.*, p. 173.

43. Manchester Central Library, *Laws of Debtors in Lancaster Castle* (Lancaster, 1804).

44. J. Hall, *Lancaster Castle: Its History and Associations* (Lancaster, 1843), pp. 15-20. This book was written for the use of Castle debtors; Hansbrow corrected the proofs.

45. *Ibid.*, p. 14.

46. Isaac Smith, *A Warder's Experiences in Lancaster Castle* (Blackburn, n.d.), p. 10.

47. *Ibid.*, p. 13.

48. LCL, scrapbook 5, *Rules and Regulations for the Guidance of Members of the Quakers Room* (printed broadside, Lancaster, n.d.).

49. Second Report.
50. Thirteenth Report.
51. PRO, PCOM 2/444.
52. Hall, p. 26.
53. *Ibid.*, p. 38.
54. Michael Ignatieff, *A Just Measure of Pain* (New York, 1978), chap. 1, "Pentonville," pp. 3-14.
55. *Ibid.*, p. 193.
56. *PP* 1845 XXIV, Tenth Report of the Inspectors for the Northern and Eastern District.
57. Second Report.
58. *PP* 1839 XXII, Fourth Report of the Inspectors for the Northern and Eastern District.
59. *Ibid.*; see also the second report.
60. Thirteenth Report. This was Frederic Hill's first report on Lancashire prisons. He had previously served as the inspector of the Scottish prisons.
61. Second Report.
62. Fourth Report.
63. Second Report.
64. *The Poor Man's Advocate*, July 21, 1832.
65. W. Hepworth Dixon, *The London Prisons* (London, 1850), p. 310.
66. Third Report.
67. *Ibid.*
68. Second Report.
69. Third Report.
70. Dixon, p. 338.
71. Eighth Report.
72. *PP* 1835 XI, Evidence Taken Before the Select Committee on Gaols and Houses of Correction, appendix.
73. Tenth Report.
74. PRO, PCOM 2/444, March 2, 1846. See Margaret DeLacy, "County Prison Administration in Lancashire, 1690-1850" (Ph.D. dissertation, Princeton University, 1980), p. 609, n. 110, for additional references to insane prisoners.
75. PRO, PCOM 2/443, July 26, 1845.
76. *Ibid.*, March-April 1843.
77. Eighth Report.
78. Patricia O'Brien, *The Promise of Punishment: Prisons in Nineteenth-Century France* (Princeton, 1982), chap. 3, pp. 75-108.
79. LCRO, QAL 1/1: proceedings of the Lancaster Castle Committee.
80. Walter Lowe Clay, *The Prison Chaplain* (Montclair, 1969), pp. 110-11.
81. *Poor Man's Advocate*, July 21, 1832.
82. PRO, PCOM 2/443, Aug. 7, 1843.
83. *Ibid.*, Sept. 14, 1844.
84. PRO, PCOM 2/444, March 11, 1846.
85. PRO, PCOM 2/443, Aug. 19, 1845.
86. *Ibid.*, Aug. 19-20, 1845.

87. For further discussion, see my article, "Grinding Men Good? Lancashire's Prisons at Mid-Century," in Victor Bailey, ed., *Policing and Punishment in Nineteenth-Century Britain* (London, 1981), pp. 182-216.

88. See Tomlinson, vol. 1, pp. 168-70.

89. Dixon, p. 312.

90. Eighth Report. Cf. Ursula Henriques, *Before the Welfare State* (London, 1979), p. 192.

91. Eighth Report.

92. Second Report.

93. Thirteenth Report.

Chapter Eight

1. John Howard, *The State of the Prisons in England and Wales* (Abingdon, 1977; orig. ed. 1777), p. 121.

2. *PP* 1819 VII, Evidence Taken Before the Select Committee on Gaols.

3. Joseph John Gurney, *Notes on a Visit Made to Some of the Prisons in Scotland and the North of England in Company with Elizabeth Fry*, 2d ed. (London, 1820), p. 419.

4. Ursula Henriques, "The Rise and Decline of the Separate System of Prison Discipline," *Past and Present* 54 (Feb. 1972): 61-93.

5. Matthew Davenport Hill became a close friend of Bentham's toward the end of the latter's life. See Peter W. J. Bartrip, "The Career of Matthew Davenport Hill with Special Reference to His Place in Penal and Educational Reform Movements in Mid-Nineteenth-Century England" (Ph.D. dissertation, University of Wales, 1975). See also David Roberts, *Victorian Origins of the British Welfare State* (New Haven, 1960).

6. "Creative anguish" is a modern phrase, used by King and Elliott to describe the regime at Albany when it opened, but it is an extremely apt description of what the prison chaplains wished to foster in Victorian gaols. For the "common-sense school" see W. L. Clay, *The Prison Chaplain* (Montclair, 1969), pp. 212-19; Philip Collins, *Dickens and Crime* (London, 1965), pp. 70-81; and Sidney Webb and Beatrice Webb, *English Local Government*, vol. 6: *English Prisons Under Local Government* (London, 1963; orig. ed. 1922), pp. 87-89.

7. *PP* 1837 XXXII, Second Report of the Inspectors of Prisons for the Northern and Eastern District.

8. Hepworth Dixon, *The London Prisons* (London, 1850), p. 253.

9. John Clay, chaplain's third report to the Preston Quarter Sessions, 1826; W. L. Clay, p. 113.

10. LCRO, QSZ/1, AGS 1821.

11. W. L. Clay, pp. 110-11.

12. HO, Prison Department, Manchester MSS., register of felons, January 1796. I am grateful to the Home Office for enabling me to see this register.

13. PRO, HO 20/2, March 3, 1827.

14. W. L. Clay, p. 114.

15. *The Preston Pilot*, Sept. 15, 1827.

16. W. L. Clay, p. 115. The dispute grew so bitter that William John Williams hinted that one of the parties should resign.

17. John Clay, chaplain's reports to the Preston Quarter Sessions. Though Clay's reports were published and widely distributed, some have vanished. The reports for 1824-26, 1828-29, 1839-42, and 1844-58 are available in the LCRO (QGR 2). W. L. Clay's *The Prison Chaplain* contains copious extracts from many reports. After 1837 they were printed in full in the schedule B returns in the *Parliamentary Papers*. The reports of the prison inspectors contain some extracts from Clay's journal. J. J. Tobias included excerpts from some reports in *Nineteenth-Century Crime: Prevention and Punishment* (Newton Abbot, 1972).

18. Thomas Batty Addison, general report on the Preston house of correction (Preston M 1827), LCRO, QGR 2/14. Clay's report for 1827 has disappeared, but it seems clear that Addison was summarizing it accurately. Clay returned to the subject in 1850, quoting the 1827 report to show that his views had not changed.

19. Chaplain's report for 1851.

20. Second Report.

21. Chaplain's reports for 1848 and 1849.

22. V. A. C. Gatrell and T. B. Hadden, "Criminal Statistics and Their Interpretation," in E. A. Wrigley, ed., *Nineteenth Century Society* (Cambridge, Eng., 1972), pp. 388-91. I would like to thank Dr. Gatrell for assistance with an early draft of this section.

23. Chaplain's report for 1851. This example has been taken at random; similar tables appear in nearly every report. Cf. Norris Pope, *Dickens and Charity* (New York, 1978).

24. W. L. Clay, p. 212.

25. Chaplain's report for 1842.

26. LCRO, QGR 3/45, Richard Appleton, chaplain's report for Kirkdale, 1850. See also S. Greg, "Notes on Criminal Statistics," MS. copy of a paper read before the Manchester Statistical Society, sess. 1837-38, Manchester Central Library, MS. F. 310. 6. m5. I am grateful to the City of Manchester Cultural Services, Archives Department, for providing me with a copy of this and other Statistical Society papers. James Phillips Kay-Shuttleworth also believed that environmental improvements and education were the only solution to the problem of crime. See *The Moral and Physical Condition of the Working Classes Employed in the Cotton Manufacture in Manchester* (2d ed. Manchester, 1969; orig. ed. 1832). On the views of the Society as a whole, see Michael J. Cullen, *The Statistical Movement in Early Victorian Britain* (New York, 1975), chap. 8, and T. S. Ashton, *Economic and Social Investigations in Manchester, 1833-1933* (London, 1934).

27. PRO, PCOM 2/445, Aug. 27, 1849.

28. PRO, HO 20/4, Williams to Lord John Russell, Wakefield, Nov. 18, 1837, and Dec. 14, 1837. Jebb was even less tactful and more disliked than Chadwick, and it is difficult to believe that his efforts alone could have had much effect on a county already resisting the New Poor Law. See Eric Stockdale, "The Rise of Joshua Jebb, 1837-1850," *British Journal of Criminology* 14 (April 1976): 164-70. I am grateful to Judge Stockdale for providing me with a copy of this article.

29. LCRO, QGR 5/1, Report of the Committee on Prison Accommodation and Discipline (1853).

30. *Ibid.*

31. *PP* 1863 IX, Report from the Select Committee on Prison Discipline.

32. *Ibid.*

Document Sources

Major Manuscript Collections

Bodleian Library
  Burdett MSS.
  Gough collection
  Howard MSS.
  MSS. Top. Oxon

British Library (BL)
  The Liverpool papers

Corporation of London Records Office
  Report from the Committee of Aldermen appointed to visit several gaols in England, 1815-16

HM Prison Lancaster and HM Prison Preston
  Miscellaneous newspaper clippings and similar materials

Home Office
  Manchester prison registers. (See also HO entries under Public Record Office below.)

Lancashire County Record Office (LCRO)
  CT. Financial papers
  DDB/74/15, 16. Parker collection, calendars of Crown prisoners, 1782-83
  DDGr. Dawson-Greene papers
  DDHe. Hesketh papers
  DDHu. Hulton papers
  DDKe. Kenyon papers
  PP. Prison plans

The Preston Chronicle

Probate records, Original wills for the diocese of Chester and the archdea-
conry of Richmond

QAF. Financial papers

QAL. Lancaster Castle Committee minutes, 1783-1848

QAV/3. Report on Manchester house of correction, 1783

QGR. Reports by governors, chaplains, and surgeons, 1823-67

QGR/S/1. Report of the Committee on Prison Accommodation and Discipline, 1853

QGV. Prison rules

QJB. Insolvent debtors' papers

QJC. Calendars of Crown prisoners

QSB/1. Recognizance rolls

QSG. MS. Annual General Session minutes

QSO. Quarter Sessions order books

QSP. Quarter Sessions petitions

QSV/11. Proceedings of the Sheriff's Board, 1661-94

QSZ. Annual General Session minutes (printed)

Rate books: CAV/3, CPV/3 (ca. 1750), DDB 64/7 (1710), DDF 5 (1645),
DDKe 2/17/9 (17ᶜ), DDN 1/64 (1624), DDP, DDPt (1622), DDRo
(1665), DDT (2d batch), DDTa 215 (17ᶜ), DDX 114/1 (1675-78), DDX
123/42 (1718), DDX 603/1 (1752), DDX 678/2, DDX 951/7, ZBR 2/2A
(ca. 1640)

Lancaster City Library (LCL)

Biographies file

D6351, no. 20, Letters on the treatment of John Bagguley (1817)

D6351, no. 24, John Higgin on his salary

D6351, no. 30a, Returns and correspondence, Lancaster Castle

Docton, Kenneth H., *Index to the Records of the Jail at Lancaster Castle*

Miscellaneous Assize calendars

Miscellaneous printed guides

MS. 6615, Debtor's rules, ca. 1772

MS. 7321, Folder on J. S. Harrison

PT 8167, "The Insolvent Debtor"

Rules of Debtors, 1804

Scrapbook no. 2

Scrapbook no. 5

Sketches of Edward Slack

Lancaster City Museum

Sketch of "The Quakers" by Edward [S]lack

Manchester Central Library
  Papers read before the Manchester Statistical Society
  Report of T. B. Bayley and S. Clowes on the Manchester house of correction
  Rules and regulations for the Salford house of correction
Public Record Office (PRO)
  DL 21/2. Duchy of Lancaster, sheriff's papers
  DL 44/271, 423, 812. Miscellaneous papers, Lancaster Castle
  HO 12. Home Office, criminal papers
  HO 17. Petitions, 1819-39
  HO 18. Petitions, 1839-54
  HO 20. Home Office correspondence
  HO 40. Correspondence on disturbances, 1812-55
  HO 42. Correspondence
  HO 43. Correspondence
  HO 52. Letters from magistrates, 1835-40
  HO 74/1-3. Letters to commissioners of inquiry
  MPC 179. Maps and drawings
  MPH 351. Maps and drawings
  MR 15. Maps and drawings
  PCOM 2/442-48. Journals and letter book, Lancaster gaolers
  PL 25. Assize rolls, Lancashire
  PL 26/27-30. Assize indictments, Lancashire
  PL 26/285-95. Coroner's inquisitions, Lancashire
  PL 27. Lancashire depositions
  PL 28/16. Crown office order book
  PL 28/22. Crown office order book
  PL 28/40/2. Sheriff's papers
  PL 28/41. Assignments of Lancaster Castle
  SPD Geo. I, II. State papers, domestic
  T 90/148, 149. Sheriff's cravings
  TS 11/1025. Treasury solicitor's papers, R. v. George Dewhurst
  TS 11/6056. Treasury solicitor's papers, R. v. Bagguley, Drummond, and
    Johnstone
St Mary Priory and Parish Church, Lancaster
  Parish registers
Salford Public Library
  Journal of Henry Fielding
  Plans and pictures of the Manchester and Salford houses of correction
University College London
  The Chadwick papers

Parliamentary Papers

Returns under 4 Geo. IV, c. 64

1828 XX	1837-38 XLIII
1829 XIX	1839 XXXVIII
1830 XXIV	1840 XXXVIII
1830-31 XII	1841 XVIII
1831-32 XXXIII	1842 XXXII
1833 XXVIII	1843 XLIII
1834 XLVI	1844 XXXIX
1835 XLIV	1845 XXXVII
1836 XLII	1846 XXXIV
1837 XLV	

Reports of the Inspectors for the Northern and Eastern District

First: 1836 XXXV	Seventh: 1842 XXI
Second: 1837 XXXII	Eighth: 1843 XXV and XXVI
Third: 1837-38 XXXI	Ninth: 1844 XXIX
Fourth: 1839 XXII	Tenth: 1845 XXIV
Fifth: 1840 XXV	Eleventh: 1846 XXI
Sixth: 1841, sess. 2, I	Thirteenth: 1847-48 XXXVI

Investigations into Individual Prisons

1812-13 V (Lancaster Castle and Lincoln)
1822 IV (Ilchester)

Other Prison Papers

1819 XVII (Number of prisoners and management)
1819 VII (Prisons in England and Wales)
1821 XXI (Returns from gaols)
1822 IV (Prison discipline)
1826-27 VI (Increase in criminal commitments)
1828 VI (Secondary punishments)
1831 XV (Prison expenses)
1831-32 VII (Treadwheel labor)
1833 XXVIII (Number of prisons, prisoners, and cells)
1833 XXVIII (Expense of prisons)
1833 XXVIII (Officers and servants)
1835 XI (Answers of governors, prison discipline, the silent system)
1839 XXXVIII (Amount spent from rates for prisons)
1840 XXXVIII (Prisoners for political offenses)
1840 XXXVIII (Abstract returns)
1843 XLIV (Prisoners for nonpayment of fines)
1843 XLIII (Salaries and size of gaols)

1843 XXV and XXVI (Prison discipline)
1850 IX (Discipline in gaols)
1851 XXII (Digest of returns)
1863 IX (Prison discipline)
General Financial and Other Papers
1813-14 XII (Lancashire rates)
1814-15 X (Lancashire treasurer's accounts, 1786-1814)
1825 VI (County rates committee)
1826 XXI (Poor Law returns)
1831-32 XXXV (Population of Lancashire)
1835 XIV (County rates)
1836 XXVII (County rates)
1839 XLIV (Expenditure on poor)
1850 XIII (County rates bill)

Index